PRAISE FOR

TO RAISE A BOY

"*To Raise a Boy* is a clear-eyed and sometimes shocking view of the world that we have created for boys, and a call for change."

—Peg Tyre, author of the *New York Times* bestseller *The Trouble with Boys*

"A stunning work of investigative journalism that looks at the systems and structures that have failed our boys."

—Soraya Chemaly, author of *Rage Becomes Her*

"So many of the problems of our times can be traced back to our suffocatingly narrow definition of masculinity. We don't talk about this nearly enough. And when we do, we talk about it badly. *To Raise a Boy* lays out the problems alongside the solutions, giving us tools we can use right now—to do better by boys and girls, men and women."

—Amanda Ripley, author of the *New York Times* bestseller *The Smartest Kids in the World*

"We talk a lot about what men do to each other and to women, but we don't spend much time thinking about why men are the way they are. This book does that. It comes along at exactly the right time."

—Tony Dokoupil, *CBS This Morning*

"This book is necessary, and the timing couldn't be more perfect."

—Mary Gordon, founder of Roots of Empathy

"Brown offers a study of what it means to be a boy in America today—and the outdated notions of masculinity that continue to let our boys down."

—*Washington Monthly*

"Insightful, sometimes disturbing . . . A groundbreaking sociological investigation [and] a vital addition to the conversation."

—*Kirkus* (starred review)

"Deeply insightful . . . Readers will leave this book inspired by Brown's vision."

—*Publishers Weekly* (starred review)

"This authoritative and accessible consideration offers insights, solutions, and hope."

—*Booklist* (starred review)

"A groundbreaking exploration with clear recommendations on how to better raise and support boys."

—*Library Journal* (starred review)

TO RAISE A BOY

CLASSROOMS, LOCKER ROOMS, BEDROOMS, AND THE HIDDEN STRUGGLES OF AMERICAN BOYHOOD

EMMA BROWN

ONE SIGNAL
PUBLISHERS

ATRIA

NEW YORK   LONDON   TORONTO   SYDNEY   NEW DELHI

ONE SIGNAL PUBLISHERS

ATRIA

An Imprint of Simon & Schuster, Inc.
1230 Avenue of the Americas
New York, NY 10020

First One Signal Publishers/Atria Paperback edition January 2022

ONE SIGNAL PUBLISHERS / ATRIA PAPERBACK and colophon are trademarks of Simon & Schuster, Inc.

For information about special discounts for bulk purchases, please contact Simon & Schuster Special Sales at 1-866-506-1949 or business@simonandschuster.com.

The Simon & Schuster Speakers Bureau can bring authors to your live event. For more information or to book an event, contact the Simon & Schuster Speakers Bureau at 1-866-248-3049 or visit our website at www.simonspeakers.com.

Interior design by Jill Putorti

Manufactured in the United States of America

3 5 7 9 10 8 6 4 2

Library of Congress Cataloging-in-Publication Data

Names: Brown, Emma (Journalist), author.
Title: To raise a boy : classrooms, locker rooms, bedrooms, and the hidden struggles of American boyhood / Emma Brown.
Description: New York, NY : One Signal Publishers/Atria, [2021] | Includes bibliographical references and index. | Summary: "A journalist's searing investigation into how we teach boys to be men—and how we can do better" — Provided by publisher.
Identifiers: LCCN 2020044541 | ISBN 9781982128081 (hardcover) | ISBN 9781982128104 (ebook)
Subjects: LCSH: Boys—United States—Social conditions—21st century. | Boys—United States—Psychology. | Child rearing—United States—History—21st century. | Masculinity—United States—History—21st century.
Classification: LCC HQ775 .B76 2021 | DDC 649/.132—dc23
LC record available at https://lccn.loc.gov/2020044541

ISBN 978-1-9821-2808-1
ISBN 978-1-9821-2809-8 (pbk)
ISBN 978-1-9821-2810-4 (ebook)

For June and Gus

Contents

CONTENTS

Prologue

My first year as the mother of a boy coincided almost exactly with the first year of the nation's reckoning with sexual abuse by powerful men in media, entertainment, and politics. My son was six weeks old when the *New York Times* and the *New Yorker* published their first stories about Harvey Weinstein's alleged predation. I read those stories on my phone as he nursed.

Then the stories kept coming. Roy Moore, Charlie Rose, Matt Lauer, Louis C.K. Stories about unnamed men, stories that women had been carrying silently for years and that were suddenly flooding social media. Stories about entire constellations of people who had helped shield alleged abusers from being held to account. The wave of all that, the weight of it, left me breathless and sometimes furious. And it left me, too, with a persistent, niggling question: How would I raise my son to be different?

It wasn't only that I wanted to teach him not to be sexually violent. (I mean: Obviously!) I also wanted him to be a person who would challenge sexist and abusive behavior instead of looking away. And I wanted him to know how to thrive in his relationships—with girls and women, with other boys and men, and with himself.

Six months after I gave birth to my son, I returned from maternity leave to my job as an investigative reporter for the *Washington Post*. And five months after that, an anonymous woman texted the *Post*'s tip line to say that she had been sexually assaulted by Brett Kavanaugh when they were both in high school more than three decades earlier. Kavanaugh was on the short list to become President Trump's next Supreme Court nominee.

The tip fell in my lap, and I called her. She wanted decision makers in Washington to know her story, but she didn't want to come forward publicly. Over the next two months, I stayed in touch with her as she wrestled with how to proceed, talking and texting whenever possible—in the windowless room at work where I pumped milk for my son, or in the driving rain on the shoulder of a mountain in Vermont while backpacking with my family. She decided not to speak out, figuring her story probably wouldn't make a difference. But then news of her allegations began to leak, without her permission, to other media outlets, and in the last few days of summer, California psychology professor Christine Blasey Ford decided that if her story was going to be told, then she would be the one to tell it.

She turned to me—the journalist "who had gained my trust," she later said—to help her do that. By now, we all know what she said: Kavanaugh and his friend, Mark Judge, both drunk, had cornered her in a bedroom during a house party in the D.C. suburbs, and Kavanaugh had jumped on top of her, held her down, and groped her. She had been unable to forget certain details of that long-ago night—the way, for example, the boys had laughed "maniacally" while she feared for her life. But there was plenty she couldn't remember, including where this had happened and how she had gotten home. To corroborate her story, she provided notes her therapist had taken about her survival of an attempted rape during high school, and her husband told me she had first mentioned the assault, including Kavanaugh's name, six years earlier.

On September 16, 2018, the *Post* published her allegations and Kavanaugh's flat denial. Perhaps naively, I did not expect what came next: a polarized political brawl that played out on cable news talk shows, on President Trump's Twitter account, and in the Senate Judiciary Committee hearing room. Ford's emotional testimony, coupled with Kavanaugh's angry rebuttal and eventual confirmation to the high court, led to inevitable questions about how much had changed for women since Anita Hill accused Clarence Thomas of sexual harassment nearly three decades earlier. The controversy also became a key Trump talking point, one he used to rally Republican voters ahead of the 2018 midterm elections.

But Ford's testimony did not just cause a political earthquake. It also opened a door to quieter conversations—some of them around dinner tables, between parents and kids—about sexual violence and substance abuse, about accountability, privilege, and consent, about how boys learn to be boys. Ford's story, alongside a cascade of #MeToo revelations, reverberated among teenagers, galvanizing many of them to speak out against sexism and sexual violence.

"We must take it upon ourselves to change," three seniors at St. Albans, a private D.C. boys' academy less than ten miles from Kavanaugh's alma mater, wrote in the school newspaper, urging fellow students to listen to the stories young women at their sister school told about being insulted and belittled. "Privilege comes with responsibility."

Elsewhere, there were signs of backlash. "I have a lot more distrust of women in my life," a wary high schooler told me.

In the days after the *Post* published Ford's story, my in-box filled with messages from people who felt moved to tell, some for the first time, their own stories of teenage sexual assault. They wrote me:

> *"I kept my secret for more than two decades."*
> *"I know what I experienced in high school was rape and blamed myself for it for years."*
> *"I remember silently crying into my pillow wishing that it would all end."*
> *"The experience is what I think about when I cannot sleep."*
> *"It has been 53 years since this happened to me."*
> *"I said no, no, no. . . . He did what he wanted and left me laying on that floor."*

Their memories taught me that sexual violence is braided into the lives of not just men and women but also boys and girls. They taught me that the hidden pain made visible by the #MeToo movement has its roots, often, in childhood. And they showed me that there is an enormous appetite for meaningful change. It turns out that a lot of people want answers to the same question I have been asking myself: How will we raise our boys to be different?

I'm embarrassed to admit that I had never given much thought to how boys learn to be boys until that moment in late 2017, sitting at home with my chubby, cooing infant son, reading about the wrongdoings of men. These men had been infants once, too. And then they had grown up.

For me, raising a boy feels a little like traveling in a foreign land. It was different with my daughter. When I gave birth to her, three years before my son was born, I had no idea how to be a mother, but after decades of navigating life as a woman, I knew unequivocally what I wanted for her.

My husband and I named her Juniper, after the hardy trees that cling to the sides of mountains. I wanted her to see herself as capable of anything, constrained by none of the old limits on who women must be and how they must move through the world. She could play with trucks and dolls. She could wear dresses and overalls. She could be an astronaut or a nurse. She could be fierce and funny and loving and steely-spined. "I am strong and fearless," I taught her to say when she was two, as she hesitated on the playground, her lips quivering as she considered crossing a rope-netting bridge strung ten feet above the ground. I took her hand and helped her across, nudging her along with that mantra, which she repeated as we inched forward.

There was nothing premeditated about that little sentence. It just appeared on my tongue, distilling what I wanted her to be and how I hoped she would think of herself. When we reached the far end, she threw her arms in the air and crowed: "I am strong and fearless!" Even now, she still says it out loud occasionally when she encounters something intimidating or difficult, and it thrills me to hear those powerful words in the voice of a little girl.

I had no such pithy motto for my son, August. Reminding a boy to be strong and fearless seemed unnecessary and maybe even counterproductive, fortifying a stereotype instead of unraveling it. What could I give him to help him ignore the tired old expectations of boys, to understand the limitlessness of his life's possibilities in the same way that I had wanted Juniper to see the limitlessness of hers? I had no idea. I didn't know how to help him resist the stresses and stereotypes of boyhood, because I had never grappled with the fact that boys face stresses and stereotypes at all.

It had seemed to me, as a girl, that things were easier for boys. Whereas their strength and competence was assumed, I was always having to prove mine. During the volleyball unit in eighth-grade gym, we girls were given a giant inflatable beach ball to play with while the boys got a real leather volleyball. The message was not subtle. I complained to the school board, and I learned the power of my voice. Yet however strong I felt, I understood that I was also vulnerable in a way my three older brothers were not. My parents pointed out newspaper stories about rapes on the local bike path, where I was not allowed to jog; my mom told me once that a police officer had warned her that my long blond hair was a beacon for bad guys. I learned as a girl to be a little bit afraid, and more than once, I wished I were a boy.

Off I went to college, to seasonal jobs as a wilderness ranger, to working as a teacher and then a reporter. I never really lost the feeling that things were simpler for boys. But then I embarked on the research for this book, and I realized I was wrong. The question I started out with, about how I might raise my son to be different, morphed into new questions. How do I need to be different to help him thrive? What have I misunderstood about boys? And what will it take to see boys more clearly?

In the course of this project, I interviewed hundreds of people across the country, including public health experts, physicians, sociologists, psychologists, neuroscientists, teachers, principals, coaches, parents, girls and young women, and—of course—boys and young men. I spoke to all kinds of boys—Black, Latino, Asian, gay, straight, bi, from rural and small-town America, from affluent families and those barely scraping by. I sifted through thousands of pages of court documents and I pored over peer-reviewed journals, relying on the literature of social science and public health to help put my reporting into context. I traveled from Maine to California, from Utah ranchlands to the suburbs of Minneapolis, and from classrooms in Washington, D.C., where I live, to schools on the South Side of Chicago. I wanted to get it right.

On these trips, in these conversations, I was forced to recognize that as a woman—and not just as a woman, but as a privileged white woman who grew up in one coastal metropolis and went to college and graduate school in another—I had been carrying deeply ingrained assumptions that clouded my view of boys and their experiences. I thought we needed to raise our sons differently in order to protect our daughters. Now, after spending time in the world of boys, I understand that we also need to raise our sons differently for their own sakes. We have failed boys, and our failure amounts to a public health crisis. Boys face staggering levels of physical and sexual violence, suicide rates that keep climbing, tight constraints on who and how they can be, and so much shame and fear.

We simply have not given boys what they need to build healthy relationships with themselves, with other boys and men, and with girls and women.

I think of the young man who told me what it was like to grow up in small-town, football-obsessed Indiana, grappling with the self-reproach he felt for competing in gymnastics—for *loving* gymnastics. "I remember feeling ashamed that my best friends were girls," he said. "I remember being chastised about that by my friends and brothers and my mother, who said, 'You need to learn to hang out with more guys, because you need to learn to be a guy.'"

I think of the clutch of well-to-do white boys about to graduate from high school just north of San Francisco, explaining what they called "guy culture": the pressure to either lose your virginity or face ridicule, the dictate not to care too deeply about anything. "You're bros, you hang out, you don't show emotion," one of them said. "You don't talk about your feelings."

I think of the middle-aged men I met on a Tuesday night in a church near the U.S. Capitol, who gather weekly to practice connecting with their own emotions and with each other, to unlearn ingrained lessons about how men are supposed to relate. "I turned fifty, and I realized I was alone," one of them told me. "I didn't have any friends to share things with."

I think of the gunshot victim I met in Chicago, a towering young man who hopes his infant son does not grow up to be too tall and strong, because in his neighborhood, tall, strong Black boys attract attacks from those who feel they have something to prove. "There's a lot to deal with living out here," he told me over coffee on a cold spring day. "There's a lot to deal with, being a male."

I did not write this book as a how-to parenting guide—I'm no parenting expert, my kids can tell you. Instead I set out to discover what my son is going to deal with as he grows up, so I stand a better chance of understanding how to help him through it—and to share my findings with other people who have a hand in raising boys, including teachers and coaches and mentors and fellow parents. When I write about "our sons" in these pages, I am speaking both about the boys in our lives and those we have never met, in whose success and health we nevertheless have a stake.

I hope that reading this book will move you to reexamine your ideas about boyhood in the same way that writing it forced me to rethink mine.

We talk about sex as if it is something boys want and boys get, but these days, teen boys are actually less likely to have had sexual intercourse than teen girls. We talk about sexual violence as a woman's problem, but boys and men are also victimized at surprisingly high rates. We talk as if we expect boys and men to respect girls and women. Respect is not optional, we tell them, even as they can see that Donald J. Trump—who was accused of sexually assaulting or harassing more than a dozen women, who was caught on tape bragging about grabbing women by the "pussy," who insulted television anchor Megyn Kelly on national television with a remark about her period—was elected president of the United States.

And we tend to talk about gender bias as something that creates particular challenges for women, leaving boys feeling as if their own challenges are somehow invisible or less important.

I am not saying that women have entirely overcome inequality—particularly women of color, who face discrimination I have never had to deal with. Women are still underrepresented in politics, business, and other realms of power. But over the last half century, the women's movement has transformed life for many girls in the United States, exploding myths about what they cannot or should not do. Girls weren't even welcome at public high schools until the 1820s; now, not only are women more likely than men to enroll in and graduate from college, but they also earn more than half of the nation's master's and doctoral degrees. Women still don't earn equal pay, but we're much closer than we used to be: we earned 82 cents for every dollar paid to men in 2019, up from 59 cents on the dollar in 1969. To be an American girl in the twenty-first century is to grow up with a chorus of voices that sing the praises of girl power and Black girl magic and a future that is female, voices that proclaim you can be whatever you dream.

The lane for boys has broadened to some degree, too. High-profile men are helping to redefine what it means to be a man: Daniel Hudson, a pitcher for the Washington Nationals, skipped a playoff game for the birth of his daughter in fall 2019, a move his teammates vocally supported before they went on to win the World Series. Chance the Rapper postponed his 2019 tour for the birth of his daughter, too. After tennis star Serena Williams gave birth, her husband—Reddit cofounder and venture capitalist Alexis Ohanian—took sixteen weeks' paid paternity leave. Since then, he's become one of the leading voices advocating not only that dads should have access to paid parental leave but that they should feel free to use it without fearing penalty at work. "That's why I took the leave in the first place," Ohanian told the journalist Kara Swisher. "I wanted other men to see it and be like, 'All right, well no one's going to accuse Alexis of not being an ambitious go-getter. If he can do it, I can do it.'"

The proportion of dads who stay at home full-time to care for kids has nearly doubled since 1989. Dads are spending three times as many hours on childcare each week, and more than twice as many hours on housework, as they were a half-century ago. The proportion of male registered nurses more than quadrupled over roughly the same period.

But those numbers disguise a truth: many boys are still growing up with a narrow view of who and what they can be, should be, are expected to be. They face intense pressure to be a certain sort of boy and to become a certain sort of man.

For all the change, still only 7 percent of fathers are stay-at-home dads, compared to 27 percent of mothers who are stay-at-home moms. Dads still spend far less time than moms on childcare and housework, and they face more pressure to earn money for their families. And while the number of male nurses may be growing, they still only account for a little over 11 percent of the field—a field that is forecast to expand rapidly over the next decade, creating hundreds of thousands of new jobs at the same time that the number of jobs in male-dominated industries, like manufacturing, are likely to shrink. (Certain other jobs that revolve around nurturing also remain largely female: men account for only 4 percent of dental assistants, 6 percent of childcare workers, and 11 percent of elementary school teachers, for example, and there are actually fewer men in teaching now than there were two decades ago.)

Many of us have encouraged our daughters to be more like stereotypical boys—to pursue professional ambitions, to become leaders in business and politics, to be, as I told my own daughter, strong and fearless. But there has been no equivalent social movement to persuade our boys to embrace the best qualities associated with girls.

Girlishness is so cringeworthy, in fact, that eight in ten adolescent American boys have heard someone tell a boy he's "acting like a girl," an insult meaning weak or emotional or gay. The result is a rising generation of young men who are still learning disdain for the things we consider feminine, and are still shaped by stubborn old stereotypes about what it means to be a man. More than one-third of boys believe that, in the eyes of society, strength and toughness are the most important qualities they can have. About the same number believe that boys are expected to suppress their feelings of fear and sadness.

We raise boys to "halve" themselves, to deny and disavow the necessary skills of feeling, expressing, and connecting with other people, according to Terry Real, a family therapist and author of a book on male depression. He sees the results of the way we raise boys in his practice: men who are unable to sustain the closeness that they and their romantic partners crave. "Women across the board want more emotional intimacy from men than we have raised boys to cherish and deliver," he told me.

But men and boys also want more emotional intimacy than we raise them to expect. Truly allowing boys to be boys would mean allowing them to admit that, actually, they want this kind of closeness—often even more than they want sex. And they want closeness not only in their romantic relationships but also in their friendships, especially their friendships with other boys.

New York University psychologist Niobe Way has tracked groups of teen boys over periods of several years, interviewing them about how their friendships, and their feelings about friendship, change over time. She found that in early adolescence, until about age fifteen, boys sound a lot like girls when they talk about their friends. They are effusive about the boys they turn to for deep companionship and intimacy, speaking often about trusting them with their secrets.

But as these children grew into men, something changed, Way found. Between the ages of sixteen and nineteen, they spoke of either losing their closest friends or feeling as if some new distance had crept into their most important friendships. Some professed not to care, but others spoke of loneliness and depression, and they admitted to craving a closeness that seemed out of reach.

The age range in which Way noticed boys losing their close friendships is the same age range in which their suicide rate spikes, from two to four times the rate of girls. And though Way cannot prove a causal link, she does not believe this is a coincidence. She told me she believes that disconnection from themselves, and from intimate connections with other boys, is the price that they pay in order to become men.

Obviously, these are generalizations. The things a white boy deals with growing up in rural Wyoming are not the same as those facing a prep school student in New England or the son of Mexican immigrants living in East Los Angeles or a Black boy growing up in Southeast D.C. But there are some common threads that run through diverse boyhoods across the United States—pressure to be strong, to be in control, to never admit weakness, doubt, or a need for help. Pressure to want sex, to get sex, and to brag about sex. Pressure for so many boys—even now, at a time when same-sex marriage is legal and attitudes about LGBTQ rights are shifting quickly—to be straight. Pressures that are reinforced by friends, music, and the media—and by well-meaning adults, including teachers and coaches and parents.

The narrative about masculinity that boys soak up in the United States is not confined to this country. Researchers at Johns Hopkins University, who are leading a massive study of gender attitudes among ten- to fourteen-year-olds in fifteen countries, have found remarkable similarities across the globe. From Baltimore, Maryland, to Cuenca, Ecuador, and from Shanghai to New Delhi to Nairobi, boys learn that they are supposed to be tough and strong and sexually dominant. Girls learn that they're supposed to be attractive and submissive. While tolerance is clearly growing in some countries for girls who play soccer and wear pants and otherwise resist gender stereotypes, the same cannot be said about tolerance for boys who paint their fingernails.

"It's like this global script. It's really extraordinary," said Robert Blum, one of the Johns Hopkins scholars who is leading the study.

The global script clearly harms girls, who face disproportionate levels of sexual violence, not to mention greater risk of early pregnancy and leaving school. But Blum, a physician who has studied adolescents for forty years, wants people to understand that it also hurts boys.

The Johns Hopkins study, which focuses on children in poor urban neighborhoods, found that boys suffered even higher levels of physical violence, neglect, and sexual abuse than girls. The more a boy was victimized, the more likely he was to do violence to others. Boys are more likely than girls to die in their second decade of life, and they use more alcohol and tobacco, habits that erode their health as they age, Blum said.

"The story about boys has yet to be told, and I think it's a really important story," Blum explained to me. "Our data suggest that the myth that boys are advantaged and girls are disadvantaged simply isn't true."

Blum and his colleagues at Hopkins and around the world believe that we can change these outcomes for boys by helping children rewrite the script when they are still young—before their ideas about gender start solidifying at around age fifteen. But it can be hard to persuade donors to invest in helping boys when they see such profound need (and when there *is* such profound need) to empower girls. "People have been sold a belief that you can create gender equality by focusing on girls," Blum said. "I don't know how you do that. I don't know how you create a gender-equal world and ignore boys any more than you can create a gender-equal world and focus on boys and ignore girls."

In this regard, the United States is lagging other countries, according to public health experts. Since the 1990s, international development workers and activists seeking to improve the lives of girls and women have increasingly turned to working with men and boys. If boys can be persuaded to expand their notions about what it means to be a man, the thinking goes, they will be less likely to be sexually aggressive, more tolerant of women's empowerment—and healthier. In countries as diverse as India and South Africa, a small but growing body of research suggests that there is merit to this theory.

In the United States, meanwhile, concern about the state of boyhood has simmered for at least two decades, since Harvard psychologist William Pollack argued in his 1998 book *Real Boys* that the "mask of masculinity" was contributing to boys' high rates of sadness, suicide, and failure at school. The following year, clinical psychologists Dan Kindlon and Michael Thompson called on parents to nurture their sons' emotional literacy in the bestselling classic *Raising Cain*. Alongside such books, organizations including A Call to Men and Men Can Stop Rape worked directly with boys and men, promoting a vision of a healthier masculinity as a way to prevent violence.

As sexual violence moved into the national media spotlight in 2017–2020, psychologists and journalists made new efforts to draw connections between how boys learn to be boys and how they navigate relationships. In 2020 alone, two notable examinations of the subject were Michael C. Reichert's *How to Raise a Boy* and Peggy Orenstein's *Boys & Sex*.

But a notion that has never held sway in this country is that we should teach our sons that they have a gender, teach them that their gender subjects them to a whole package of stereotypes and assumptions, and teach them that they can resist and transform those stereotypes and assumptions.

Neither has the argument that gender equality is as much about breaking down barriers for boys as it is about expanding opportunities for girls.

Now there is a new momentum toward change. From troubled public schools in the heart of the nation's biggest cities to elite all-male prep schools, a growing number of institutions that serve boys—not to mention the parents who care for them—are examining how we have been teaching boys to be men, and how we can do better.

This change comes in the wake of two big shifts: the #MeToo movement, which ushered in a broad cultural examination of masculinity, and the growing visibility of transgender and nonbinary people, which created more space for all of us to consider what gender *is*, and what impact gender norms and gender stereotypes have on our lives.

But efforts to rethink gender norms have run up against intensifying resistance, part of a deepening polarization that has seeped into so much of American life. It's not as if gender and politics have ever been separate, but the issues were memorably fused by Trump's election, given his record with women. The #MeToo movement has only seemed to widen the divide between those who defend masculine norms and those who question them. And that is trickling into boys' lives. Educators and coaches told me that it is much harder, compared to just a few years ago, to talk to boys about gender norms and sexual violence. They now show up to those conversations already knowing what they believe, already having picked a side.

An eighteen-year-old Texan was one of many boys who admitted to me that he feared an awkward or drunken hookup would be twisted into a false rape accusation that could derail his life. He figured that once he was out of college, his maleness would make it harder to get a job. The victims of sexism these days, in his eyes, are not women but men. "You can always say, well, men have come out ahead for so long, this is what they deserve, but I don't think that's fair. I was born at this time with this genitalia and I'm a man. What am I supposed to do?" he said. "Does my opinion not matter because I'm a cisgender heterosexual male?"

We can do a better job of making the case to the boys in our lives, including our sons, that they have something to gain in this conversation, and—I want to say here, right at the top, before we go any further—we can start by laying off the term "toxic masculinity." It's easy shorthand for the pressures boys face, but it is freighted with connotations that shut down discussion and invite backlash. Many of the boys and men I have met interpret "toxic masculinity" as an attack on maleness, as a declaration that something about men is essentially poisonous. "It feels bad to be a guy," a high school senior from a suburb of San Francisco told me. Start talking about toxic masculinity, a junior from St. Louis told me, and "no one is going to hear a word you say."

Some of the white boys I interviewed objected to "toxic masculinity" with particular vehemence and defensiveness. Aware that they are growing up at a time when Americans are attuned not only to sexism but also to racism, white supremacy, and a rising movement of white nationalism, they felt singled out and scrutinized for traits they were born with. They found comfort online, watching YouTube videos that assured them that they were essentially good, and that attacked liberals and feminists for trying to demonize whiteness and manhood. "They're constantly talking about how evil white men are, and I don't like it," one fourteen-year-old white boy from Minnesota told me. "The system is rigged to tell us that we're wrong for existing."

Roll your eyes, if you want. But eye-rolling doesn't help engage boys and young men who are looking to develop a sense that they belong, that they are appreciated, that they are cared for—and that they have something worthwhile to contribute. If we want boys to listen, it helps to try to empathize with what the world looks like through their eyes—and to use language they might be willing to hear.

Well, what do we *do*?

On a trip to Seattle a few months ago, I met an old friend who works in international public health and is the mom of a little boy. We sat in a park, and she described the straightforward way research unfolds in her field of work, moving from exploratory science through clinical trials to the development of vaccines and medicines that effectively counter infectious diseases. Preparing boys for respectful and fulfilling relationships is not nearly so simple. There is no one cause of sexual violence or emotional disconnection, and there is no vaccine.

Instead, it's a lot of things that add up—levers we can pull, ways we can do things better. As I'll explain in the coming pages, some of those levers are inside our own homes, within the private sphere of our families. Starting when our sons are babies, parents can refrain from denigrating "feminine" toys and pursuits and can work on building close, warm relationships that give our sons safe harbor to be their real selves—so that even if boys have to put on a certain armor to navigate the outside world, they don't lose touch with who they are and how they feel. We can protect our sons from witnessing or experiencing violence in our homes, which puts a boy at far greater risk of doing violence to others later on. And we can talk much more to our sons about sex and bodies, teaching them starting in early childhood that everyone has personal boundaries that deserve respect. Later, we can buffer the messages embedded in pornography and other media by sharing our values around sex and by opening the door to questions and discussion.

But many of the levers are outside of our homes, in the world at large. As a former middle school teacher and education reporter, I may be biased, but I believe that K–12 schools—where our children live so much of their social lives—have the potential to be a powerful engine of change. Sexual harassment and assault are astonishingly common not just among teenagers in middle and high school but among children in elementary school. Yet many teachers and administrators don't know how to address these issues, because they haven't been trained to do so.

Meanwhile, sex education—which may be one of our best tools for helping boys build healthy relationships—has been disappearing from classrooms even as online pornography has become ubiquitous in our children's lives. Public health experts have long called for the K–12 education establishment to take sexual violence as seriously as it has taken bullying, and for sex education—long viewed as a political and ideological football—to be reframed as a critical issue of public health and safety. It's time to heed those calls.

When I started this project, I had some trepidation about what the world might hold for my children. But to my surprise, I am finishing it having discovered a well of hope—largely because of the boys I have met. They are trying to adapt to the new sex and power dynamic in relationships, a dynamic that they describe as both terrifying and ever-changing. Many of them are earnestly grappling with this feeling that they have not only a pressing responsibility to avoid doing harm to women but the freedom to redefine what it means to be men. And many of them are seeking guidance.

At Lincoln-Sudbury Regional High in an affluent suburb of Boston, I asked a group of student athletes which sports they played. When I got to a dark-haired, muscular senior named Jack Garrity, he smiled. "I play lacrosse, football . . . and cello," he said, clearly taking some pleasure in frustrating the assumptions a stranger might make about a guy like him.

A few minutes later, he stepped up to a podium in the school auditorium to kick off a daylong assembly on dating violence, telling his fellow students that he did not want to make boys feel blamed but to remind them that, as he put it, "These are not just women's issues." Afterward, Jack told me he is eager to help reshape the ideals to which boys and men aspire. "Being a man doesn't mean solving problems with violence or getting the most hookups," he said. "It means being my brother's keeper and respecting women."

As earnest as he was about being a better man, he was equally earnest about his fears that he would inadvertently screw up. He worried about sex in college—about drinking, misunderstood hookups, hurting someone without meaning to. In a way, he had been set up. He knew the basic rules of consent: as a slide projected during the assembly read, "No always means no!" and "Yes doesn't always mean yes!" But he didn't know how the rules were supposed to work in real life. He didn't feel like he knew how to keep himself and his partners safe from the specter of sexual misconduct. It seemed to him that the only way to learn was by trial and error, and yet in 2019, he felt there was no room for error.

"I'm excited to grow up and grow into a real man," he told me. "I hope I can do it safely, without any trouble."

CHAPTER ONE

What We Don't See

The Invisible Epidemic of Sexual Assault Against Boys

The first I heard of *brooming* was in one of those interstitial moments, a busy day on pause, waiting for my car to be repaired at an auto shop before racing to work. It was pouring outside, so I huddled along with a half-dozen other harried customers in a small room where a television blared a local news show. Five boys, football players at a high school just outside D.C., had been arrested for allegedly raping and attempting to rape their teammates with the end of a wooden broomstick.

Not only had I never heard of such a thing, but I had never even imagined it. Raped with a broomstick? Long after I left, I was still trying to wrap my head around it, and as details emerged in the following days and weeks, I could not look away.

It had happened on the last day of October, Halloween, at Damascus High, a diverse public school with a powerhouse football program in Montgomery County, Maryland. My colleagues at the *Washington Post* reported the wrenching details of the attack. Freshmen on the junior varsity team had been changing in a locker room after school when suddenly the lights went out, and they could hear the sound of someone banging a broomstick against the wall. The sophomores had arrived. "It's time," one of them said. They went from freshman to freshman, grabbing four of them, pushing them to the ground, punching, stomping. They pulled the younger boys' pants down and stabbed the broom at their buttocks, trying—and at least once succeeding—to shove the handle inside their rectums. The victims pleaded for help, the attackers laughed at them, and a crowd of other boys looked on, watching the horror unspool.

Whenever I learn of something unconscionable, I find myself looking for clues that it could never happen to me or the people I love. That's human nature, I guess. But like any other kind of sexual assault, brooming is not a phenomenon confined to this one high school, or to any particular type of school or community. It cuts across racial and socioeconomic lines, shows up in elite private boys' academies and coed public schools, in big cities and rural villages and small towns that dot the heartland.

Gatlinburg, Tennessee, 2015: Three members of a visiting varsity basketball team were arrested after ramming a pool cue into their teammate's rectum, perforating both his colon and his bladder. La Vernia, Texas, 2017: Thirteen boys were arrested for allegedly penetrating their teammates' anuses with objects including a Gatorade bottle, the cardboard tube from a coat hanger, and a flashlight. Bixby, Oklahoma, 2018: Four boys were arrested for raping their teammate, again with a pool cue.

What do you think you know about boys and sexual violence? I thought I knew that boys are victims only rarely, and I automatically equated "child sexual abuse" with adults preying on kids. But I was wrong on both counts.

Many boys are molested by adults, that's true. But there are strong signs that children are even more likely to be sexually abused or sexually assaulted by other children. In one study of thirteen thousand children aged seventeen and under, three-quarters of the boys who reported being sexually victimized said the person who violated them was another child. In a little more than half those assaults, the violator was a girl. Most boys who had been aassaulted had never told an adult.

Though sexual violence mostly affects girls and women, it is still astonishingly common for males to be victims. I was shocked to learn that as many as one in six boys is sexually abused during childhood. About one in four men is a victim of some kind of sexual violence over the course of his lifetime, from unwanted contact to coercion to rape. LGBTQ men are at greater risk than heterosexual men: more than 40 percent of gay men and 47 percent of bisexual men say they have been sexually victimized, compared to 21 percent of straight men.

In 2015, a national survey by the Centers for Disease Control and Prevention (CDC) found that nearly 4 million men (and 5.6 million women) had been victims of sexual violence just in the previous year. More than 2 million of those men were subjected to unwanted sexual contact, and more than 800,000 said they were "made to penetrate" another person— an awkward term that doesn't show up much in the media or in public debate. It means that a man was either too inebriated to consent or was coerced or threatened into oral, vaginal, or anal sex.

Just as with girls and women, violation of men and boys can involve physical force or emotional coercion. Just as with girls and women, boys and men sometimes have sexual experiences to which they cannot consent because they are underage or blackout drunk—experiences that we might reflexively call sex but that we should really understand as assault. And though the perpetrators in those cases can be other boys and men, they can also be girls and women. The overwhelming majority of male rape victims say that the person who violated them was another male, but most male victims of other kinds of sexual violence—such as sexual coercion, unwanted sexual contact, and being made to penetrate another person—say they were violated by a female.

Boys and men who survive sexual violence can experience serious psychological and emotional fallout, including post-traumatic stress, symptoms of depression and anxiety, suicidal thoughts, substance abuse problems, and sexual dysfunction. A boy's body can respond to unwanted stimulation—that is, he can get an erection when he's being abused—an experience that may leave him feeling guilty and ashamed, or utterly confused about his sexual orientation and his masculinity.

We rarely hear about any of this on the news. We hardly ever talk about it. Stories of sexual misconduct are everywhere, but the tellers of those stories are mostly girls and women. The stories of men and boys still remain mostly hidden, unacknowledged and undiscussed.

The default in discussions about sexual violence is to think of boys and men as perpetrators and women as victims. But that is an oversimplification that is built on a damaging stereotype about male invulnerability, and it obscures the truth: boys can be victims, and boys can need help. We've just built a world that makes it hard for them to admit it—and for the rest of us to acknowledge it. If we want to raise boys differently, we must start believing that they are equally capable of feeling pain and doing violence.

In Gunnison, Utah, in a valley of farms rimmed by steep mountains, a sixteen-year-old boy—a high school football player, baseball player, and wrestler—admitted in January 2019 that he had sexually abused eight of his teammates.

The following month, his victims spoke through tears as they stood up in court to tell the judge what had happened to them, and how it had hurt. He had crushed their testicles. Some said he had penetrated them, shoving his thumb up into their anus. He had laughed as they screamed for him to stop. After the attacks, they had suffered in silence, humiliated and too afraid to talk about it. They had been haunted by shame.

"The worst of it all is when he squoze and twisted my testicles hard enough to pop them. I've never felt so much pain in my life," said the first boy who testified. "I didn't tell my parents, but they knew something was wrong when I couldn't get out of bed and was peeing blood. The pain was unbearable in my stomach. They took me to the hospital, and I was scared. The doctor at Primary Children's asked me if I had any trauma to my testicles, but I told him no. I knew I needed help but was too scared to admit what really happened."

At the hospital, scans showed swelling of his internal organs, he said. The doctors, stumped, prescribed medicine and sent him home. Eventually the pain dissipated. The same boy had attacked him two other times, he said, but he had never told anyone what happened. Instead, he tried to avoid his tormentor. He didn't want to go to wrestling practice anymore, even though he loved it and was good at it. He tried to quit football, but his parents urged him to keep playing. Though he'd always excelled at school, now he didn't want to go.

"We had no idea what was going on," the boy's mother said in court that day. "As his parents, we felt helpless."

Twisted testicles. Peeing blood. Foreign objects shoved into anuses. Sickening harm. Why am I starting here, with wrenching details of sexual violence against boys?

The simple answer is that I have found no clearer window into the pressures and violence of American boyhood, and no more visceral way to understand my own misapprehensions about what it means to be a boy. I dove into research for this book asking why boys hurt other people; now I know that I was missing something vital. Boys can be victims, too, and we won't be able to make headway for our daughters—or for our sons—until we see that full picture.

Why Boys Don't Ask for Help (or, "Don't Be a Pussy!")

When I first began learning about locker room assaults, I wanted to know what motivated a boy to hurt another boy in this way. But along the way, I became even more puzzled—and troubled—by the victims' experiences. They had so much difficulty identifying what had happened to them as sexual assault, and felt too much shame to admit they were hurting.

One boy was so distressed about the prospect of being attacked by his basketball teammates during a tournament trip that he called his mother, intending to ask her for help. As frightened as he was, when it came down to it, he couldn't bring himself to tell her what was going on. "I was going to tell her when I first got on the phone with her, but I ended up not saying nothing," he later said. "I was going to tell her, but I didn't know how to say that."

I'll call him Martin. He was a freshman on the varsity team at Ooltewah High School, near Chattanooga, Tennessee. In December 2015, he and his teammates drove two and a half hours from their homes to a Christmas tournament in Gatlinburg, in the Great Smoky Mountains. They stayed in a two-story cabin called JJ's Hideaway, where there was a pool table downstairs in the boys' quarters. The coaches stayed upstairs.

By their fourth day at JJ's Hideaway, Martin knew the upperclassmen were coming for him. They had already gone after the other three freshmen; every evening, he had seen the brandishing of a pool cue and he had heard the screaming. He knew he was next; that's when he called his mother. And yet he didn't know how to ask for help without embarrassing himself and violating an unwritten code of silence. He just couldn't get the words out.

Girls who are victimized face their own horrors. Boys contend with the stories they have heard about what it means to be a man, strong and invulnerable and in control. And boys don't get the benefit of stories that they have never heard, about the sacredness of their bodies, and the privacy and personal autonomy they deserve.

Soon after the phone call with his mother, three of Martin's teammates grabbed him and pulled him into a bedroom, onto a bed. One of them rammed a pool cue into Martin's anus, tearing a hole in his pants, his underwear, his rectum, and his bladder.

"Don't be a pussy!" the same boy had yelled while attacking one of Martin's teammates. "Take it like a man!"

Martin tried to "take it like a man." Even after the attack—which ultimately landed him in the hospital with a monthslong recovery ahead of him—he did not immediately tell the truth about what had been done to him. He told his coach that he and his attackers had been "wrestling," and he insisted he was fine—until he peed blood, then collapsed and had to go to the emergency room. It was only because of his extreme injury that the truth came to light.

Later, during a sworn deposition, Martin was asked why he thought the older boy had penetrated him. The lawyer wanted to know if it had to do with sexual orientation. Was the older boy gay? No, Martin said. It wasn't that at all. "I feel like he tried to make me—belittle me," he said. "Tried to make me feel like less than a man, less than him."

The freshman intuitively understood and endorsed the argument that scholars make in academic circles: this kind of sexual assault has nothing to do with sex. It's about power. It's about older boys establishing their place at the top, putting younger players in their place, humiliating them in a raw and fundamental way. It's about older boys using sodomy to simultaneously prove their own manhood and emasculate their teammates.

This particular way of flexing power depends on the cluelessness or tacit acceptance of the adults who are paid to keep boys safe. It also depends on the silence of victims, who—like most teenagers—want desperately to belong, which means bearing pain, handling it and definitely not snitching. But it's dangerous and unfair to expect boys to bear the responsibility for protecting themselves, Monica Beck, one of the attorneys who represented Martin in a civil lawsuit against the school system, told me. Boys, like girls, deserve the protection and help of their coaches, their teachers, their parents, and their principals.

After Martin collapsed and underwent surgery, he spent six days in the hospital and nine months recovering, including relearning how to walk. One of the attackers was convicted of aggravated rape, the other two of aggravated assault.

Even with these horrifying facts, not everyone agreed that what happened to Martin should actually be considered sexual violence. The police officer who investigated the crime filed charges of aggravated rape, a crime that in Tennessee does not require sexual motivation. But he suggested in state court that what happened was not in fact a sexual assault. It was instead, he said, "something stupid that kids do" that "just happened" to meet the definition of aggravated rape.

"To me it was an assault. It wasn't sexual really in nature. His pants weren't pulled down. They weren't doing it for sexual gratification. This was something stupid that kids do that shouldn't have been done," Gatlinburg detective Rodney Burns said. "There was no rape or torture, no screams of anguish. . . . What this case actually is, is much smaller than what it's been blown up to be."

Later, Martin sued Hamilton County Schools for failing to protect his civil rights. As the trial approached, lawyers representing the school board asked the judge to prohibit Martin's legal team from using certain terms in front of a jury: rape, aggravated rape, sexual battery, sexual assault.

The judge never had to decide, because the school district's insurance carrier settled with Martin for $750,000, avoiding a trial. But it's notable that this was even a potential issue of debate. Imagine that a girl was attacked as Martin was, violently penetrated and seriously injured. Would anyone doubt that it qualified as a sexual assault?

The Culture of Sport

For me, sports were always a refuge. I played soccer growing up—a lot of soccer—and my teammates were my friends and my support network, girls who valued strength and skill and who reminded me to appreciate my body for what it could do instead of worrying so much about what it looked like.

I'm not alone. Sports is a refuge for so many children, and an engine for so much good. Kids can learn to communicate and depend on each other. They can learn to push and surpass their own athletic limits. They can learn to win, and to lose, with humility and grace. Kids who play organized sports tend to do better in school than kids who don't, have stronger social skills and higher self-esteem, and are healthier physically and mentally, according to the American Academy of Pediatrics.

But as anyone who has spent much time on the sidelines of a youth soccer or basketball or football game can tell you, sports can also be destructive. Coaches and parents can be verbally abusive, teaching kids that winning is more important than integrity and that disrespect is part of the game. Kids can learn to prize the use of force and violence. And in especially sports-crazed communities they can learn that, if they don't make the team, they don't much matter.

It's this darker side of sports that turns it into a breeding ground for hazing, initiation rituals that older players use to belittle and humiliate junior teammates. For boys who find themselves on teams with such a poisonous culture, sports are not a refuge. They are a nightmare.

Over the past generation, hazing pranks that once seemed innocuous—think dressing up in silly costumes or singing an embarrassing song in public—have evolved, becoming increasingly dangerous and sexual, according to social scientists who study hazing and consultants to high school athletics teams. Sexualized hazing, some argue, is an expression of a narrow version of masculinity that is celebrated in sports—a version of masculinity that is not just about strength but about dominating at all costs, about hiding pain and enduring weakness, and about degrading anyone or anything that seems feminine or gay. Even as a growing number of alternative niches gives boys places to thrive as proud geeks and artists and gender nonconformists, many sports have remained staunchly macho in this way.

We don't have comprehensive data on how common it is for boys to sexually assault other boys in the context of athletics. In 2000, researchers from Alfred University, a small private school in western New York, conducted the first and so far only national survey of high school hazing. They wanted to ask about sexualized hazing, but they were stymied. In those early days of the internet, they had to send their survey out to students in the mail, and they got access to a database of student addresses only on the condition that they not ask any questions having to do with sex or sexuality. (In general, researchers have trouble getting permission to ask children under eighteen questions about anything related to sex, sexual violence, or abuse—which is understandable, but which also hobbles our understanding of kids' experiences.)

Norm Pollard, one of the lead researchers on the Alfred University survey, found students' replies to one open-ended question shocking. "They talked about being sexually assaulted at away matches, in the back of the bus and in locker rooms," Pollard said. "It was devastating to read those reports from kids that were just trying to be part of a team or a club."

Psychologist Susan Lipkins has studied hazing since 2003, when she traveled to a small town near her home in New York to interview the parents and coach of high school football players who had been abused by teammates at a preseason training camp. The players had been sodomized, including with broomsticks and with pinecones covered in the pain reliever Icy Hot. In the cabins the boys shared during the camp, the older players had pummeled their teammates with full bags of ice and hung them by their underwear on hooks. None of the victims reported the abuse to a coach, a parent, or any other adult. It came to light only because one of the boys, still bleeding from his rectum days after returning home from football camp, sought medical help—and the cover story he told doctors to explain his injuries didn't make sense.

She and other experts said that they have seen noticeably more media reports and court filings alleging penetration and other ritualized sexual violence among high school boys, leading them to believe that it is becoming more common and more severe. Boys tell each other and themselves that they are taking part in a tradition: this is what it takes to be part of the team, this is what it takes to belong. First you are assaulted; then you become a bystander, watching as others are brutalized; finally, you get your turn at the top, your turn to attack.

Boys who report being sexually assaulted face the humiliation of having to describe how they were violated out loud, to another person, and then they face what Lipkins calls a "second hazing"—a blowback of harassment and bullying not unlike that heaped on female victims of rape. Lipkins noted she has seen parents and students band together to protect their team, their coach, even local real estate values against allegations of sexualized hazing. "Communities support the perpetrators and say you're a wimp, why did you report it," she said.

As a result of all that pressure, she said, it's common for boys to remain silent even after being assaulted. Not only do boys not want to tattle on their teammates, but they often don't even recognize that they're victims of an unacceptable violation and of a crime. No one has told them. "Hazing education is in the dark ages," Lipkins said.

Lipkins said she believes that young people and adults, including parents, coaches, and administrators, need much more training to recognize this kind of behavior as an unacceptable form of harm rather than a tradition to be upheld. And she believes it won't end until groups of players stand up together to stop it, either as active bystanders who protect victims or as victims who together find the courage to speak out.

Of course, when they speak out, they need grown-ups to hear them and protect them. Coaches must understand that building a healthy team culture and guarding players' safety are crucial parts of their job. And we parents must tell our boys the same thing we tell our girls—that their bodies are their own, that no one should touch them without their consent, that we will not tolerate violation of their physical autonomy.

Lipkins recalled a football player from St. Amant, Louisiana, who did manage to speak up after he was attacked. On his birthday, his teammates had stripped him naked, taped him to a bench, and beat him. One of them shoved an empty roll of athletic tape into his buttocks. It was a birthday tradition.

Years before, when he was a preteen, his mother had given him a magazine article about hazing. They had talked about it and about his right to maintain his personal boundaries. His mother had made clear that if anyone ever touched him without his permission, he should speak up. Armed with that awareness, he did. "I had enough of this birthday thing," he told the coach, according to Lipkins. And he quit the team.

Sexual Assault Is Not "Horseplay"

Boys who are raped or sexually assaulted face a particular kind of disbelief. They may not be accused, as girls often are, of reinterpreting a consensual sexual encounter as nonconsensual. They're perhaps less likely to be accused of straight-up lying, or of being crazy. Instead, they're accused of taking things too seriously. Sexual assault? No! It was just messing around. Just a joke. Just boys being boys. Just hazing.

The language we use to describe what happens to boys helps feed the problem, argues Adele Kimmel, who has become one of the leading lawyers for male and female victims of sexual assault.

Hazing sounds innocuous, and being penetrated against your will is the opposite of innocuous. Even when it feels like something is wrong, boys often don't have a word for what they experience or what they see happening to other boys around them. And that—coupled with the shame that boys feel about admitting that they've been sodomized—makes it hard to report.

"Terminology matters," Kimmel, a wiry woman with jet-black hair, told me on a rainy day in downtown Washington at the sleek offices of the nonprofit firm Public Justice, where she is a senior attorney. "Some of these boys don't even recognize that they've been sexually assaulted because it's been normalized by the adults. They call it these euphemistic terms—they call it horseplay, roughhousing, poking, hazing. They don't call it sexual assault. They don't call it rape."

One of Kimmel's clients, David Smith, was met with this kind of disbelief when he reported his experience to authorities. His story is important because it shows how boys exist in a world that often refuses to acknowledge that they are capable of the same degree of pain as girls. Is it any wonder that they grow up believing they can't show vulnerabilities?

David's family arrived in the tiny town of Washington, Oklahoma—a half-hour south of Oklahoma City—a few months into his sixth-grade year. They had moved to escape the wreckage of their home in another town, which had been leveled by a tornado. David's parents told me that they were drawn to what seemed like a tight-knit community in Washington, with shared Christian values. On one of their first visits to the middle school in the weeks before Christmas, "Silent Night" and "Joy to the World" played over the intercom, they told me. Teachers set aside time for prayer, and they didn't call it a moment of silence—they called it prayer.

"We thought we would be comfortable there," said David's mother, Carla.

But a few months after David enrolled, three of his football teammates turned on him in a very public, very non-Christian way, according to the Smiths. During music class, when the teacher was out of the room, in front of dozens of other students, one of the football players held David down. One of them watched, laughing, as David struggled. And a third stuck his fingers into David's rectum, through his clothes.

Afterward, David called his mother in tears, furious and humiliated. He and his parents reported the assault to Stuart McPherson, the school principal, who responded with what seemed to the Smiths like little concern. The football player who had shoved his fingers into David's rectum was suspended for five days. David was branded as a tattletale, the target of constant taunting and bullying from classmates who called him, according to the Smiths, "prison snitch" and the boy who was "butt-fucked." He was threatened, including by the football player who had penetrated him, who according to the Smiths texted "Fuck you, I am going to kill you."

The bullying continued into David's seventh-grade year. More than a year after David was penetrated in the music room, his father, John, asked the principal to help protect his son from that harassment. The principal responded: "What do you want me to do, hold his hand?"

John was disgusted. "It's no easier humanly for a boy to handle something like this than it is a girl," he told me. "But we're oh so willing, you know, to tell the boys, 'Suck it up, be a man and get over it.'"

Later on the same day that John pleaded for his son's protection, David reported that in the preceding months he had been sexually assaulted two more times by two different boys. He hadn't told anyone at the time. First local law enforcement got involved, then the Oklahoma State Bureau of Investigation (OSBI). And the Smiths sued the school district, McPherson, and A. J. Brewer, the superintendent of schools, arguing that they hadn't taken David's complaints seriously because he was a boy.

Both McPherson and Brewer described David's experience in the music room as normal "horseplay" among boys, according to the Smiths. In sworn depositions, the superintendent said he'd called it horseplay based on the principal's description of what happened, and the principal stood by his initial assessment: horseplay, not sexual assault. Why? "I did not think it was sexual," he said.

The Smiths also accused both the principal and superintendent of acknowledging that if the same thing had happened to a girl—if it had been a girl who was anally penetrated, rather than a boy—they would have seen it differently. They would have considered it sexual assault.

Responding in court, the defendants argued that they had taken the incidents seriously. But they said they didn't have enough information to know whether the superintendent and principal had in fact admitted they would have treated a girl differently. "I don't remember saying that," Principal McPherson responded when he was questioned under oath during a deposition.

But McPherson did say it, according to an OSBI agent who testified in a sworn deposition that the two school officials had been clear. They didn't believe that what happened to David qualified as sexual assault. But they would have felt differently if he was a girl.

"During my interviews with them, I asked them both that question, if—you know, if this had occurred to a female student, would it have been handled the same way," the agent, Josh Dean, said.

"What was their response?" one of David's lawyers asked.

"That would have been considered a sexual assault. But their opinion was that this—these were just boys horseplaying, and not a sexual assault in nature."

That was a mistake, according to Dean. They should have treated it as sexual assault and handed it off to law enforcement for investigation.

Ultimately, after the OSBI investigated, two students were criminally charged with rape by instrumentation, according to documents filed in the Smiths' civil lawsuit. One of those students—the boy who had admitted to sticking his finger into David's anus—pleaded no contest. The other stipulated to a charge of simple assault and battery.

The notion that what happened to David should be considered sexual assault is a novel one not only for school officials in Washington, Oklahoma, but for anyone who grew up seeing such behavior among boys as unremarkable and acceptable. As a mom, I hope that more people will come to see it as unacceptable—not because I want more middle schoolers branded juvenile offenders, but because my son and all boys deserve to be safe, both at school and in the rest of the world.

When we convey to boys that unwanted touch is a serious issue of sexual assault only when it affects girls and not when it affects boys, we are sending a message that only girls' bodies are worthy of protection. That message leaves our sons vulnerable to abuse, and it presents them with a knotty question: Why should boys treat other people's bodies with dignity and respect if their own bodies are not also treated with dignity and respect?

The Smiths' lawyers argued that the failure of school officials to treat David's penetration as a sexual assault—and their direct acknowledgment that they would have responded differently if the victim had been a girl—was a textbook case of sex discrimination.

Washington Public Schools denied that but settled the lawsuit in July 2020. The district did not admit wrongdoing, and neither did McPherson or Brewer, neither of whom works for Washington schools anymore. But the district did agree to pay the Smiths and their lawyers $550,000. It also agreed to overhaul the schools' handling of complaints about bullying and sexual harassment, including by training staff, tracking complaints, and providing mental health services for students. The settlement also gave the Smiths a role in making sure the district makes good on its commitments: every year for three years, district officials must report on their efforts to the Smiths' lawyers, who can ask a judge to intervene if progress falters.

Andy Fugitt, a lawyer representing the defendants, said the school system wished the Smiths well. "Middle school is a difficult time and middle school kids make lots of mistakes. The school district and school officials attempted to do what they thought was best at the time. Could they have done things better? Absolutely. But in the end they did their best."

The Smiths said they filed the suit because they wanted to make a difference for other parents and their sons. John Smith told me that he believed it would take a long time to change the culture in the schools and the community. But the settlement was a step. "I couldn't rewind time. I couldn't go back and prevent the things that happened to my son. Now it has to be, what are they doing moving forward?" he said. "The hope is the community changes, the culture changes, and people stand up and say you know what? That's unacceptable."

The Smiths have moved two and a half hours east, to a community where David can just be a normal kid instead of the kid who got buttfucked. His parents said his demeanor changed almost immediately after he went to school in his new town and realized that he no longer faced a constant threat of violence and harassment. For the first time in years, they said, they heard him giggle.

The Myths About Boys We Still Believe

Violence prevention programs often focus on debunking rape myths about women victims. No, wearing a short skirt is not the same thing as consenting to sex. But they less often delve into the myths we continue to believe about male victims—particularly those men who are violated by women. The idea that a man would have to be forced or coerced into sex with a woman runs counter to our cultural scripts about how sex works. How can a woman coerce a man into sex if men are supposedly down to fuck anytime?

But that's just another misleading stereotype, and one that makes it hard for boys and men to recognize and deal with their own experiences.

By now, for example, stories about college campus rape have firmly established that some men assault women who are too drunk to consent. There's no counternarrative about men being raped when they have had too much to drink—usually, that's just called sex. But whether they consider it assault or not, men on campus can and do have unwanted sex. One student at the Massachusetts Institute of Technology told me how uncomfortable he felt when he was pursued by a woman he wasn't interested in. He found himself unable to say no to her persistent advances, even though he knew he didn't want to have sex with her because he still wasn't over his ex. "You don't want to be rude," he said. "You don't want to be weird."

College fraternities have a reputation for tolerating and even encouraging sexual violence against women, and there is some evidence that fraternity brothers are at greater risk than other college men of committing assault. But there is also other, perhaps less widely known evidence that fraternity members are at greater risk than other students of being assaulted themselves. In a study of fraternity men at one midwestern college, more than a quarter—27 percent—said that someone had had oral, anal, or vaginal sex with them without their consent, either through the use of force or by taking advantage of them when they were drunk. The study was small, with only 108 respondents, but unlike most other research, it asked questions tailored to capture men's experience of nonconsensual sex—that is, it didn't just ask men whether they'd been penetrated against their will, but also about whether they were made to penetrate someone else when they didn't want to or were too inebriated to decide.

But many people do not define a man pushed into nonconsensual sex as a person who has been sexually assaulted. A 2018 survey of twelve hundred adults found that one in three would not quite believe a man who said he was raped by a woman, and one in four believed men enjoy being raped by a woman. There's a belief that men cannot be raped because women aren't strong enough to physically force them, and a conviction that straight men want sex so much and so consistently that they just aren't that bothered by a woman who refuses to listen when he says no. These ideas are embedded in our institutions, from media to medicine and law and scholarship.

It wasn't until 2012 that the FBI recognized that men could be raped. Until then, the bureau defined rape as "the carnal knowledge of a female, forcibly and against her will." Now it uses gender-neutral terms; rape is defined as "the penetration, no matter how slight, of the vagina or anus with any body part or object, or oral penetration by a sex organ of another person, without the consent of the victim."

Scholars studying sexual violence have often asked men only about their own sexual aggression and women only about being violated, an approach that fails to acknowledge—much less measure—the existence of male victims, female perpetrators, or same-sex assault. When researchers *have* asked about sexual violence in gender-neutral terms, they have made some startling discoveries. One survey of three hundred college men found that half had experienced some type of sexual victimization, and an astonishing 17 percent—nearly one in five—had been raped, meaning they had unwanted intercourse because they were threatened, physically forced, or taken advantage of while too intoxicated to consent.

The media also seems unable at times to conceive of the fact that sexual violence causes men real harm. Take, for example, a 2006 Associated Press story about a serial rapist who had attacked five men in a suburb of Houston. Despite describing how the rapist stalked young men before attacking them at gunpoint or knifepoint at their homes, the story went on to claim that "no one has been seriously hurt." It's hard to imagine a journalist claiming that female victims of a serial rapist were not "seriously hurt."

And then there are the prison rape jokes, which persist even as hundreds of thousands of people, mostly males, are raped in detention each year. In April 2018, television host Bill Maher noted that Michael Cohen, President Trump's onetime fixer, had once said he'd take a bullet for Trump. "Now that he's looking at prison time," Maher said of Cohen, who was embroiled in a campaign finance and bank fraud scandal, "we'll see if he's willing to take a dick." The audience laughed.

Lara Stemple, an assistant dean at UCLA School of Law, is a feminist who has focused some of her research on highlighting the large number of men who have experienced sexual violence and the institutional biases that have obscured their experiences. She told me that her efforts to bring attention to male victims—and to the surprisingly high rates of female perpetration of such violence—have at times triggered false accusations that she is aligned with men's rights activists, who believe that we live in a "gynocentric" world that discriminates against men, and who are known for antifeminist and misogynistic language and ideology.

Men's rights activists argue that male victims of sexual assault are invisible because feminists refuse to recognize that sexual violence is anything other than a women's problem. The men's rights website A Voice for Men—where writers and commenters describe women with terms such as "cunts," "whores" and "feminazi scumbags," and where a person who identifies as feminist has been deemed "a loathsome, vile piece of human garbage"—argues that feminists refuse to recognize male victimhood because doing so would threaten their funding, their political power, and their "monopoly on perceived victim status."

But you don't have to be a men's rights activist, or buy into their misogyny and antagonistic view of women's rights, to be troubled by the hiddenness of male victims and the illegibility of their experiences. As Stemple argues, acknowledging the invisibility of men's suffering does not mean dismissing or doubting violence against women. It is not one or the other. Both problems are tangled up in some of the same deeply ingrained notions about what it means—or what we think it means—to be a man.

A brunette twentysomething told me in the echoing atrium of a hotel in downtown Washington, D.C., that he was still unsure how to interpret his first sexual experience. He said his father pressured him into having sex with an older woman when he was just fifteen, a year too young to legally consent in the state of Georgia, where he lived at the time. She was part of a small group of people who had come over for drinks with his dad one evening after school. "My father was saying, 'Do you like my son?' He was creating this pressure. I felt I would be disappointing him if I didn't take action," he said. So he lost his virginity that night to a woman he didn't know. "I felt detached from the experience," he told me. "I went upstairs and had sex with a woman much older than me. I kept thinking, this is what men do. Now I'm a man." But looking back, he wishes he hadn't begun his sexual life that way. He wishes his father—who he thinks was seeking reassurance that he was straight—hadn't put him in that position. "I wasn't ready," he said.

I was not able to independently confirm his account. But imagine the disgust and rage you'd feel if you learned about a father who pressured his fifteen-year-old daughter to lose her virginity to one of his drunk adult male friends. And now ask yourself: Do I feel the same degree of disgust about a father pressuring his teenage son to have sex with a woman?

I'm not sure I do. And I feel a little sick admitting that. Believing that such a violation would not trouble a boy quite as profoundly as a girl is a sign that I have bought into sexist stereotypes about boys. It's a sign that, without even realizing it, I have made my own narrow assumptions about who boys are and how they feel.

Why Men's Stories Matter

Richard Rosenthal was a baseball-crazy seventh-grader when his mother gave him a memoir by R. A. Dickey, a Major League knuckleballer who won a Cy Young Award in 2012. In the book, the pitcher disclosed that when he was eight years old, he was repeatedly assaulted by a female babysitter, and that later, he was violently raped by a seventeen-year-old boy.

Richard read Dickey's book while lying on his bed at home in Florida— the same bed where he had once been molested by his middle school principal, who was babysitting one evening when Richard's mother was out of town.

Richard had been too ashamed and confused and fearful to tell anyone about how his principal had touched him that night. But when he learned that a pro athlete he admired had been sexually abused as a child, something in him shifted. He felt less doomed, he told me. He found the courage to tell his mother what had happened. Then he told police. The principal pleaded guilty to sexually abusing both Richard and another adolescent boy—and now he is a former principal, serving a ten-year prison sentence.

I told Richard I was going to call R. A. Dickey, and I asked if there was any message he wanted me to deliver. "Just tell him thank you for sharing his story, because it changed my life forever," he said. "It was really that book that drilled into my mind that I'm going to be okay. There are people that understand what I'm going through, and I'm not going to be alone."

The #MeToo movement has been built out of stories, one after the other, a flood that helped us see how men in positions of power abuse women and then keep their violence secret. In those stories, the world saw evidence of a sprawling problem in urgent need of solutions. Women found solidarity in acknowledging what had happened to them and in declaring that it was not tolerable and was not their fault.

Now boys need to hear more of these stories from men.

Dickey, who is now retired from baseball, said he'd been forced to come to terms with his abuse decades after it happened because the shame of it had driven him into a corner where the only ways out seemed to be suicide or hurting the people he loved. "I was at the end of myself," he told me. He spent years in therapy before he wrote his memoir, and he said he found it both cathartic and nerve-racking to finally share his history. He was pitching for the New York Mets at the time, and the locker room was a "petri dish of machismo and bravado," he said. When an excerpt of his book (including the portion about his abuse) ran in *Sports Illustrated*, he steeled himself for tasteless ribbing about his sexuality. But no one said much of anything—except for two teammates who privately confided that something similar had happened to them when they were younger. They had never before told a soul.

That's the power of a story.

Media coverage of high-profile cases of sexual violence against men and boys has helped opened Americans' eyes to the fact that the sexual victimization of boys is not just possible but deeply scarring, psychologist

Richard Gartner, who specializes in treating male victims, told me when I reached him by telephone. When Gartner began speaking publicly about male victims in the 1990s, he was often greeted with blank stares and disbelief.

But then came revelations about widespread abuse by Catholic priests, by Penn State football coach Jerry Sandusky, by Boy Scout troop leaders. Those stories forced people to begin to recognize the vulnerability of young boys. When actor and former NFL player Terry Crews came forward to say he had been groped by a male Hollywood executive, it forced people to consider the vulnerability even of strong adult men. And it made room for more boys and men to come to terms with their own experiences as victims of abuse, Gartner said.

"Every time that happens, some boy somewhere says, well, if he can come forward, maybe I should be talking to someone," Gartner told me.

Perhaps it is starting to happen more often. Over the last few years, the women who came forward in droves to speak out about sexual violence were joined by men who said they had been abused, including by powerful, high-profile men such as actor Kevin Spacey and film director Bryan Singer. In one remarkable reckoning, more than three hundred former Ohio State University students said they had been sexually abused by an Ohio State doctor, Richard Strauss, and sued the university for failing to protect them.

Ron McDaniel, one of the many plaintiffs, told me he was a freshman on a tennis scholarship when he first went to see Strauss in the fall of 1981. Strauss asked him to drop his pants and then inspected his private parts for what seemed like an awfully long time. When McDaniel told a few athlete friends later that evening what had happened, they just laughed, he recalled. They had dubbed Strauss "Dr. Nuts" because of his penchant for genital exams. As in the case of seventh-grader David Smith, they didn't doubt that what McDaniel said was true; they just didn't think it was a big problem. "You knew something was wrong, but it was like, well, I guess it's normal. And we just took it," McDaniel recalled in an interview.

He tried to avoid Strauss but ended up seeing him after he hurt his ankle. Again, Strauss asked him to drop his shorts, and when McDaniel asked why that was necessary, Strauss then grabbed his waistband and tried to pull his shorts down. McDaniel left the office, hobbling out on crutches. He said he told a tennis coach and other officials in the athletic department about Strauss's attempt to examine his genitals for an injury that had nothing to do with genitals, but they just laughed it off.

"It was a running joke," he said, to the point that a coach threatened to send players to Dr. Nuts if they screwed up or didn't run a mile in under a certain time.

It was no joke for McDaniel, who said he was so determined to avoid doctors—and especially male doctors—that he didn't have a full medical examination for more than a dozen years after college. He developed a tumor in his left testicle, but because he stayed away from doctors, he didn't know about it until a bike accident—which sent him flying into a telephone pole crotch-first—forced him to finally seek care. By then, the tumor was large enough that his testicle had to be removed. He said the doctors told him that if he had sought help earlier, they likely would have been able to do a lumpectomy instead.

Strauss killed himself in 2005. In 2019, an independent investigation commissioned by the university found that Ohio State officials knew of complaints about him as early as 1979, but allowed him to continue practicing until he retired with honors two decades later. As people laughed off his abusive behavior, Strauss committed nearly fifteen hundred acts of sexual abuse, including forty-seven acts of rape, the university told federal authorities in 2019. His alleged abuse included unnecessary genital exams, fondling to the point of erection and ejaculation, and performing unwanted oral sex on at least two male athletes.

The stories that McDaniel and other Ohio State graduates tell about Strauss bear remarkable similarity to the stories that hundreds of women told about the abuse they suffered at the hands of Larry Nassar, the former Michigan State University physician and USA Gymnastics national team doctor. If the collective power of Nassar's victims forced the nation to confront the ways in which institutions ignore girls and young women who report sexual assault, then the graduates of Ohio State may help force us to see how we have dismissed boys and young men.

For now, though, many men still see reasons to keep their stories to themselves. Gartner has written extensively about the shame, trauma, and confusion that his patients struggle with as they try to make sense of how they were victimized. Many fear that admitting violation will be seen as evidence of personal weakness. They fear they won't be believed. And they fear they were somehow complicit, especially when unwanted touch leads to erection and ejaculation.

Boys who report assault or abuse need to hear from their parents and the people close to them that they are unconditionally loved. "The most important thing to say is, 'I believe you, and it wasn't your fault . . . and we still love you,'" Gartner said. And parents who want to prevent their boys from being abused, he said, should be telling their sons all the same things they tell their daughters about their right to control access to their bodies.

I have taken Gartner's advice to heart. Now that I understand how common it is for boys to be victimized, I am as concerned about protecting my son from sexual violence as I am about protecting my daughter. I tell them both, frequently, that they have the right to say no to touches they don't want.

When we fail to recognize and address violence against boys, not only are we failing to protect boys, but we also may be stoking violence against women. These problems are to some extent intertwined: while most do not go on to lives of violence, criminality, or delinquency, victimized children are at greater risk of doing harm to others.

R. Kelly, the acclaimed singer and songwriter whose alleged abuse of multiple underage girls was detailed in the Lifetime docuseries *Surviving R. Kelly,* has said he was himself the victim of childhood sexual abuse. From the time that he was eight, an older girl molested him regularly and threatened to hurt him if he told anyone, according to his 2012 memoir, *Soulacoaster.*

In 2016, he told *GQ* that he had forgiven her because he understood that she had herself been the victim of abuse. "I looked at it as if there was sort of like, I don't know, a generational curse, so to speak, going down through the family." But even as he acknowledged the long-lasting impacts of sexual abuse, he said he had avoided them. The allegations against him were false, he insisted as he was held in custody, facing more than two dozen state and federal charges including child pornography, sexual assault, and kidnapping.

A Town Hurts

To a traveler headed south on the two-lane highway from Salt Lake City to Utah's famous red-rock canyons, Gunnison is a blink-and-you-miss-it blip: a state prison on one end of town, a Subway and a grocery store and a gas station. But to the people who live there, it is a world, and the world was undone by allegations of sexual violence. A group of boys told police that for years they had experienced assaults by their teammate Brad. His family, prominent in town and in the local Mormon church, defended him ferociously. The parents of the victims were equally fierce in their desire for accountability. Everyone took sides, at the expense of longstanding friendships.

Brad's alleged abuse had come to light when he and another football player held down a freshman named Greg Liefting while a third player—Brad's brother—rubbed his naked buttocks and genitals on Greg's face. Though Greg was upset by it, he went on to practice without mentioning what had happened. But someone anonymously tipped off a police officer, Carl Wimmer. The revelations that emerged in the following months ripped the social fabric of this small town, affecting not just the many boys involved, and not just their school, but their families and their whole community.

Wimmer, a former state legislator, had moved to Gunnison Valley after a failed bid for U.S. Congress in 2012. Now he was an evangelical pastor who led worship services out of his house and worked as a school resource officer for the local police department. His office was tucked away off a corridor in the local high school, decorated with photographs of his family, trophies from his days as a competitive powerlifter, and a couple of banners—one for his alma mater, Jerry Falwell's evangelical Liberty University, and another for his favorite pro football team, the Miami Dolphins. I visited at the end of track season, when kids from the track team—which he helps coach—kept popping in to sign thank-you cards for their other coaches.

It was here in this windowless room that Wimmer had asked Greg about what happened at football practice. Greg told him, and gave him the names of witnesses. Not long afterward, Greg's mother overheard another boy confessing that something similar had happened to him. Wimmer followed the trail, calling the boys into his office one by one, asking each to name witnesses and other victims. According to the twenty-three-page report he eventually compiled, more than a dozen boys told Wimmer that Brad had attacked them, twisting or squeezing their testicles or sticking his fingers into their anus. When they screamed, he laughed, they said.

In his report, Wimmer noted the demeanor of the boys he interviewed: "visibly nervous," "very uncomfortable," "clearly shaken." Most of the boys told him that they had never told anyone because they were afraid. "There's a stigma of shame that is so strong," Wimmer told me.

He said he did not find a similar pattern of complaints against the other two boys involved in Greg's assault, who were ultimately charged with one count each of forcible sexual abuse.

Brad's parents would not agree to talk to me, and neither would his lawyer. His parents told Wimmer that they felt their son was being unfairly singled out, according to his report. A lot of boys were grabbing each other's testicles and penetrating one another's anuses, they said; it had happened to Brad, too. But Wimmer said they never offered any names, and his interviews turned up no information about children who were hurting others in the same way.

The local prosecutor charged Brad with eleven felonies, including six counts of object rape. Though he and his family had forcefully denied that he'd done anything wrong, Brad admitted to eight felony counts of sexual abuse, a deal that spared everyone the ordeal of a trial.

Brad was sitting at the defendant's table on Tuesday, February 26, 2019, when Judge Brody Keisel invited the victims to speak. The courtroom was packed. Later, Keisel would say that he was surprised by what he heard that day. The boys' stories, raw and full of shame, were filled with echoes of the stories so many girls and women have told about their own experiences with sexual assault. The boys feared that they would not be believed, and that they had brought the attacks on themselves.

One boy explained that he had kept Brad's behavior secret because he was terrified of the backlash that speaking out might bring. But he hadn't been able to keep up appearances. He had stopped wrestling and he had contemplated suicide. "After it happened I just quit caring about everything," he told Judge Keisel. He hadn't been able to tell his parents, which drove a wedge between them and made him feel even more alone. "I hate on myself every day because I feel like I didn't fight hard enough to get [Brad] to stop. This makes me feel weak."

His father—I'll call him Robert—spoke to the judge through the clench of tears. He had grown up in Gunnison, he had been close with Brad's family—and he was heartbroken. So many people in his community believed his son should be able to shrug off his pain. They couldn't see how deep the hurt was, the hurt that Robert faced every day when he went home and tried to reach a boy who had become unreachable. "I have lost friends over this, saying we're making too big a deal out of this and that it's just kids having fun. Well, it isn't fun. It's a struggle every day," Robert told the judge.

A few months later, in May, I traveled to Gunnison to try to understand what had happened and what it meant. Robert agreed to meet me at a playground on the north side of Gunnison, close to the state prison where he works as a corrections officer and case manager. We sat at a picnic table together, shivering as we talked on an unseasonably cold morning. The night before, the temperature had dipped into the thirties and passing snow squalls had left the mountains dusted white. Robert was stout and soft-spoken, and still wearing his uniform from the prison.

In middle school, his son had been a straight-A student, an enthusiastic football player and wrestler, and always on the move. But a few weeks after the start of his freshman year he'd become inexplicably withdrawn and let his grades slide. By then, Robert's son had endured at least three assaults. "He'd get home from school and go sit in his bedroom," Robert said. "It wasn't even a thought in my mind that something like that could be going on. . . . I know that that happens to boys. But I just thought it would never happen here in Gunnison Valley, and especially to my son."

As an assistant football coach at the high school, Robert knew all the players, and he said he had no idea about the attacks and never would have suspected Brad, a short, compact boy he described as "over-the-top charismatic." He claimed that Brad's family had accused the victims of concocting stories in a jealous plot to oust their athletically gifted son from sports. But Robert believed the boys. Their shame was so visceral, they couldn't have been lying.

"All in all, this has been an experience I would never want to go through again, for sure," Robert told me, speaking slowly, his words measured and careful. "But it's an experience that has helped me understand better, understand that there's stuff like this that goes on and goes unreported for a long time—and especially with boys."

His son had been seeing a therapist, he said, and the darkness had started to lift. He was grateful the Gunnison boys had been able to finally say what had happened to them and start to get the help they needed. He hoped that anyone struggling with what they had been struggling with would have the same chance to be heard, and the same chance to heal.

Juvenile court cases usually unfold out of sight, behind a shield of well-intentioned confidentiality that is meant to protect the privacy of minors—and that also prevents us from hearing stories that would force us to acknowledge the extent to which criminal sexual violence affects the lives of boys and girls.

But in Gunnison, I had a window into the allegations against Brad thanks to a Utah law that allows some public access to the most serious juvenile cases, and thanks to Greg Liefting—the freshman whose willingness to honestly answer questions about being assaulted at football practice led to a broader investigation—and his mother, Misty Cox. Cox described herself as a sexual assault survivor who was horrified by the persistence of Brad's abusive behavior, apparently over a period of years.

She told Greg, over and over, that what happened to him was not his fault and he should not be ashamed.

I met her at her home on a quiet street in Mayfield, Utah, a few miles outside Gunnison, during the last week of the school year, nearly seven months after Greg was assaulted. After class let out for the day, Greg took the bus home and then came sweeping through the kitchen to ask his mom if he could go hang out with friends. It was an unusually chilly 50 degrees outside, but they were planning to go swimming in an irrigation pond, which I thought sounded torturous—and which Greg thought sounded pretty fun. He paused to talk with me briefly, keeping his backpack on and pushing his sandy blond hair out of his face while he recounted the assault. In the moment, he said, he was utterly confused. He could not believe what was happening to him. Afterward, he had gone to practice and tried to shrug it off. I asked him when he realized he'd been sexually assaulted. Not until Officer Wimmer had told him in that windowless room, he said. Until then, he hadn't had a name for it.

His friends pulled up in a truck and he bounded off. He was tired of talking about the assault and tired of thinking about it. "I'm at the point where I just want to get past it," he told me.

Cox offered me a cup of coffee spiced with cinnamon. Small and irreverent, wearing eyelash extensions and a quick grin, she has taken it upon herself to force Gunnison to confront not only Brad's behavior but why it remained hidden for so long.

With Greg's blessing, Cox had spoken to a Salt Lake City television news reporter, an interview that drew statewide attention. Then she sued the school district, South Sanpete, for failing to protect Greg's civil rights, claiming that school officials were aware of previous complaints about Brad's sexual misconduct and did nothing to stop it. The district agreed to settle for a total of $48,000—$30,000 going to Cox's attorneys and $18,000 into a trust fund for Greg.

I don't know whether South Sanpete School District knew of Brad's behavior and shrugged it off, as Cox claims. The district has denied it, and Superintendent Kent Larsen told me that he couldn't speak about the litigation—and didn't have any desire to discuss with a reporter an

issue that had so fractured his community. But Cox's clamoring almost
certainly means more families in this valley now know that boys can be
victims of sexual violence.

Maybe I finally know it, too.

If you had asked me, before I started working on this book, whether
I believed that boys and men could be victims of sexual assault, I would
have said *of course*. If you had asked me whether I bought into the notion
that boys and men always want sex, I might have rolled my eyes: *Um, no*.
But listening to the stories of male victims taught me that I didn't completely believe what I thought I believed. I noticed my own knee-jerk
resistance—especially to the idea that boys could be traumatized by unwanted sexual contact, to the idea that it would *matter* quite as much to
them. Deep down, somewhere under my skin, I was holding on to some
seriously wrongheaded assumptions—ideas so ingrained I did not even
notice them, and that rendered boys as something less than human.

CHAPTER TWO

Boys Will Be Men

Nature, Nurture, and Rethinking Boyhood

My son desperately loves his plastic fire truck—the same truck that his older sister mostly ignored when she was his age. She preferred caring for her stuffed animals, lovingly pretending to tuck them in and put them to sleep. He does none of that, and instead is so intent about wheeling around his fire truck that one grandmother recently gave him a second fire truck. His other grandmother gave him a dump truck, and his aunt gave him a school bus. He's delighted by pretty much anything with wheels.

Some people would look at my son and see a typical boy, born to prefer boyish things. Others would say he learned his preferences from the world around him, including the adults who choose which toys he grows up with. This is, in miniature, the never-ending debate about gender: Are boys born "boyish," or do we make them that way?

You can find data to support either view. Scads of studies show that mothers and fathers shape their children in ways they may not even realize by interacting with sons differently than daughters. We pay more attention to boys' anger and less to their fear; we are less likely to talk with them about how they feel; we treat them as if they are stronger and more physically capable than they really are. Then there's the media, of course. The more television a four-year-old watches, the more likely he is to think that most people believe boys and men are better than girls and women. There is evidence that watching more TV nudges teen boys to tolerate sexual harassment, and that video games featuring busty, scantily clad women nudge them to believe in rape myths.

So it's clear that what boys learn as they grow up matters. A lot.

But the notion that socialization is the *only* thing that matters is not right, either. There *are* some biological differences between the typical boy and the typical girl, though many of these differences are not nearly as large or as clear as they're sometimes made out to be.

Consider a famous experiment that psychologist Edward Tronick conducted in the 1970s, called the "still face" experiment. The study involved pairs of babies and their mothers. The mothers were instructed to first smile and coo at their infants and then to go stone-faced and expressionless, refusing to respond to their babies' appeals for attention. Inevitably, the babies cried and fussed and shrieked, trying to get their mothers to notice them. Eventually the babies gave up, dejected. Video recordings of the tiny boys' and girls' distressed reactions to their unresponsive parents have helped scientists understand the impact of neglect on children. They are hard to watch.

I first learned of the still face experiment from Niobe Way, the developmental psychologist at New York University who has studied male friendships for more than two decades. She sees it as evidence that all people, regardless of gender, are born with an inherent need to connect. That is why she was so bothered when one of the boys in her studies declared: "It might be nice to be a girl, then you wouldn't have to be emotionless." In Way's view, boys and girls are fundamentally alike, but only boys are forced to disown their own desire for emotional intimacy as they grow up.

I called Tronick, now a distinguished professor at the University of Massachusetts–Boston, to ask what he had learned about gender from his classic study. He agreed with Way on one point: he said that the babies' universal distress showed a "primordial" need for connection that is not masculine or feminine but human.

But Tronick sees the sexes as fundamentally different in important ways, a theory that is also supported by the results of the still face experiment. His team found that girls were better at dealing with their stress and self-soothing, while boys became more upset and needed more help to calm down. "Infant boys in my lab were referred to as fussy little things," Tronick said. "They demand more attention from their mothers."

Tronick believes that these differences persist as boys grow up, making it more likely that they will struggle to regulate their own behavior and will need more intensive parenting from their mothers and fathers.

But what does that tell me about my son? Not so much. Just because boys tended to be fussier in Tronick's lab doesn't mean I should expect my son to be fussy—or that I should expect my daughter to be serene. Everyone is born with aptitudes and inclinations, as well as limitations. Whether or not my kid has a penis doesn't predict much of anything useful about what those aptitudes and inclinations and limitations will be.

In fact, on measures ranging from empathy to verbal and spatial skills, differences between the average boy and the average girl tend to be minimal, and the overlap between all boys and all girls is substantial. Knowing a child's sex does not tell us who they're going to be or what they're going to excel in any more than it tells us whom they're going to fall in love with.

We do know, however, that stereotypes and assumptions about boys play an important role in shaping their mental and emotional health, their academic success, and their approach to sex and relationships. We do know that boys who grow up believing there is only one right way to be a man are at greater risk for a whole host of poor outcomes.

Scientists do not talk about nature versus nurture but nature *and* nurture, powerful forces that can't be easily separated from each other. If we want to give our boys the best shot at healthy and happy lives, maybe we should focus on the only thing we have any shot at controlling: what we teach them and how we treat them.

Clearly there is growing interest in rethinking how we teach boys to be boys. You can see it in the media's coverage of masculinity, in the growing number of schools offering programs aimed at giving boys space to talk about the pressures they face, and even in the toy aisle, where industry leaders now see a business case for investing in broadening the definition of "boyish."

There's no telling how long this moment will last, or whether it will transcend consumer culture into deeper changes for men and boys. I was born in the 1970s, when gender-neutral parenting was in vogue. The feminist record *Free to Be . . . You and Me* played on repeat in the living room at our house: Alan Alda and Marlo Thomas sang about William, a little boy who desperately wanted to play with a doll, and the former pro football star Rosey Grier reassured boys that "It's alright to cry." But those messages gave way in the 1980s and 1990s to a popular culture that blanketed boys in action figures and superheroes and implicit warnings to stay away from everything pink and princess. Now the pendulum seems to be swinging again.

Hormones, Brains, and How Parents Treat Boys Differently—Without Even Realizing It

I am wary of the ways in which supposedly essential differences between boys and girls have been used to justify discrimination for generations. But the truth is, biology does shape all of us. My son's devotion to trucks is, I think, something he was born with. He always had his sister's dolls around, and as parents we tried to entice him to play at caring for them. But he was never very interested. I eventually bought a new doll just for him—which he promptly set aside in favor of a toy Metro bus. You can give your son options, but you can't force him to love what he doesn't love.

It turns out that play is one of the clearest ways in which boys and girls differ, and looking at what drives that difference offers a glimpse into all the forces that make a boy "boyish"—including both biology and socialization.

Studies suggest that infants begin to show divergent toy preferences when they're as young as nine months, before they are even aware of gender. Boys are more likely to prefer trucks and balls, and they'd rather play with other boys than with girls, while girls are more likely to choose dolls and anything pink. As they grow up, boys are also more active and do more rough-and-tumble play.

These differences seem to be rooted at least partly in the testosterone that washes through boys' bodies before they are born, while they are still in the womb. That wave of testosterone, which masculinizes their genitals, also seems to encourage "boyish" play.

Researchers have come to understand the effects of prenatal testosterone by studying girls who have a rare condition known as congenital adrenal hyperplasia, or CAH. In utero, these girls' bodies make much more testosterone than usual. Sometimes they have an enlarged clitoris or other "intersex" characteristics. After they're born, they can be treated with hormones, correcting the imbalance. But their exposure to so much testosterone in the womb sets up an experiment. By comparing CAH girls to their sisters, who were not exposed to the same high levels of prenatal testosterone, scientists can try to tease out some of the effects of nature versus nurture.

They have found that when CAH girls are presented with toys to choose from, they are more likely to choose "masculine" options—cars, trucks, and Lincoln logs—than their sisters who didn't get the same big dose of prenatal testosterone. They are also modestly more aggressive, and some studies suggest that they may also have higher activity levels. These studies and others tell us that prenatal exposure to testosterone does seem to shape some of kids' interests and behaviors.

So hormonal differences may in part explain "boyish" and "girlish" behavior. But experts say the raging testosterone that people love to blame for boys' behavior is overhyped, particularly when it comes to what it's famous (or infamous) for: allegedly fueling uncontrollable urges for sex in boys and men.

Just as prenatal testosterone appears to give little boys a bias toward trucks over dolls that is then encouraged and exaggerated by parents, peers, marketing, and media, scientists believe that the flood of testosterone at puberty is just one factor that shapes a boy's sex drive.

Developmental psychologist Carolyn T. Halpern tracked about one hundred seventh- and eighth-grade boys over the course of three years, regularly testing the testosterone levels in their saliva and interviewing them about their sexual thoughts and activities. She found that having higher testosterone levels didn't mean a boy was more likely to think about sex, and was only weakly associated with being more sexually active.

In the same research project, she also discovered something about the power of social expectations. The boys who were most sexually active were those with two factors that may have pushed them toward sex. One was biological—high levels of testosterone. And one was social—they didn't go to church regularly. The boys who were least sexually active had two factors discouraging sex: low testosterone and regular church attendance. Neither result was particularly surprising.

But what I found fascinating was that churchgoing seemed to help control the supposedly uncontrollable hormonal urges. High-testosterone boys who went to church were *less* likely to be sexually active than low-testosterone boys who didn't go to church. Whether because church leaders delivered strong messages about abstaining from sex, or because church provided boys with a sense of identity, or for some other reason, that connection to a religious community was a powerful influence that had nothing to do with DNA. Nature mattered, but so did nurture.

Halpern said she is tired of arguments that either biology or culture plays a bigger role in shaping our attitudes, our behavior, and our lives. It's both, in concert. "People really do overplay the role of hormones," she said.

What I take from this research is that we should resist the temptation to blame boys' bad or wild behavior on testosterone. When we do blame raging hormones, even jokingly, what we are saying is that boys are biologically predisposed to be out of control—that because of their gender, their genitalia, they just can't help it. That's an attitude that sells boys short, and that relieves the rest of us of our responsibility to teach them to do better.

If boy hormones matter less than we might think in determining "boyishness," then boy brains hardly matter at all. That's the argument that neuroscientist Lise Eliot laid out in *Pink Brain, Blue Brain*, her 2009 book that pushes back against the notion that men are wired in fundamentally different ways than women.

Eliot has examined hundreds of studies involving millions of images of brains, and she has found that there are indeed some average differences between the sexes. Males have slightly larger brains, corresponding to their larger bodies, for example. But Eliot sees no evidence that the differences we see in men's and women's behavior can be explained by what we currently know about their brains. She sees no evidence that men and women use different circuits in their brains to process the world and the information in it, including language, math, and emotion. Male and female brains, she argues, are no more different than male and female kidneys—organs that are so similar that they can be successfully transplanted between the sexes.

Eliot is a professor at Chicago Medical School, part of the Rosalind Franklin University of Medicine and Science. I met her at her childhood home, near Lake Michigan north of Chicago, where she was helping her elderly parents with a few tasks. Sitting in the living room, Eliot explained how her curiosity about the differences she noticed among her own children—two boys, one girl—led her to dig into the science of sex differences. What she learned, she said, was that differences between male and female infants start out small and are then amplified by a world in which kids can clearly see what is expected of them based upon their genitalia, from toys and play to verbal and math skills to empathy and competitiveness.

"We dunk these kids in this two-gendered culture, and we do everything possible to emphasize it," she said.

Even in realms where there are relatively significant differences between the average boy and the average girl, there is still plenty of overlap, Eliot said. Take physical aggression, which, along with toy preferences, is one of the larger sex differences that scientists have identified. The average male is more physically aggressive than two-thirds of females, Eliot said—but that means one-third of boys are *less* aggressive than the average girl. So a baby boy *might* be born with a more aggressive predisposition than his sister—or he might not.

Similarly, girls and women show slightly greater empathy on average, but as the still face experiment illustrates, all children crave deep connections with other people—and there are plenty of men who are more empathetic than the average woman. Science has shown the same about a long list of other traits usually associated with one gender or the other, including nurturing, competitiveness, and risk-taking. There are differences between the sexes, but they are generally small, and the overlap between girls and boys is substantial.

Eliot is an expert in neuroplasticity, or the capacity of brains to change depending on environment and experience. In her book, she writes that under the "hot sun of our highly gendered society," our plastic brains get better at the skills they get more practice at—often, whatever the world tells us we're supposed to be good at, as boys or girls—while other skills atrophy. If our brains are hardwired for anything, she argues, it's to adapt to our surroundings.

As babies, we are born with the potential to learn any language on earth, but we only learn the languages to which we are actually exposed. We are born with the potential to see, but it takes months of visual experience to wire the brain circuits that give us full visual perception. Brains can also learn both "masculine" and "feminine" skills, Eliot argues, if we give them a chance.

As a parent, this means that I have to realize I can't predict who my son is going to be—what his disposition will be, what he will like to do and be good at—based solely on his gender. You're thinking, *Of course you can't.* But this is what so many of us do, without even realizing it. In ways we may not even recognize, Eliot argues, we are prodding boys and girls down different paths, helping to create many of the differences we see between adult men and women.

Boys learn to tough it out from the obvious messages they get from the media, and from the teasing and policing of their friends, but also from their parents, who—often unwittingly—respond to boys and girls in subtly distinct ways. Moms and dads are more likely to rate newborn boys—even those less than twenty-four hours old—as strong and hardy, and newborn girls as softer and littler, even when there are no measurable physical differences. With toddlers, parents tend to help girls who ask for help, but they rebuff boys, perhaps teaching boys to eventually stop asking.

Parents also see boys as tougher and more capable of navigating the world on their own. In one remarkable study, mothers were asked to predict how steep a ramp their eleven-month-old babies would be able to crawl down. Compared to mothers of girls, mothers of boys predicted that their babies would be able to crawl down much steeper slopes—but they were mistaken. There was no difference in the boys' and girls' ability to crawl down steep inclines, or in their willingness to take risks. The researchers concluded that the difference in mothers' beliefs about their children's abilities was so stark that they "expect their girls to fail when the probability of success is 100 percent and expect their boys to succeed when the probability of success is 0 percent."

We have limited girls throughout history by underestimating their abilities. But this study makes me think about the ramifications of overestimating what boys are capable of. What happens when we expect boys to succeed even when there is zero chance that they will? What happens when we fail to see that they need help?

Then there's emotion and entitlement. Parents tend to subtly discourage boys from expressing pain and toward using anger as a strategy to get what they want. Fathers of young children are more likely to be attentive to girls' sadness and anxiety and to boys' anger, for example, whereas mothers tend to give in to the demands of angry sons more often than those of angry daughters. In one study of toddlers playing in a group, mothers intervened when their child disagreed with another child over a toy. For the most part, moms told their own kid to give up the toy and let the other kid play with it—but moms of boys were more likely to tell their own kid to stand his ground. Without seeing that we are doing it, we may be teaching our sons that they have a right to get and do whatever they want.

These are just a few of the ways that we tell boys and girls that they are fundamentally different beings, bound by fundamentally different rules.

It's not hard to see how simple assumptions about the essential nature of boys can snowball. Boys who play with trucks and guns tend to play with other boys who play with trucks and guns, enforcing gender stereotypes about what boys do and don't do, and reinforcing their parents' assumptions about what they like and how they behave. Boys who are rewarded when they're angry (and ignored when they're sad) tend to learn to express anger (and hide sadness). And boys who hear over and over that men always want sex learn to behave as if they always want sex.

My task as a mom, I figure, is partly to examine my own language and behavior for these hidden assumptions and then work to undo them, whether by making a conscious effort to talk to my son about feelings, asking him if he needs help, or organizing coed play dates. But I also need to call out these hidden assumptions for my children, so that they can start to see and challenge the messages they are getting about an allegedly wide gulf between girls and boys.

When my daughter, Juniper, was the age my son is now, about two and a half, she looked out the window of our home one day, watching a construction crew at the house across the street. She asked why there was a woman on the porch roof. My husband explained that the woman was one of the workers, and—to my horror—Juniper said that couldn't be true. "Women can't be construction workers," she said. That was absolutely logical, in her experience. She had seen a lot of construction workers in her short life, and they had always been men.

Juniper's declaration gave me a glimpse of how early children start to see gender, and how efficiently they translate their observations of the world as it *is* into strict rules about how it *must always be*. (If I only see men on construction sites, then women don't belong. If I only see girls wearing pink, then boys cannot. And, later on: If I only see men have orgasms in porn, then women's pleasure doesn't really matter.) If we don't want our children to be trapped by the social rules they perceive for boys versus girls, then we have to talk with them a lot about the silliness of those rules—and we have to flout them ourselves.

How to Help Boys Succeed

Inside a classroom at the Sheridan School, in one of the most expensive neighborhoods of Washington, D.C., a couple dozen middle school students munched on salad, pita bread, and hummus and considered the way the world tells them how to be.

It was the first joint meeting, in this progressive private K–8 school, of two occasionally warring factions: the school's female empowerment club, which girls founded to fight sexism, and a boys' group. Established originally as a group with no agenda other than to complain about girls, the boys' group had become, under the guidance of counselor Phyllis Fagell, a rare place for preteen guys to talk about the pressures they face.

After many months of separate meetings, the two groups were ready to find common ground. Fagell decided to launch this attempt at integration with an activity. As she read a list of adjectives rapid-fire, the boys and girls called out whether the words belonged or did not belong in the Man Box. This was the cage of stereotypes about how boys and men are supposed to act and what they're supposed to aspire to: making money, suppressing emotion, taking control, getting sex, and not being girly or gay.

"Dominating?" Yes.

"Careless?" Yes.

"Angry?" Yes.

"Wishful?" No.

Their answers came almost in unison, as Fagell called out words like "outspoken," "competitive," "tough," "possessive," "ambitious," "disruptive," and "obnoxious"—all added to the Man Box.

The words that did not go in, unsurprisingly, ended up being unanimous choices for the Woman Box.

"Delicate," "soft," "dreamy," "shy," "anxious," "insecure." The kids knew reflexively, without thinking, which words went where.

"Isn't it amazing how much you internalize?" Fagell asked. She wanted them to see how everyone in the room is always contending with expectations. She asked the students to write five adjectives describing themselves on pink and yellow sticky notes, and then she read them out loud. Who wrote *strong, independent, opinionated, smart,* and *competitive*? A girl. *Friendly, generous, awkward, creative,* and *moody*? A boy. Real people don't fit into stereotypical categories, Fagell wanted them to see.

"When we try to act like we're supposed to act," a bespectacled girl said earnestly, "we're really limiting ourselves."

Sheridan exists inside a left-leaning, affluent, urban bubble, and the conversation happening here is certainly not happening everywhere in America. But in the course of my research for this book, I found that versions of Fagell's gender box activity—all descendants of the "Act Like a Man Box," a notion first articulated decades ago by California activist Paul Kivel, who organized men to prevent violence against women—have sprouted up in a wide range of places. In public schools and private, in small-town Ohio and rural New England, in Chicago and in low-income parts of D.C., home to mostly Black and Latino boys, a few miles and a world away from the Sheridan School. In these pockets around the country, children are being guided to recognize and challenge the gender norms that shape not only girls' lives but boys' lives, too.

Children can still see the walls of the Woman Box, but they also know those walls are thin. Over the last half century, feminist activists have campaigned to wipe away stereotypes about women, replacing old rules about who they are supposed to be with acknowledgment that they can do and be anything they want. Yes, men still disproportionately hold corporate and political power. Yes, girls still grow up feeling pressure to meet impossible standards of beauty, to be sexy without being slutty, to be passive and willing and nice, to avoid appearing too smart or too ambitious. But girls are also growing up in a world where there are many ways to be a woman and many different examples of "feminine."

As the 2019 *Sports Illustrated* Sportsperson of the Year, soccer star Megan Rapinoe wielded a sledgehammer on the magazine's cover—while wearing a flowing Valentino gown. Supreme Court Justice Ruth Bader Ginsburg was brilliant in court and terrible in the kitchen; her husband, Marty, also a successful lawyer, was the chef who fed their family. Beyoncé grew from a teen R&B star into one of the world's most powerful women, a totemic figure in art, music, and culture. Engineer and computer scientist Katie Bouman played a key role on the team that captured the first-ever image of a black hole.

The Man Box, on the other hand, has proved sturdy.

Efforts to dismantle it have faced fierce resistance from those who argue that broadening our sons' choices about who they might be, and how they can be, is akin to ignoring differences between the sexes and trying to turn men into weaklings.

In January 2019, the American Psychological Association (APA) publicly promoted new guidelines for working with men and boys. The guidelines emphasized the importance of clinicians understanding the particular pressures that men feel to live up to traditional masculine norms, and the mental and physical health threats that men suffer as a result. The backlash was immediate on Fox News ("The Left's War on Men," read a chyron during a Laura Ingraham segment that mentioned the guidelines as part of an allegedly antimale movement among Democrats) and in online communities that saw the report as an attack on men.

Ronald F. Levant, a psychologist at the University of Akron who helped develop the guidelines and was frequently quoted in news coverage, told me he was doxxed and threatened. He installed a home security system on the advice of university police. One particularly offensive email that he received wrongly accused the APA of promoting pedophilia as normal and masculinity as abnormal, and called for the National Guard—white guardsmen only, though—to round up Levant and his ilk in "windowless vans."

"Are you a filthy juden and a faggot or just a filthy juden?" the email, full of white supremacist language, read. "You filthy cocksuckers! Inverting right to being wrong and wrong and disgusting to being right!"

That same month, the razor company Gillette released an ad asking men to call out sexual harassment, bullying, and misogyny. The ad was titled "We Believe: The Best Men Can Be," an updated twist on its classic slogan, "The Best a Man Can Get." It went viral, accumulating eight hundred thousand likes on YouTube and twice as many dislikes.

A slew of think pieces followed, many arguing that these two events were a sign of a growing assault on masculinity—and a flat-earth denial of the supposed fact that men are essentially different from women. "Let boys be damn boys & men be damn men—and stop this damaging war on masculinity," British television broadcaster Piers Morgan tweeted, peeved about the razor ad.

A similar fight erupted over a far less weighty issue in 2015, when

Target announced that it would do away with gender-specific labels for boys' and girls' toys. The notion that corporate America would try to blur the distinct pink and blue worlds of kids' toys struck a nerve with people who felt it violated a deeper natural order, and they promised to boycott the company's stores. "God's wrath and judgement is coming . . . There will be a whole lot of people who will be very sorry they did this to our country," one woman wrote on Target's Facebook page. "I'll shop where they don't cave to the PC Nazis," another commenter wrote. "What in the world is wrong with a boy being a boy and a girl being a girl?"

The outrage underlines deep convictions in some quarters that boys are the way they are because they are born that way—and to encourage them to play with dolls, or to ask them to call out sexual harassment, is somehow contrary to and dismissive of their fundamental boy nature.

At stake in this debate is so much more than the toys boys play with. The stereotypes and pressures that boys face threaten their physical and mental health, their ability to navigate their inner lives and interpersonal relationships, and even their academic success.

Consider how boys are doing in school. The average boy lags behind the average girl in reading. Boys are more likely to drop out of high school and less likely to enroll in college. Journalists and activists have been calling attention to this "boy crisis" in education for two decades, attributing it to teaching styles ill-suited to boys and more generally to the assumption, among feminists and educators, that the students most in need of attention and help are girls.

But research suggests that boys are limited in part by the commonly held belief that girls are better than boys at reading. In classrooms, where many children firmly believe that stereotype, boys have less confidence in their own reading skills, less motivation to read, and weaker reading skills, according to a longitudinal study that tracked more than fifteen hundred students as they moved from the fifth to sixth grades. A stereotype about boys in this case became a prophecy.

The results of that study show that to help our sons succeed, we have to wage a war on the assumption that boys are naturally less skilled at reading. While we are at it, let's take on and destroy the rest of the negative assumptions that people carry around about boys: they're violent, dirty, impolite, unfeeling, disengaged. These are damaging, destructive generalizations that have a real impact on our sons. George W. Bush famously spoke of the "soft bigotry of low expectations" in education, the pernicious belief among adults that poor children and children of color aren't capable of academic excellence. Well, there is a bigotry of low expectations when it comes to boys, too. It is not boys who are flawed and in urgent need of fixing; it is our ideas about boys.

The Man Box and Men's Health

The boys in our lives are constantly making decisions about whether they're going to conform to stereotypes about how boys are supposed to be or not be. This is not just some theory. This is also what boys say, when you ask them what it feels like to grow up male in America.

"I was told a lot to not cry and suck it up, by my mom, my brother, pretty much my whole family," twenty-year-old Ezekiel Clare told me by phone, after we first met at a conference in downtown Washington, D.C. Ezekiel had been invited to the conference to speak about a high school mentorship program that had opened doors to him as a teenager in New York City.

Slight and self-possessed, Ezekiel grew up in Harlem sensing he was different from other boys. When he was little, he liked animals and bright colors and playing with girls, and he didn't like sports or roughhousing. As he got older, he found a niche in art, drawing, and piano. He wore his hair long, in dreadlocks. He was always talking back to bullies. "People would call me gay for whatever reason," he said. "There was never really a reason."

Ezekiel was not gay, but he wasn't "boy" enough, according to the kids who teased him. He also wasn't "Black enough" for the other boys, who taunted him by calling him white. He guessed it had something to do with the kind of music he listened to, the Beatles and the Dave Matthews Band. "At my school, I was this white, gay kid with locks. I was like, this doesn't make sense." If the box white boys must fit inside to be a "real man" is small, then the box for Black boys can be even smaller.

Now Ezekiel is studying film at SUNY-Purchase, where he has a girlfriend and a group of friends who get him—and space, he said, to be himself. He is among the many boys who have found ways to resist messages about how they are supposed to be on the way to figuring out who they are.

But there are also plenty of American boys who still subscribe to old-fashioned ideas about manhood, according to a 2017 survey of young men aged eighteen to thirty by the international nonprofit Promundo. One-quarter believe that "men should use violence to get respect." One-quarter believe that gay men are not "real men." An even greater number—about four in ten—believe "men should figure out their personal problems on their own without asking for help," and that men who get pushed around and don't fight back are "weak." Six in ten believe "guys should act strong even if they feel scared or nervous inside."

Buying into gender stereotypes comes with some advantages. The Promundo survey found that guys who live inside the Man Box—who say they are hypersexual and homophobic and believe they should be aggressive, in control, and self-sufficient—are significantly more likely than other men to say that they feel satisfied with life overall. Which makes some sense: it is comfortable, in many ways, to live in sync with the world's expectations.

But a growing pile of research in psychology, sociology, and public health suggests that boys and men who believe that they must live up to these stereotypes—especially those who believe that men should control and dominate women—are more likely to sexually harass women, more likely to commit sexual violence, and more likely to physically or sexually abuse their dating partners.

In one recent study, a research team from Georgia State University and the CDC asked 208 men in their twenties and thirties how often they had coerced a partner into sex against their will, whether through insistence or physical force.

Then they measured how vehemently men felt that they should avoid girlishness. Using an approach developed and refined over many years by Ronald Levant, the psychologist who helped develop the controversial APA guidelines, they asked the respondents to rate how much they believed in eight basic gender stereotypes:

> Boys should play with action figures not dolls.
> Men should watch football games instead of soap operas.
> Boys should prefer to play with trucks rather than dolls.
> A man should prefer watching action movies to reading romantic novels.
> Men should not wear make-up, cover-up, or bronzer.
> Boys should not throw baseballs like girls.
> Men should not be interested in talk shows such as "Oprah."
> A man should avoid holding his wife's purse at all times.

These statements were proxies for how rigidly men defined masculinity—how much shame and wrongness they saw in edging into girlishness. The men who believed staunchly in these statements were more likely to be freaked out by the idea that they might have to submit to a woman's authority or that someone might see them as feminine—and also more likely to be sexually aggressive. Their aggression was a way of showing their dominance over women, researchers concluded.

This doesn't mean that boys who prefer trucks and action figures to dolls and tea sets are going to grow up to be rapists—far from it! But it does suggest that if we don't take care to help boys see that the gender stereotypes beamed at them from birth are stereotypes, and not ironclad rules—that they *can* love trucks, but need not feel that they *must* love trucks, that they can be stoic and competitive sometimes and other times upset and in need of help—then we miss an important opportunity to teach them that there is more than one acceptable way to be a man. And we reinforce a dangerous disdain for girls, women, and femininity.

When I think of my own son, I don't care whether he ever takes to the baby doll we finally gave him. But I do care deeply about whether he feels like he has the option to play with that doll, if he wants to. I care that he understands that there's nothing disgusting about girls or girlishness, and in fact plenty to admire. And I care that he has the space, as he grows up, to be comfortably himself—whoever that turns out to be.

The pressure boys feel to be appropriately "masculine" obviously undermines the health and safety of girls. But what I found eye-opening was the evidence that it can be equally destructive for *boys*. Guys inside the box are more likely than other guys to report symptoms of depression, according to the Promundo survey, and twice as likely to say that they'd thought about killing themselves within the previous two weeks. They were more likely to binge-drink and two or three times as likely to get into traffic accidents. They were four times as likely to say that they had been the victim of physical bullying and six times as likely to say they had physically bullied someone else.

"There is this framing about masculinity as being harmful for women, but . . . it's also really important to talk about masculinity in terms of what it does to limit men and boys," said Holly Shakya, an associate professor and public health researcher at the University of California–San Diego.

Perhaps the most notable way in which boys pay a price for buying into traditional masculine norms is that their health suffers. This showed up during the COVID-19 pandemic as a refusal to wear masks. One large-scale study found that people wedded to sexist beliefs—those who said they were uncomfortable having a female boss, for example, and were unwilling to believe women are able to think as logically as men—were less likely than nonsexist people to be concerned about the virus. They were also less likely to wear masks and take other precautions against infection—and they were much *more* likely to report falling ill with the virus. Only 3 percent of the least-sexist survey respondents had contracted the novel coronavirus, compared to 28 percent of the most-sexist.

Experts believe that the pressure men face to act like men is literally toxic, pushing them toward dangerous behavior and away from professional help—and putting their lives at risk.

Compared to women, men in the United States are more likely to be victims of violent crime. They are also more likely to die from heart disease, cancer, and ten of the other thirteen leading causes of death. Men are four times more likely than women to kill themselves and four times more likely to be killed by someone else. Men die earlier than women across the globe; in the United States, their life expectancy is five years shorter.

I did not recognize these remarkable disparities between the sexes until I became the mother of a boy. Now they worry me deeply. And while I can't control everything that affects my son's mental and physical health—I can't control the economic forces, for example, that have displaced so many jobs and unmoored so many men from their sense of self—there are two important things I can do now. I can rethink my own stereotypes about boys, and I can help my son broaden his ideas about what it means to be a man.

Shakya led a team of researchers who analyzed data from nearly twenty thousand people who were tracked over two decades starting in the mid-1990s, when they were adolescents, through 2009, when they were in their twenties and thirties. Those who behaved in more stereotypically "masculine" ways as teenagers were more likely to report depressive symptoms in adulthood, and to smoke, drink, and use drugs. According to a different analysis of seventy-four studies involving nearly twenty thousand men, guys who believe they must be self-reliant, have sex with lots of women, and exercise power over women are also more likely than their peers to struggle with mental health and less likely to seek psychological help.

California psychotherapist Will Courtenay, a pioneer in the field of men's health, argues that these disparities can be traced not only to ideas about masculinity that shape the behavior of boys and men but to the assumptions the rest of us make about the boys and men in our lives—especially the assumption that they don't need help. In his 2011 book *Dying to Be Men*, Courtenay points to a study showing that while early detection is important for treating both breast cancer and testicular cancer, 86 percent of doctors instruct girls and women in how to examine their breasts for signs of cancer, compared to just 29 percent who tell boys and men how to examine their testicles. Consciously or not, we all help build the walls of the Man Box.

Fostering Boys' Emotional Literacy

Judy Y. Chu, a developmental psychologist who teaches at Stanford University, spent two years observing and interviewing a group of four- and five-year-old boys. In *When Boys Become Boys* (2014), she described watching her subjects as they learned to hide their real selves in order to fit in and be accepted as one of the boys at school.

The main requirement for acceptance: don't be like a girl.

The don't-be-a-girl rule seeped into every part of boys' lives, from the toys they allowed themselves to play with to the affection they allowed themselves to show parents when they knew other kids were watching (at best, a grudging hug). The boys were able to articulate, even at such a young age, that they had to sacrifice what they really wanted in order to fit in with their friends. One little boy told Chu that he wanted to be friends with girls in the class—that he liked them but had to pretend he didn't, or he'd get kicked off the "Mean Team," a group of boys led by Mike, the most powerful and popular boy in the class. Another boy confessed that he didn't like being mean to other people, but he had no choice but to do whatever Mike told him. He understood if he didn't, he'd be "fired" from the team—kicked out of the sense of belonging he so craved. "There's no way to get off the Mean Team," he lamented.

Chu argues that boys don't lose their emotional acuity or a desire to connect deeply with other people, but they cover those things up in the swirl of peer pressure that begins as early as preschool. Nevertheless, they are often willing to reveal their real feelings within the safety of a close relationship where they can be themselves. This is the job of parents and other adults in a boy's life, Chu says: to give him a space where he can stay connected to his own feelings and interests and abilities. We know, from surveys of thousands of adolescents, that this is one of the most important things we can give boys. Having a close confidant—whether a parent, a coach, or a friend—is a powerful shield for teenagers against, for example, the risk of violence, substance abuse, and depression.

A young man named William taught me something both about the ways we fail to teach boys how to navigate their feelings and about the protective power of a caring relationship with a parent.

I met him when he was in his early twenties, working his first job out of college in Washington, D.C. A handsome, clean-cut guy who dressed in the preppie office uniform of the nation's capital, he told me that a mental health crisis in college had forced him to revise his ideas about what it means to be a man, what it means to be strong, and what it means to be successful. He was trying to unlearn some of the lessons he had learned as a boy. He was getting somewhere, he said. But it was not easy.

He had grown up wanting nothing more than to please his parents, and he worked hard to meet their high expectations. He was particularly desperate for approval from his father, a man who, in refusing to cry or ever say "I love you," efficiently delivered the message that displays of emotions were not acceptable for him or for his sons.

Gifted and ambitious, William did well in school and on the soccer field. But he was hobbled by an uncontrollable anger that fueled violent, throwing-things tantrums, episodes that gripped him in a way that he found frightening. Looking back, he sees a child who hadn't learned any other way to deal with anxiety, frustration, or disappointment. "Very small sparks sent me into a tirade," he told me. "I would just be unhinged."

Obviously, William was born into a body, with predispositions embedded in his DNA. But he was also born into a family and a society that told him who he should be. He felt pressure to succeed on their terms, he said. And he had no idea how to deal with the well of emotions he felt when he failed.

In college, he pledged a fraternity in search of friends and belonging—and after a period of hazing, he felt he had found both. But then his grandmother, with whom he was very close, died just before Christmas, and he didn't know what to do with the intense grief that followed. When he returned to campus on New Year's Eve, he didn't know how to tell his friends that he was sad. He couldn't even say that his grandmother was gone. So he just drank—a lot. And kept drinking. One night at a bar, he presented a fake ID that got him a citation. Shame overwhelmed him, and on the way home, when he passed a tall building, he decided he should jump.

When I think about how boys become boys, I think of how much William wished he could understand what was going on inside himself, how badly he wanted to connect with other people—and how ill-equipped he felt to do either.

He was lucky on the night he contemplated suicide. There was someone he could call: his mother, with whom he was close. And there was also a police officer nearby. William told the officer that he needed help—an option he may not have had if he were not confident that the officer would see his clothes and fair skin and guard his safety instead of treat him as a threat. The cops got him to a hospital.

He stayed for a week. He learned that the word for what he was feeling was depression. And that one of the antidotes was coming to terms with his feelings—as well as authentic, vulnerable connection to other human beings.

He went to therapy and joined a grief group, where it was safe to admit he was sad and sometimes felt lost. He went to youth ministry every week, and it too offered a haven where he could drop his mask and share how he was really doing. He found relief in those times and places where he could finally be honest about the ways he struggled.

As he told me his story, over the din of a busy café in downtown Washington, his face flushed and his eyes grew teary. He told me he keeps a journal now, to stay in touch with how he's feeling, to stay healthy. He finds relief there, and he knows it is good for him. But he doesn't admit this to many friends. He still finds himself fearing, sometimes, that this work of trying to understand his inner life is unbecoming, somehow. An unmanly way to spend his time.

How do we show boys that building emotional literacy and connections with other people are not unmanly pursuits but essential human skills? Teenage boys told me they're tired of being lectured at by adults who say that they need to be more vulnerable. Chu, the psychologist who has studied younger boys, says what is not constructive is to swap out one list of traits that we expect boys to have (stoic, strong, competitive) for another (emotional, sensitive, and compassionate). Boys can be all of the above and more. There are plenty of stereotypical masculine qualities that are positive, that we have been pushing girls to adopt for half a century.

The problem is not when boys act "boyish" but when they bury how they feel and what they want because of powerful social rules that dictate how they are supposed to be. My goal, as a mom, is not to force my son to be more vulnerable or less "masculine." It's not to tell him how he must be but to make sure he is not shamed out of being himself.

Fred Rogers had it right, closing episodes of *Mister Roger's Neighborhood* with a reminder to his young audience that each of them was unique, and he cared for all of them. "There's no person in the whole world like you, and I like you just the way you are," he told the children who looked up to him.

"It's so simple," Chu said. "But we haven't really managed to accomplish it."

How Fathers Build the Man Box—or Tear It Down

Today, boys face calls to challenge traditional ideas about masculinity, but that's not something they can do by themselves. We have all had a hand in pushing boys to stay inside the box—including girls and women, who send powerful messages about what boys and men must do (or refrain from doing).

Take the way *Good Morning America* host Lara Spencer made fun of Prince George—the six-year-old son of Prince William and Kate Middleton, the Duke and Duchess of Cambridge—when reports surfaced that he liked ballet. "We'll see how long that lasts," Spencer chuckled. She later apologized, but she couldn't take back her reflexive, dismissive laughter. It said more than words about the stubborn stereotypes boys still face.

Seared into my own memory is a little boy I had a crush on in fourth grade, waving goodbye to me as he stepped off the school bus. He had sandy brown hair and a gap-toothed smile, and he was slight and kind, and the other kids teased him mercilessly, calling him a "girl." I don't recall joining in, but I know that I never stood up for him.

But if we all have a part in deciding whether to fortify or tear down the Man Box, dads seem to have an outsized role. And even when dads wholeheartedly believe that men and boys should be able to buck stereotypes, they can feel torn when it comes to deciding how to parent their own sons. Often, fathers' desire to support their boys runs up against a desire to protect them from cruelty in a world that doesn't show much tolerance for gender-nonconforming boys.

Stephen Hoffman, a fifty-year-old podcast producer, lives in California now. But he grew up in 1980s Chicago, where the rules were clear: you could not be gay or feminine, and you had to be tough and strong and willing to fight. Hoffman recalled standing up once for an effeminate boy who was being bullied during class, and a withering retort from a girl who questioned whether Hoffman was standing up for the boy because he himself was gay. "I was humiliated. I thought I was doing the right thing, but I felt terrible about it," he said. "I don't want my son to feel that way. I don't want him to be singled out."

He said his eight-year-old son had recently asked to go to the mall because he had seen a boy doll at the American Girl store, and he hadn't been able to stop thinking about it. Hoffman said he knows there's nothing wrong with boys having dolls—he truly believes that. But still, it felt "weird" being in that store with his son. He said the weirdness probably comes in part from his own desire to measure up, to be masculine enough. But it also comes from his desire to protect his son from a world that Hoffman believes still has very clear rules about what's appropriate for boys— and those rules don't allow for playing with American Girl dolls.

"I want my son to be as free as he wants to be and be exactly who he wants to be without having to worry about judgments from other people. But I'm desperately and deeply afraid of those judgments and what it could do to him," Hoffman said.

Despite his fears, this very openness could help his son grow up to be a happier, healthier man, less likely to scorn "girly" things or feel shamed into practicing a certain sort of masculinity, better equipped to explore a broad range of passions and pursuits.

Hoffman's fears are common among parents of boys. In interviews with dozens of parents of preschoolers, the sociologist Emily Kane found that moms and dads wanted to support their boys in exploring activities and feelings beyond those that have been traditionally considered masculine—but only up to a point. They believed in encouraging empathy among boys, and felt it was acceptable for boys to practice domestic skills like cooking and caregiving. But parents—and fathers in particular—were much less willing to accept more decidedly "feminine" behavior, like crying or painting fingernails. They saw a baby doll as appropriate for boys to play with, because they saw the value in building skills for future fatherhood. But a Barbie doll? No way.

Some parents said they wanted their son to act in conventionally masculine ways so they would fit in and not have to deal with teasing or social rejection. But some fathers admitted that they policed their sons' behavior to bolster their own sense of masculinity.

"I don't want him to be a little 'quiffy' thing, you know," the father of a five-year-old with "girly" interests told researchers.

The interviewer asked: "Is it a reflection on you as a parent, do you think?"

He replied: "As a male parent, yeah, I honestly do."

Parents who spoke to Kane weren't concerned that their daughters' tomboyish behavior meant they were lesbians. If anything, they were proud of the way their girls had broken free of gender stereotypes. But many, especially fathers, drew connections between boys' interests and activities and their sexual orientation, and worried that boys who want to take ballet are going to grow up to be gay. They felt responsible for steering their sons in what they saw as a more "masculine" direction.

One father, an upper-middle-class straight white man, told Kane's team that if his five-year-old son turned out to be gay, "I would probably see that as a failure as a dad . . . because I'm raising him to be a boy, a man."

His answer is a reminder of the pressure that some fathers still feel to raise boys who are heterosexual, and who conform to a certain idea about what it means to be masculine. But other fathers—including some with huge public platforms—are moving out of their comfort zones to embrace their sons as they are.

When Magic Johnson's teenage son came out as gay in 2013, the basketball legend warned him that there would be people who would judge him, who would make his life harder. "I wanted to prepare him," Johnson said four years later, "and let him know that I would always support him." Since then, Johnson has become an enthusiastic public supporter of his son, EJ, a reality television show and social media influencer known for a fashion sense unconstrained by gender—leather miniskirts, gowns with plunging necklines, and dramatic eye makeup.

We have no evidence that allowing boys to pursue interests traditionally considered "feminine" makes them more likely to be gay. But it's a belief that just won't die. Rebecca Melsky has seen this dynamic in action as cofounder of Princess Awesome, a clothing company that makes dresses for girls emblazoned with trucks, airplanes, and dinosaurs. When Melsky and her friend and business partner Eva St. Clair launched the company in 2013, they got very little negative feedback. People understood, appreciated, even loved the idea that girls should not be limited to "girly" tropes.

Then Princess Awesome started bringing in a million dollars a year, and the pair decided to launch a complementary line of clothing for boys, dubbed Boy Wonder. People were not so willing to accept that boys should not be limited to "boyish" clothes. Press coverage of Boy Wonder's inaugural line—featuring shirts with cats and unicorns and pants with pink flamingoes—drew vitriol that Melsky described as homophobic, transphobic, and misogynistic. "This is child abuse," one person told them through a survey on their website. On Facebook, others decried the "pussification of men," the "little fags we are raising," and the "little pansy-asses in the making."

My husband and I can't protect our son from the judgments of strangers, but we can make sure he knows that he is safe and loved at home no matter what. And we can make sure that the refrain he hears from us is that boys can be and do and wear anything they want—just like girls.

Why Your Own Relationship Matters

Angel Duran, a nineteen-year-old native of east Los Angeles who now studies at Humboldt State University, told me what it felt like to be on the receiving end of fatherly disapproval as he was growing up. "Growing up, my dad used to always tell me, you can't cry because you're a guy," he said.

Angel liked to dance, but his dad shut that down. Angel played football, even though he didn't like football, because he wanted to live up to his father's expectations. "I always wanted to make him proud," Angel said.

It was only after a crisis—when his father became physically abusive, and Angel and his mother moved out—that Angel could see how his father's expectations weren't serving him well. "I tried so hard to fit into the stereotypes he had that I kind of lost who I was," he said.

His father, Johnny Duran, told me he'd grown up gang-banging in Los Angeles, the oldest of seven kids in his family, in charge of protecting everyone. He wanted something different for Angel, but the only way he knew how to love his son was to show him how to be tough and take care of himself. "I told him, 'Don't do that shit, it looks gay,'" Johnny recalled of Angel's dancing. He acknowledged that he became abusive as his marriage to Angel's mother fell apart. "I was a hardass on him," Johnny said. "I could have shown him a lot more love."

Through their own romantic relationships, parents send powerful messages to their children about what it means to be a man—and when their relationships are abusive, as Angel's parents' was, those messages are dangerous. When fathers inflict harm on their partners or children, it can have long-lasting effects on their sons' ability to build healthy relationships. Boys who witness violence in their home or who are themselves abused are at greater risk of perpetrating interpersonal violence. Boys are also more likely to abuse their dating partners when their parents have a habit of getting angry, yelling, criticizing, and using physical punishment.

This research tells me that the energy my husband and I put into nurturing our partnership is not just for us but also for our son's vision of how marriage works. He is watching and learning from the way my husband and I solve problems, from the way we disagree, from the way we show affection. Every day, we are drawing a road map for relationships that he will carry with him.

We are also, by the way, feeding our children every day. And doing dishes. And changing diapers. And taking out the garbage and reading books before bedtime. And, and, and . . . in how my husband and I share this everyday work of parenting, too, we are shaping our son's imagination of his future life.

Dads who challenge the traditional family model—who, apart from working for pay, also share in the work of caring for their family—are more likely to have sons and daughters who envision an egalitarian marriage for themselves, in which both partners are involved in childcare. College men who can recall their own fathers caring for them as children—by planning and preparing meals or taking them to the doctor—say they feel significantly more competent to care for their own future children than their peers who don't remember their dads being involved.

Megan Fulcher, a psychologist at Washington and Lee University in Virginia who studies gender development, argues that this is a sign of the power that parents have to either reinforce or interrupt the pressure that men feel to earn money and women feel to prioritize taking care of kids.

A boy who grows up seeing his dad uninvolved in caring for kids is less likely to see himself as a caregiver, Fulcher says. So when he starts a family, he keeps going to work full-time, and at home he falls into the role of mother's helper—a babysitter who can go to the store if his spouse provides a grocery list, but not a parenting decision maker himself.

A boy who does watch his dad care for kids is more likely to be able to see himself doing the same thing someday—the first step in the confidence he needs to carve out his own role as an expert at home, freeing up his partner to pursue her ambitions at work.

Division of labor matters equally, of course, in families headed by same-sex partners. No matter the sexual orientation of parents, inequitable division of home parenting and housework conditions kids to model stereotypical behaviors: sons see themselves doing so-called masculine jobs when they grow up, while daughters envision "feminine" work. On the other hand, when parents divide work equitably, their kids benefit from a broader range of imagination about what they might do someday.

In other words, one way we parents can give our kids a willingness to buck gender norms is by bucking those norms ourselves. As Fulcher and her colleagues write: "Fathers' most important task may be to be seen, by their children, their employers, and their peers, doing daily domestic tasks and doing them well."

Signs of Change

It's hard to figure out what, exactly, is going on with Americans' views of gender and masculinity.

There are signs of a growing willingness not only to reimagine what it means to be a boy and what it means to be a girl but to get rid of the notion of two genders altogether. An increasing number of people see gender as fluid and dynamic rather than binary and hitched to sex. Half of millennials see gender as a spectrum and say that some people "fall outside conventional categories," according to a 2016 poll. Younger people may be even less tied to traditional ideas about gender. In 2017, the Williams Institute at the University of California–Los Angeles found that more than a quarter of California teens were gender-nonconforming.

Oddly, at the same time, more young people appear to believe in traditional ideas about the roles of men and women. A survey of high school seniors administered annually over the past four decades shows that, since the mid-1990s, the vast majority say that men and women should have equal opportunities in the workplace. But a steadily growing number have endorsed the idea that, in a family, it's better for everyone if men work and make important family decisions while women take care of the home. Sociologists believe that this seeming contradiction may be explained by the fact that there's a gap between what young people will accept out of economic necessity (women, including mothers, need to work to support their families because one income isn't enough) and what they would like for their own lives (a more traditional arrangement in which moms stay home). Whatever the explanation, the trends show that people who support gender equality in public life don't necessarily support it in their own personal lives.

"We're in a contested moment, and I'm not quite sure where it's going to go," sociologist Elizabeth Sweet told me. But Sweet, who studies gender and toys, sees reason to believe that corporations—who have huge investments riding on guessing right about where the culture is headed—are betting that customers want to live in a world in which boys have more latitude to be "girlish."

Toy companies have made huge profits in recent decades by sending children strong signals about what is—and is not—for them, coding oceans of products either for girls (pink and princess) or boys (blue and black and red and superhero). Sweet found that by 1975, only 2 percent of toys in the Sears catalog were marketed to either boys or girls. But two decades later, in 1995, fully *half* the toys in the Sears catalog were clearly aimed at one sex or the other. By the first few years of the twenty-first century, gender-neutral toys had all but disappeared on the websites of major toy manufacturers and in the aisles of big-box stores, and toys were more gendered than they'd ever been.

But now things are changing again.

Target's 2015 decision to get rid of boys' and girls' toy aisles presaged other moves toward gender neutrality in the toy industry. The industry stopped giving out separate awards for boys' and girls' toys in 2017, and while Disney used to separate the toys for sale on its website into gender categories, these days, shoppers who seek only toys "for boys" or "for girls" end up seeing the same products.

In 2019, Hasbro started marketing Baby Alive—a popular doll that eats, drinks and poops—to both boys and girls on the doll's packaging and on its website. On the site, a little girl feeds her doll Play-Doh spaghetti alongside a boy who excitedly changes a diaper. A Hasbro video advertisement from

Brazil shows boys (and girls) tenderly feeding and comforting their dolls. "What is a child doing with a doll?" reads the text on the screen. "Practicing caring. Developing responsibility. Becoming a better person. If a girl can discover so much taking care of a doll, why couldn't a boy?"

Mattel—the company behind Barbie, the prototypically stereotypical doll—has taken its own steps toward meeting what it perceives as demand for blurrier lines between boy and girl products. In September 2019, the company launched what it described as the world's first gender-neutral doll collection, featuring bodies and faces that could be interpreted as female, male, or nonbinary. Speaking to a *Time* magazine reporter, Mattel executives described the "Creatable World" dolls as an effort to reach members of a younger generation who reject rigid gender norms and embrace the notion that gender is a spectrum rather than a binary choice between male and female. "I think if we could have a hand in creating the idea that a boy can play with a perceived girl toy and a girl can play with a perceived boy toy, we would have contributed to a better, more sensitive place of perception in the world today," Mattel president Richard Dickson told *Time*. "And even more so for the kids that find themselves in that challenging place, if we can make that moment in their life a bit more comfortable, and knowing we created something that makes them feel recognized, that's a beautiful thing."

To Sweet, these changes are astonishing, and a sign that broader cultural conversations about masculinity are making their way into the concrete things our kids play with every day—and may ultimately soften the gender rules we convey to our children when they are very young.

"There's something happening right now," she said. Marketing special dolls just for boys is one thing, she said. But it is a step further to market dolls as toys that anyone can enjoy, regardless of gender. It challenges the usual walls that we put up to separate little boys and girls and show them that they're different. Says Sweet: "It's a radical shift."

Toys are just one arena in which we are seeing this shift, this appetite to give boys more space to question assumptions and stereotypes about who they are, how they act, and what they're interested in. We also see it in retired NBA star Dwyane Wade and his public, enthusiastic, and unequivocal support for his twelve-year-old child, Zion, as he came to terms with Zion's gender identity. In June 2019, Wade shared photos with his 15 million Instagram followers of Zion attending a Pride parade in Miami Beach. Months later, Wade posed with Zion, who wore a crop top and manicured nails, for a family photograph posted to social media. Finally, praising Zion's strength and courage, Wade started using the pronoun "she" to refer to his second-youngest child. She wanted to be called Zaya, Wade announced.

"I've watched my son, from day one, become into who she now eventually has come into," Wade said on a sports podcast in December 2019. "Nothing changes with my love. Nothing changes with my responsibilities. Only thing I got to do now is get smarter and educate myself more."

Wade's willingness to publicly embrace his trans daughter made a powerful statement, and not one that was always cheered: "Gay ass son," someone wrote on Instagram, commenting on photographs of Wade and Zaya grinning in Christmas pajamas. "You are hurting your son more than you think." Commenters like these seemed to believe that it is a father's job to keep his child in line, to keep his child straight and "masculine." But Wade had already articulated a different vision for fatherhood: to love his children unconditionally, to get to know each of them, and to help them grow into their true selves.

"My job as a father is to facilitate their lives and to support them and be behind them in whatever they want to do," he told *Variety*. "It's my job . . . to let them know you can conquer the world. So, go and be your amazing self and we're going to sit back and just love you."

We also see a push to give boys more space to be themselves on the red carpet, where actor Billy Porter showed up to the Golden Globes wearing a pink cape over his suit and to the Oscars wearing a tuxedo over a full-skirted black velvet gown. We see it in the media, in movies like *A Beautiful Day in the Neighborhood*, lionizing impossibly kind and compassionate Mister Rogers, and Disney's *Frozen II*, featuring two sisters who risk their lives to save the world while men play the role of loving supporters, waiting in the wings.

And we see this shift in some boys' real lives. In D.C., the boys' group that Phyllis Fagell runs at the Sheridan School has become a fixture for middle school boys who want to talk about the pressures they're facing. At nearby Georgetown Day, a private high school, male students founded Boys Leading Boys, a group for talking about resisting social pressure that contributes to sexual violence. At public schools across the city and in several states, Men of Strength clubs—an initiative designed by the organization Men Can Stop Rape—encourage boys to reject the "dominant story of masculinity" and become allies in preventing violence against women. In California, a summer camp for boys as young as eight is focused on questioning stereotypical masculinity. And in Maine, middle schools are now taking class time to help boys examine gender stereotypes, build empathy, and understand sexual consent.

"In our culture right now we're wrestling with these issues that we haven't openly in the past," said Ryan Tardiff, twenty-seven, who facilitates programs for the nonprofit Maine Boys to Men, which runs the middle school program. "This is fairly new territory."

The Maine Boys to Men curriculum is full of hands-on activities, and one of the most popular introduces the concept of gender stereotypes by asking boys to think about toys they loved as children. They discuss what toys they would buy as a present for a second-grader who is a boy (cars and video games) versus a girl (dolls and kitchen sets), and they talk about differences in the ways toys are marketed to boys and girls. The toy activity also begins a conversation about the ways in which boys don't buy into all the stereotypes they're fed—a rare opportunity in a world where many boys assume that they are alone in their discomfort with the messages they get about who they are supposed to be, said Matt Theodores, the executive director of Maine Boys to Men.

Boys are always hearing the same old stories about how they are supposed to act and what they're supposed to like, he said. They also need to hear the counterstories, the ways in which real boys and real men don't fit into those small boxes. I've realized that is one of the most valuable gifts I can give my son: a narrative about who men are, and who they can be, that undermines the messages he will undoubtedly hear from friends, teachers, and the media. I can give him the space and encouragement to decide for himself who—and how—he wants to be.

CHAPTER THREE

The Sex Ed Crisis

Why Silence About Sex Is Dangerous for Kids

In a memorable scene from the racy HBO series *Euphoria*, two teenagers hook up for the first time. The guy puts his hand around the girl's neck and starts to choke her. She struggles, then screams at him to stop.

"Why would you grab me like that? I couldn't breathe," she says.

"I don't know, I thought you liked that," he replies.

She's perplexed. "Why the fuck would I like that?"

The narrator explains the roots of the boy's misunderstanding: all the choking he's seen in online videos. "Everyone on the planet watches porn," she says, against a backdrop of the sounds and images of aggressive sex. "This shit is not out of left fucking field."

It's a good scene for starting important conversations with boys about sex, consent, and pornography, which they are almost certainly watching, even if we'd rather pretend otherwise. Way too many of us parents have been dodging these conversations, and it's not like schools are doing any better: kids are actually getting less in the way of sex education than they were a generation ago. And so this is what we are doing in America, according to scholars and activists of wide-ranging political and ideological stripes: raising a generation of young people whose understanding of sex and bodies is, in the absence of alternative education from parents or teachers, fundamentally shaped by free online porn.

Meet Corey, a high school senior in Boston. He started masturbating to porn in fifth grade, when friends tipped him off to the existence of Pornhub. It taught him that sex begins wordlessly, suddenly, and passionately, with no negotiation and little foreplay. It taught him that the man is in charge and sex ends when he orgasms. Whatever thin version of sex ed he got from adults at school and at home did nothing to dispel those misunderstandings. "In porn videos, they don't show consent. You kind of grow up thinking, oh, when I first have sex, I don't need to ask," he told me. "You can do whatever you want, like go crazy."

We are not doing our sons any favors when we leave them with the impression that they can "go crazy" and do whatever they want. And yet, in homes and schools across much of the country, that's what is happening.

In 1999, the massacre of twelve students and one teacher at Columbine High School led to a national movement to treat bullying not as a childhood rite of passage but as a serious school safety issue. The explosion of pornography over the past two decades, and the long-lasting, slow-moving tragedy of widespread sexual violence—which is not only happening among adults in some far-off future but here and now, among children—should finally prompt a new understanding that the dearth of sex education also poses a risk to children. Our refusal to talk to young people about sex and sexuality is a public health problem in urgent need of attention.

Sure, some boys luck into parents or teachers or mentors or church leaders who are either comfortable talking about sex, gender, and bodies or are willing to brave their own discomfort in order to start necessary conversations. But huge numbers of boys are growing up fending mostly for themselves as they figure out how to navigate physical and emotional intimacy. For many of these boys, pornography fills the vacuum left by the grown-ups in their lives.

Six in ten young adults have never had a conversation with a parent about "being sure your partner wants to have sex and is comfortable doing so before having sex," according to a survey of more than three thousand eighteen- to twenty-five-year-olds by Harvard University's Making Caring Common project. Around the same number of young people said they had never spoken to a parent about why you should not keep pressing a partner to have sex after they have said no, or about why you should not have sex with someone who is too drunk or otherwise intoxicated to consent, or about how to be a caring and respectful sexual partner. Nearly one-third of young people had never spoken to their parents about *any* of these and other core concepts of sexual consent. That echoes the findings of another national survey on sex ed, which showed that one-third of young men aged fifteen to nineteen (and one-quarter of young women) have never spoken to their parents about birth control, sexually transmitted infections, or how to say no to sex.

The picture is just as bleak when you ask boys about what they've heard from their mothers and fathers about sexual misconduct. In a 2018 national survey of a thousand young people aged ten to nineteen, only 28 percent of boys said they'd spoken with their parents about how to prevent or stop sexual harassment.

Meanwhile, boys start watching porn at age thirteen, on average, according to a national survey of more than twenty-five hundred adults conducted by sex and media researchers at Indiana University. Most of them grew up seeing a wide range of pornography, featuring gang-bangs, double penetration, and face-fucking. One in five had watched simulated rape.

That same study, published in 2020, found that the more porn boys watch, the more likely they are to use dominant behaviors in sex, such as choking their partners, calling their partners "slut" or "whore" or "bitch," and pressuring their partners into doing things in bed that they don't want to do. Fifteen percent of men admit to exerting such pressure, and 22 percent—more than one in five—admit to trying to put their penis into a partner's anus without asking.

The problem, psychology and public health experts say, is not that boys are having kinky sex. The problem is that adults are failing to talk to boys about what it means to have *consensual* sex, kinky or otherwise. Far too many of us have not been offering our sons guidance on the most basic tenets of safe, respectful relationships. Far too many of us have been silent.

And in many parts of the country, especially in rural areas, teachers have not been picking up the slack. Whether because of the nation's Puritan history or the strength of the Christian right in politics, U.S. schools have never been known for embracing sex education. But what you may not know—what surprised me, even after working as a teacher and covering education for years—is that not only are children getting little in the way of sex education. They're getting much less than their counterparts did two decades ago.

National survey data collected by the Centers for Disease Control and Prevention show a remarkable evaporation of sex education from the nation's K–12 schools. In 2000, two-thirds of K–12 schools taught about human sexuality. By 2014, it had dropped to a little less than half. Even in schools where kids are lucky enough to learn about sex, instruction is often dominated by a litany of reasons not to have sex. When I ask teen boys what they learned in sex ed at school, they usually either roll their eyes or laugh. What sex ed?

Instruction has dwindled not just on topics that we might think of as controversial, like sexual orientation and condom use, but also on uncontroversial subjects. The number of K–12 schools that teach children about "resisting peer pressure to engage in sexual behavior" fell 20 percent between 2000 and 2014; by the end of that period, just one in three schools was teaching this skill. We see the same decline in the number of schools that are teaching kids to understand the impact of the media on our ideas about sex. Even lessons on puberty have fallen off and are now taught in only one in five elementary schools. For many young people, formal sex ed has been reduced to a brief session on sexual-violence prevention during freshman orientation at college—an approach that has been shown to be singularly ineffective at changing much of anything.

Why is this happening? It's not necessarily that the country has become more conservative. In fact, the number of schools that teach about abstinence—the approach to sex ed generally favored by conservatives—has also taken a nosedive since 2000, according to the CDC.

Laura Lindberg, a scientist at the Guttmacher Institute and one of the nation's leading researchers on what children are being taught about sex, believes that sex education may be a casualty of standardized testing, squeezed out of the school day, along with recess, art, music, and social studies, by a narrow focus on math, reading, and writing. Quite possibly, many of our elected leaders—from members of Congress, who pass federal education laws, to state and local officials, who exercise enormous control over what schools actually teach—don't think offering sex education in school is all that important.

But in refusing to educate our children about bodies, sex, consent, and healthy relationships, we're setting them up to be both victims of and perpetrators of sexual assault.

I've talked to a lot of moms and dads who worry about their sons getting into trouble with sex in college, given the combination of freedom and alcohol and new vigilance on sexual assault. A spate of high-profile stories about sexual violence—including that of Brock Turner raping an unconscious Chanel Miller behind a dumpster at Stanford—have imprinted themselves on anxious parents of boys.

College is undoubtedly a risky time. But it is startlingly clear that college is way too late to start teaching boys about sex. By then, they have already absorbed eighteen years of messages about the world from Disney princesses and superheroes, from video games with scantily clad female characters, from romantic comedies and internet pornography, from joking with their friends. They have settled into their beliefs about how men and women are supposed to relate, how bodies are supposed to look, and how sex is supposed to go. And by college, some boys have already developed a pattern of troubling behavior that could have been interrupted.

Consider this: in a recent survey of eleven hundred incoming freshmen boys at thirty colleges across Georgia, 19.3 percent admitted to having already committed some act of sexual violence, from kissing forcibly against someone's will, to having oral sex with someone who didn't want it, to penetrating someone without their consent, whether by force, coercion, or intoxication. That is, before ever setting foot on campus, nearly *one in five* teenage boys pushed past another person's boundaries in a way that may have altered both their lives while in high school. "It's not just once in a while, here or there. It's an epidemic of sexual violence," said Laura Salazar, a public health expert at Georgia State University who led the study.

That study's one-in-five figure is no outlier. Lurking in academic journals, behind steep paywalls that keep readership low, is other evidence that boys are committing sexual assault and rape at disturbingly high rates long before high school graduation. Girls are, too, though less frequently.

Of eight hundred incoming male freshmen at one college in the southeast U.S., 22 percent said they had already committed sexual violence. At a different college, it was 14 percent—and of those 14 percent, *four in five* went on to commit at least one more act of sexual violence while they were in college.

What about the broader population, including boys who don't go to college? Though teenagers are less likely to be having sex than they were a generation ago, an alarming number of them are hurting each other or having sex they either don't want or aren't sure about. Just 41 percent of young women and 62 percent of young men who had their first sexual encounter when they were teenagers describe that experience as "wanted." In a national sample of a thousand adolescents between the ages of fourteen and twenty-one, 12 percent of males (and 8 percent of females) admitted that they had coerced someone into sex, attempted or committed rape, or forced some other kind of sexual contact. Perpetration rates were low among the youngest teens, and then suddenly spiked at age sixteen—the time of a boy's life when he is most likely to sexually assault someone for the first time is when he is still in high school.

The litany of disturbing data points is exhausting. But the numbers should serve as a clanging alarm bell. The problem of sexual violence—against girls and against boys—begins years before college, and our efforts to address it must start years earlier, too.

Instead, as of 2019, only twenty-nine states in the nation (plus the District of Columbia) required that public schools teach sex education. Even in states where sex education is required, it mostly focuses on plumbing: who has which body parts, how they work, and what you can do to avoid pregnancy and disease. Among the states that require sex ed, only eleven (plus D.C.) required that sex education include discussion of consent, sexual assault, or healthy relationships.

Sex ed is particularly poor for LGBTQ kids, the very same kids who face the greatest risk of victimization. More than half the states don't require any mention of sexual orientation in sex education. Seven states, whose schools together enroll nearly 10 million children—Texas, South Carolina, Arizona, Oklahoma, Louisiana, Alabama, and Mississippi—mandate that sex education courses portray homosexuality in a negative light. Alabama law, for example, requires teachers to emphasize that homosexuality "is not a lifestyle acceptable to the general public and that homosexual conduct is a criminal offense under the laws of the state."

Democrats are generally more supportive of sex ed than Republicans, and some topics—like gender identity—are wrapped up in the culture wars that can fire up the base of both parties. But even as the media covers sex ed as a battleground between conservatives and progressives, public opinion polling shows that broad swaths of such instruction are not all that controversial. Most parents, regardless of their party affiliation, believe that schools should teach kids about puberty, healthy relationships, birth control, abstinence, sexually transmitted infections, and sexual orientation.

So what if we considered sex education less a political litmus test than a safety issue? What if we considered the possibility that a fulfilling and healthy sex life starts with learning about sex, bodies, and boundaries?

How to Start the Conversation

Talking with my own son about sexuality has, to date, mostly meant making sure he understands that no one has a right to touch him unless he gives his permission, and that he doesn't have a right to touch anyone else unless they say it's okay. He also knows and proudly uses the anatomically correct terms for genitals; recently, he learned that his sister has eggs and that someday he'll start producing sperm.

But it's easy to teach a toddler to say "penis" and "vulva," and I know it's only going to get more complicated as he grows up. Parents of older boys are always joking that their sons recoil at any mention of physical intimacy or bodies. "He wants to talk with me about sex as much as he wants to have a root canal without anesthesia," a St. Louis mother told me of her teenage son.

What I have learned, though, is that parents have much more influence on their sons—including their teenagers—than they might think. From mental health to sex and birth control and alcohol and drugs, parents can make a difference in their sons' lives by communicating warmly and openly. We know this from a stack of studies based on decades of data from the National Longitudinal Study of Adolescent to Adult Health, which has surveyed twenty thousand men and women for more than twenty years, starting in 1994 when they were teenagers and continuing to the present.

Feeling close to parents and connected to school helps protect teen boys, shielding them from many of the obstacles we hope our sons will avoid: emotional health struggles and suicidal thoughts, violent behavior, substance abuse, and early sexual debut.

"I sometimes think that parents get lulled into thinking it's all about their peers and they don't care what I think or what I say. That's just not true," said Carolyn T. Halpern, a developmental psychologist at the University of North Carolina–Chapel Hill, who serves as deputy director of the massive survey project. "They actually are listening. They're just pretending not to."

Talking to kids about sex and sexual health can make a difference specifically when it comes to mitigating the effects of watching porn. One research team found, for example, that teens who watch a lot of porn—in which actors rarely use condoms—are more likely to have sex without condoms. But that's not true of teens who watch a lot of porn and whose parents talk to them about birth control and sexually transmitted infections. Pornography carries powerful messages, but parents can counteract them.

First, though, parents need to understand what the messages are. I graduated from high school in 1996, when teenagers ogled photographs of naked women in *Playboy*, hiding issues of the magazine under their mattresses. When I was a teenager, I was still using the house landline to dial into the World Wide Web and to chat with friends on AOL Instant Messenger. I think the raciest thing I saw in high school was the *Sports Illustrated* swimsuit issue.

Now, of course, kids have access to the internet and its riches pretty much any time—including a vast library of video porn in every category you can imagine (and perhaps a few you cannot)—amateur, webcam, blow job, hardcore, threesome, anal, MILF, big ass, big tits, big dick, bondage, bukkake, lesbian, gang-bang, hentai, ass-to-mouth, double penetration. If you have not perused online porn recently, and you spend some time looking, you might be surprised at how easy it is to stumble onto rough sex, even if you're not looking for it.

One frequently cited analysis, published in 2010, found that 88 percent of scenes from popular porn movies showed physical aggression, mostly spanking, gagging, and slapping. Twenty-eight percent of the scenes showed choking. Nearly half the scenes showed verbal aggression, like name-calling. Most of the aggressors were men, the vast majority of targets were women, and in almost all cases, the woman either seemed to enjoy the abuse or didn't seem to mind.

Researchers are finding reason to worry that some boys are picking up habits from what they see on-screen. One seventeen-year-old boy told researchers: "If I watch porn, and like, I see a male porn star, and sometimes like, if I'm with a female, I try to do the exact same thing as they're doing, 'cause I figure that they're stars." Another seventeen-year-old said he'd been inspired by amateur porn to videotape his girlfriend while they were having sex, without her consent. "She really couldn't tell me no, ya know?"

It's easy to blame pornography for what these boys have learned about sex: the pressure the first boy seems to feel to perform, for example, and the casual disregard the second shows for his partner's feelings and desires. But it is hard—maybe impossible—to divorce the effects of pornography from our failure to teach boys some basic lessons about respect: that each of us has the right to control our own body and our own sexuality, and that sex is something you do with, and not to, another person.

A pair of Columbia University professors, anthropologist Jennifer Hirsch and sociologist Shamus Khan, call this "sexual citizenship." It means having a sense of respect for both one's own and other people's dignity and sexual self-determination, and it has become the way I think about what I want to teach my own children as they grow up.

With psychologist Claude A. Mellins, Hirsch led a massive study of campus sexual violence at Columbia known as SHIFT—the Sexual Health Initiative to Foster Transformation. Khan was one of many faculty members involved in the project, which involved a survey of sixteen hundred students and in-depth interviews with and observations of more than one hundred fifty students who shared unvarnished accounts of their sexual experiences and their feelings about those experiences. Hirsch and Khan unspooled the findings of that research in their book *Sexual Citizens* (2020).

As with the Georgia study that found one in five incoming male students had already been sexually violent, what I found most startling about SHIFT was not so much what it revealed about college life but what it revealed about middle and high school. Twenty percent of Columbia students—one in five—said they were assaulted before they ever set foot on campus. Most of those coming to college with a history of sexual victimization were women and gender-nonconforming students, but there was also a significant number of men—9 percent, nearly one in ten.

One woman told the SHIFT team of her efforts to persuade a gay male friend to have intercourse with her, a goal she achieved over his objections. Another woman said that after a night of drinking, an older male student had taken her to his room and pushed right past her objections to his unbuttoning her pants. "It's okay," he'd said. A guy told of having sex with a blackout-drunk woman as she drifted in and out of consciousness; she'd invited him to her sorority formal, and he said he figured sex was expected. These were sexual assaults that happened not because of sociopathic tendencies, Hirsch and Khan argue, but because a young person didn't understand their right to control access to their body, or didn't respect their partner's right—or both. They didn't have a sense of sexual citizenship.

Our collective failure to instill a sense of sexual citizenship in our children is one reason why, Hirsch and Khan argue in *Sexual Citizens*, "sexual assault is a predictable consequence of how our society is organized, rather than solely a problem of individual bad actors." Weak sexual citizenship, they say, lays the groundwork for situations in which a person doesn't believe he or she has the right to say no; or feels that putting up with a blow job is preferable to ending the evening awkwardly; or keeps pushing past polite refusals, seeing a partner not as a human being so much as a means to a sexual end. When we fail to teach our kids fundamental values of bodily autonomy, we set boys up to experience sexual violence as both perpetrators and victims.

Sexual citizenship is a positive vision for how boys can aspire to be in the world at a time when many say they feel as if the only thing they get from adults, when it comes to talk about sex, is lists of cautions and finger-wagging no-no's. When I think about what I need to do for my own son now, and in the years to come, building his sexual citizenship is at the top of the list. I have learned it is one of the most fundamental things I can do to set him up for a satisfying, safe intimate life.

And I have learned that I can't do that with one big heavy lay-it-all-on-the-table talk about sex. Instead, sex educators say that we parents should look for openings in everyday life to share our values around sex, ask questions about what's on our children's minds, and treat sex and bodies as a normal thing to think and talk about.

My son's life is already filled with conversation starters. When he goes to the bathroom, we talk about how his penis is only for him to touch, and no one else except a doctor, as long as a parent is there. When he pushes his sister in frustration, or when he keeps trying to hug her after she says no, my husband and I remind him that he may not touch anyone without permission. When he is wrestling or roughhousing, he is (I hope) learning with our help how to figure out where the line is between having fun and going too far.

It is possible that I go overboard with the teachable moments. He likes to insist, loudly, that I let my hair out of a bun or get rid of my sunglasses or hat. "Take it off!" he yells. "I don't like it." In such instances, it may not be necessary for me to remind a toddler that he does not get to decide what to do with my body or anybody else's. But that's what I do. I want him to get used to dealing with other people's boundaries.

As he gets older, there will only be more openings for conversation. Tween and teen boys scroll past girls' butt selfies ("belfies") on Instagram, they read *Teen Vogue*'s guide to anal sex, they watch middle schoolers discover masturbation in the Hulu series *PEN15,* and they listen to music filled with references to pussies, dicks, clits, and cum. They also read (or hear or watch) the news, where there is no shortage of fodder for discussion about sex and power.

Chandra White-Cummings, the mother of two young adult sons, said she learns a lot from her boys by using everyday media as a jumping-off point for discussion. An episode of *Law & Order: Special Victims Unit* provided one such conservation starter. The show centered on a sexual encounter between two high school students that the girl described as rape and the guy said was consensual, since she never verbally said no. "I paused it, and I said, 'What do you think of this?'" White-Cummings told me. "You could have heard a rat walk on cotton, it was so quiet."

Finally, her twenty-two-year-old told her that he didn't want to get "beat down" for saying the wrong thing. She prodded, and he eventually relented. Guys don't always pay attention to their partners' messages, he told her—but girls aren't always clear. He thought that boys needed to learn more about being emotionally intelligent, and that they needed to be held accountable for picking up on signs of discomfort. But he also thought that girls might need to hear how they shouldn't try to be subtle. The conversation gave White-Cummings a way to learn what her son believed and what he worried about, and it gave her an opening to talk about how he might handle situations in which he wasn't sure how his partner felt. "The more I parent them, the more I realize it's so important to listen," she said.

My own parents did not talk to me or my four siblings about sex, except to tell us that they didn't approve of our having it before marriage. But besides sharing that value of theirs, they also gave us access to information. They made sure we had a copy of the feminist guide *Our Bodies, Ourselves* around the house, which is how I learned that I had a clitoris—a startling fact that somehow never came up over the dinner table or in health class at school. They also raised us in a Unitarian Universalist church, and in eighth grade, Sunday school became a yearlong coed sex education class that covered pretty much everything: boy bodies, girl bodies, relationships, pornography, pregnancy, birth control, pleasure. Twenty-eight years later,

I cannot remember a single particular moment or fact from that year of sex ed Sundays (except that, because of a soccer game, I missed the class where everyone put condoms on bananas). But I remember that we were allowed to ask questions about anything we were curious about, and that the two teachers, a husband-and-wife pair, always answered without embarrassment.

I share this as a way of saying that we parents don't necessarily have to be comfortable talking about the nitty-gritty details of sex and sexuality to give our kids a strong sense of sexual citizenship. But we do have to come up with some way to give our sons more than silence.

Sexting: Translating Offline Etiquette to Online Life

Experts say that sexting has become so common now that they consider it an "emerging, and potentially normal" part of teen sexual development, as long as it's done respectfully and with consent. So what does it mean to respect someone else's sexuality online? At the moment, many boys don't know quite how to answer that question, and they're making up the rules as they go along.

Over pepperoni pizza in an empty English classroom at San Rafael High, in California's Marin County, I listened as a group of seniors discussed the etiquette of sharing nude photographs. They spoke derisively about the kind of people who collect and post their classmates' nude photographs on anonymous Instagram accounts. Forwarding and reposting nudes is downright malicious, one female student said, declaring it "not okay."

The boys in the group agreed. But then things got muddy. They said that when they'd received nude photographs from girls, they'd shown their friends, even though those photos hadn't been meant for any eyes but their own. And their friends had reciprocated. I asked the boys if the two things were all that different, posting a girl's photo online without her consent versus sharing her photo with another guy without her consent. "My automatic reaction is, yeah, it's completely different," said one of the boys who acknowledged showing nudes to friends. "But when you really think about it, it's not."

Did they have any adults in their lives with whom they could talk about this stuff, hash out what's right and wrong when it comes to sending, receiving, and forwarding nudes?

"We kind of figure it out on our own. I don't think we talk about it with our parents," one boy said.

A girl chimed in: "They don't really know how it works."

We may not know how the sharing of nude photographs works, but we can ask our kids to explain it to us. And if we can listen without freaking out, we might hear where they need guidance. Helping boys translate respect and mutuality from in-real-life to online interactions is clearly one of those areas. If people should have control over their own bodies in real life, then they should also have control over images of their bodies—which means sharing a nude photograph without consent is wrong, whether posting it online to show the world or forwarding it to a group chat, or even showing the picture on your phone to a friend.

Yet one in three teen boys either thinks it is okay—or isn't quite sure whether it's okay—for a boy to ask a girl he's not dating to send him a nude picture. Among young people generally, one in eight has forwarded a sext without consent, and about one in twelve has had his or her own image forwarded without consent, according to a review of the few studies that have examined nonconsensual image sharing.

Some teen boys are also under the mistaken impression that a girl who posts or shares sexy pictures is signaling that she wants to have sex. Megan Maas, a Michigan State University professor of human development, heard this claim from boys in focus-group discussions about nude photo sharing, and believes this misperception is one reason why girls who post sexy pictures online have a higher than average risk of being sexually assaulted.

Maas suggests that adults should be explicit. Just as you can't assume that a girl wearing a short skirt wants sex, you can't assume that a girl who sends a nude—or even three or four nudes—wants sex in real life. Just as it's wrong to keep pressuring a girl who says no to sex, it's wrong to keep pressuring a girl who says no to sending nudes. If it would be weird and creepy to ask a girl you're not dating to disrobe in real life, then it's weird and creepy to ask her to send you a naked photo. And if it's wrong to expose your penis to another person in real life, it's wrong to send an unsolicited dick pic.

Why Boys Should Practice Masturbating Without Porn

Maas had one other piece of advice for parents: encourage your sons to masturbate without pornography.

As the use of porn has increased over the past two decades, the amount of sex Americans are having has declined, giving rise to concern about a "sex recession" fueled in part by a generation that has grown up masturbating to porn instead of seeking real human companionship. The sex recession is most pronounced among young men between the ages of eighteen and thirty. Between 2008 and 2018, the proportion of men who said that they had been celibate in the previous year nearly tripled, to 28 percent.

The degree to which the decline in sex can be blamed on pornography has been—and surely will continue to be—a matter of great debate. Neuroscientists and others who study pornography disagree vehemently about whether a person can truly become addicted to porn; pornography addiction is not listed in the American Psychiatric Association's bible, the *Diagnostic and Statistical Manual of Mental Disorders (DSM-5)*. But clearly, porn can become a noxious preoccupation. And even boys and young men who have far less disruptive porn habits can get so used to getting off on pornography that they lose the thrill of sex with in-the-flesh human beings.

One thirty-eight-year-old man from Nashville told me that he quit porn cold turkey after a string of ho-hum dates that made him question whether his habit of using porn to masturbate three or four times a week was getting in the way of good sex with another human. "Even though rationally, I know that porn is unrealistic, it desensitizes a man to the real act," he said. Six months later, he said sex feels thrilling again. And research suggests that his experience is not unusual. A survey of nearly five hundred college men found that the more porn a guy watches, the more he needs porn to become and stay aroused—and the less he actually enjoys real-life sexual intimacy.

Yet boys who are just beginning to explore sexuality are depending on porn to get turned on. Maas sees this in college freshmen who show up on campus not knowing how to masturbate without porn—not knowing, even, that it's possible. Even as academics continue to debate the effects of pornography on young people's brains and sexuality, Maas believes there's enough evidence to be concerned that young people who have their first orgasms to moving images on a screen are being conditioned to need those images to climax, and therefore to choose porn over sex with another person.

At the start of the semester, Maas tells her students that one of her goals is that they each learn how to give themselves orgasms the old-fashioned way, by pairing imagination and fantasy with close attention to what feels good. She doesn't put it on the syllabus, but, she says, "that is a skill you should be able to do."

Ideally, Maas said, boys would get this advice before they get to college, as they're exploring their sexuality: Practice masturbating to the words, images, sounds, and ideas in your own mind. Take a break from images of strangers' hairless bodies. Get to know your own body. Explore what turns you on. Be self-centered, realizing that this is the time to think only about yourself; when you're with another person, what you want must take a back seat to what you're both comfortable with.

A nudge to find sexual pleasure without porn might come as a relief to boys who have their own concerns about and discomfort with pornography. I met Jacob Greene when he was a senior at the private Georgetown Day School in Washington, D.C. By then, he was watching much less porn than he had a couple of years earlier. A group of guys at his school had started getting together to talk about masculinity, sex, and sexual violence. He realized that when he watched pornography, he was analyzing its hidden and not so hidden messages—and that they were not making him feel very good.

"I think most guys are sensitive about how they're performing, like are they lasting long enough, is their penis large enough," Jacob said. Porn feeds that anxiety, he said. Even guys in the group who resisted the idea that porn is harmful agreed that it shapes what they consider to be hot. "I've found that using your imagination is definitely a better solution," he said.

Teaching Sexual Citizenship in Schools

Virtually every expert on sexual violence I have met argues that if we want to make a dent in sexual harassment and assault among young people— and if we want to help our kids have sexual encounters that they want, instead of those that they think they should be having—improving sex education in K–12 schools is critical.

Hirsch and Khan, the Columbia professors who came up with the notion of sexual citizenship, argue that a person has sexual *projects*—reasons for having sex, like seeking status or seeking experience or wanting to have a child. They might be shaped by their parents' values, but they are intensely personal and should be off-limits from judgment or intervention by others. At the same time, Hirsch and Khan say, we all share a public interest in making sure that our children develop a strong sense of sexual citizenship. And we can't give our children that understanding without good sex education that starts early in their lives.

The research out of Columbia has already lent support to the notion that sex education can help young people avoid becoming victims. SHIFT found that teenagers who learned how to say no to sex as part of a comprehensive sex education course were less likely to be assaulted in college. Women who were taught how to refuse sex were *half* as likely to be raped.

But can sex ed also stop young people from doing sexual harm to others? The SHIFT team argues that it can, if it helps teach young people how to set and respect personal boundaries, and if it begins early—ideally in kindergarten, or even before.

"Sex ed" for kindergartners is in some ways misleading, as if little kids who aren't yet old enough to ride an amusement park roller coaster are going to go straight to practicing the proper use of condoms. So set aside any doubts you may have when you hear the term and consider the National Sexuality Education Standards, a blueprint for what kids need to learn when. Developed in 2012 by a coalition of organizations, these standards broadly describe what children should learn and when. The SHIFT team argues that the approach laid out in the blueprint also gives young people tools to figure out how to have the sex they actually want rather than the sex they think they're supposed to have.

By the end of second grade, kids should understand what makes for a healthy friendship and what constitutes bullying and teasing. They should understand that their ideas about how boys should act, and how girls should act, are shaped by their parents, their friends, and the media. And they should be able to use proper terms to describe male and female anatomy.

A quick aside here on the importance of teaching anatomical terms. Experts believe that children who know and use proper names for genitals are less likely to be targeted by sexual predators, who may be deterred from choosing victims who are comfortable talking about body parts. Children who know the terms *vagina* and *vulva* instead of *hoo-ha*, and *penis* and *testicles* instead of *pee-pee*, also have a better shot at clearly explaining what happened to them if they are molested, and they are more likely to know how to prevent and report sexual abuse.

The National Sexuality Education Standards call for children to know about personal boundaries before they reach third grade. Sex educators and sexual violence experts agree that this is one of the most important things we can do for young children to set them on a path to healthy sexual development: Teach them not only that they have a right to decide whether they want to be touched, and a responsibility to respect other people's autonomy, but also what to do if they feel uncomfortable with the way someone's touching them. Teach them the fundamentals of sexual citizenship long before they become, or even dream of becoming, sexually active.

I learned why these lessons need to be embedded in the classrooms of even the youngest children when my daughter was in preschool. Late one afternoon, when I arrived to pick her up from her aftercare program, I discovered her locked in a boy's bear hug. She looked stricken—uncomfortable and unsure what to do. When she and the boy saw me, he leaped off her and she leaped toward me. She was flushed and sweating; it is always too warm inside the school in wintertime. We gathered her things and walked into the hallway, where I bent down to talk to her. *Was that boy hugging you?* Yes, she said, looking down. *Did you want to be hugged?* No, he was hugging me too tight. *Has that happened before?* Yes.

I told her there in the hallway that her body is hers, and that she is in control of it, and if she doesn't want to be hugged or touched, she could say—should say—*I don't like this.* And if he doesn't listen, she should tell a teacher.

It was all stuff we'd talked about before, though I wished in that moment that we had talked about it much more often. I could see, in the way she turned her eyes away, that she felt embarrassed. I worried that I'd made her feel as if this was somehow her fault, and so I asked the principal if anyone was talking to the boy—and to all kids—about their responsibility to keep their hands off each other.

I was surprised and delighted to learn that there were already plans to teach students about personal space and consent. Starting with the three- and four-year-old preschoolers, every kid in every class at my daughter's public school got lessons in consent in 2019. I observed one of them: a school counselor spent fifteen or twenty minutes in my daughter's classroom, sitting with the kids in a circle on the carpet, talking and singing about how your body belongs to you and no one has a right to touch it without your permission. Want to give someone a hug or a high five? Ask for permission. Someone touches you without your permission, especially in your "bathing suit area"? Tell a trusted adult.

It was not perfect, but it was something—and it was much more, much earlier than in most U.S. schools.

If we followed the National Sexuality Education Standards, this kind of education would become routine for little kids. Older kids in upper elementary school would learn more directly about sex and sexuality, including about puberty and hygiene and sexual orientation. They would learn more about gender stereotypes, more about what it means to have a healthy relationship, and more about what consent is, what rape and sexual assault are, and how alcohol and drugs affect decisions about sex.

Middle school is where kids make the leap to gender identity, sexual intercourse, pregnancy and infection, abstinence and contraception. The National Sexuality Education Standards don't directly address pornography, but they do suggest that children should learn about the effect that the media has on their ideas about gender and sex. They call for challenging the stereotype that boys must always pursue sex while girls act as coy gatekeepers.

Is middle school too early for kids to be learning about all of this? It may instead be on the cusp of too late. Even though the number of teens having sex has dropped over the last three decades, a substantial proportion of boys are still having sex for the first time when they are very young—before age thirteen, long before they are legally able to consent, according to researchers from the Guttmacher Institute and Johns Hopkins University.

They examined two sets of survey data, from questionnaires answered by nearly twenty thousand high school students and by nearly eight thousand boys aged fifteen through nineteen. Eight percent of boys in the first survey, and 4 percent in the second (which asked only about heterosexual intercourse), said they'd first had intercourse before their thirteenth birthday.

Those averages masked huge variation in early sexual initiation by geography and race, from 5 percent of boys in San Francisco to 25 percent in Memphis. For Black boys and boys whose mothers had not graduated from college, the proportions were even higher. In Milwaukee, San Francisco, and Chicago, more than a quarter of Black boys reported having sex before thirteen. "Whether fucked by older females and males or raped by male peers in childhood, the widespread sexual abuse of Black boys receives little or no attention," wrote author bell hooks in *We Real Cool*:

Black Men and Masculinity (2004), describing how young Black boys are trapped by the belief that they are supposed to want to have sex. There is little space for them to refuse sexual advances from girls or women without calling their own manhood into question. And if they are assaulted or raped by another boy or a man, there is little space to admit it so that they can begin to heal.

The startling number of boys who are having sex before they turn thirteen—again, years before they can consent—underlines the need for sex education that starts early and that helps children see and resist gender stereotypes, including the stereotype that boys always want sex.

In the Guttmacher/Johns Hopkins study, nearly one in ten boys who reported early sexual initiation described their first experience as unwanted, and nearly four in ten said that they had mixed feelings about it. The rest of the boys who had intercourse before age thirteen, about half of them, described their experiences as "wanted"—perhaps because they believed they were supposed to want it as a mark of masculinity.

According to the most recent national data available, sixth-grade boys are now less likely to have received any formal instruction in saying no to sex than they were two decades ago.

The Problem with Abstinence-Only Education

By underlining what happens when we fail to teach children about personal boundaries, the #MeToo movement reinvigorated efforts to improve sex education in public schools. In the first half of 2019, six states across the political spectrum—from blue Maryland and Rhode Island to purple Colorado and bright-red Oklahoma—passed bills adding consent, sexual assault, or healthy relationships to their standards for K–12 sex ed.

But it's too soon to know what these bills will really mean for the conversations children are having in their classrooms.

Sex educators say—and it is common sense—that teaching about sexual consent and communication requires acknowledging that young people have a right not only to say no, but also to say yes. It requires acknowledging that they may make their own decisions about what they want to do, sexually, and when and with whom they want to do it.

But this country has for years favored teaching young people that there's only one right choice when it comes to sex—not having it until marriage.

Since the 1990s, abstinence-only sex education has displaced comprehensive approaches in many schools, helped along by laws in twenty-eight states requiring that when sex ed is taught, it must stress abstinence. One sign of its spread: in 1995, 81 percent of teen boys received formal instruction about birth control; by 2013, it was only 55 percent. The decline was steepest in rural America.

There is no strong evidence that abstinence-only education keeps young people safe. In systematic reviews of dozens of studies, scientists—including at the CDC—have repeatedly concluded that the evidence doesn't support claims by abstinence-only advocates that this approach gets kids to wait longer to have sex or have sex with fewer partners. The American Medical Association, the American Public Health Association, and the American Academy of Pediatrics all oppose it. "Research has conclusively demonstrated that programs promoting abstinence-only until heterosexual marriage occurs are ineffective," the American Academy of Pediatrics advised in 2016.

Teens who get comprehensive sex ed—including information about birth control—report less sexual activity, fewer sex partners, less unprotected sex, and fewer sexually transmitted infections. And there is no evidence that giving kids information about sex encourages them to lose their virginity earlier, as abstinence-only advocates claim. As it turns out, teaching young people about sex does not endanger them. It seems to protect them.

Advocates for abstinence-only education argue that sexual health experts who are pushing for more progressive sex ed are exaggerating when they claim that their approach can prevent sexual violence. There is no conclusive proof to support that claim, they say. And they are right: most research on sex education has studied its impact on things like the age at which teens first have sex and whether, once they start having sex, they use contraception. We have no empirical evidence that sex education starting in kindergarten can prevent a person from committing sexual harassment or assault.

But we do know that the teaching outlined in the National Sexuality Education Standards—which goes beyond reproductive plumbing—is aimed at transforming the way boys think about gender stereotypes, consent, and healthy relationships. Such transformation is intended in part to put boys at less risk for committing sexual violence than they otherwise would be. And as I'll explain in Chapter Eight, this kind of instruction in other countries has successfully transformed boys' attitudes toward women and sex, as well as their behavior.

The New Sex Ed: Porn Literacy

The National Sex Ed Conference, like any conference, brings people together in windowless hotel meeting rooms with mustard-yellow carpet and taupe walls. But the topics on its agenda tend to be more interesting than most. Here, at the airport Marriott in Newark, New Jersey, in April 2019, a few dozen educators were settling into their chairs for a workshop on teaching "pornography literacy" to young people.

"Today is a beautiful day to discuss porn!" said Jess Alder, the director of an after-school leadership program that offers Boston teens the chance to learn about—and teach their peers about—porn literacy. The audience let out a little whoop.

This is the leading edge of sex education, an approach that doesn't whisper around the edges of pornography but addresses it head-on—and not with a lecture on all the ways porn will mess you up, as many programs and activists do. Instead, porn literacy aims to give young people the tools they need to understand what they see on-screen: not a real sexual encounter but a performance for pay that is saturated with unrealistic scenarios and gender stereotypes. The idea is not to tell young people what they should think about porn, or whether they should watch it, but to arm them with information, acknowledging that they're going to need to make their own decisions.

"We're not going in and saying porn is awful," Alder said. "We're also not saying porn is amazing. We're sharing the research with young people."

The people in the audience were nurses, middle school counselors, and social workers who serve homeless kids and teens in foster care; they were university lecturers and prep school health teachers and people in charge of ensuring compliance with Title IX of the Education Amendments of 1972, the federal law that is widely known for forcing schools to let girls play sports, but that also governs how schools must respond to sexual violence. They worked with teenagers on the front lines, where they saw a huge disconnect between the reality that young people are living—with easy access to free online pornography—and the inability or unwillingness of adults to talk about it.

The curriculum they were here to learn about was developed by Alder, dating-violence expert Nicole Daley, and Emily Rothman, a public health scholar at Boston University. The three of them teamed up with two big goals. They wanted to figure out how to help teens interpret the online porn that was becoming so common in their lives, and they wanted to use porn, an irresistible topic of conversation for teens, as a vehicle to talk about things that might otherwise feel a little academic— dating violence, consent and sexual orientation, body image and gender stereotypes. They came up with a curriculum, taught it to twenty-four young Bostonians aged fifteen to twenty-four, and then evaluated the impact.

Turns out that just as talking about sex doesn't push kids to start having it, talking about pornography didn't persuade them to start watching it, the Boston crew found. But the curriculum did change what young people knew about porn, as well as what they thought about it. They were less likely to believe that porn is a good way for people to learn about sex and more likely to believe that it promotes unhealthy expectations of male and female sexuality. Specifically, after the program fewer young people believed that "calling a girl 'nasty' or 'slut' during sex is something that everyone does" or that "a lot of people think it is sexy when a girl cries, chokes, gags, or vomits during sex."

Ever since this new approach and its promising results were described in a viral 2018 *New York Times* magazine article, the women who created it have been fielding a barrage of requests to train educators across the country. In the winter of 2019, they traveled to New York City to train staff from more than a dozen private schools who were eager for guidance but cognizant of the public relations risk of embracing porn education.

"It was safety in numbers. If there was blowback, it wasn't like one weird school," said Jeannie Crowley, who organized the training and is director of technology at Ethical Culture Fieldston, a K–12 prep school with campuses in Manhattan and the Bronx. Crowley said schools are hungry for help addressing porn and sexting, both of which enter many kids' lives early, before they are formally taught about consent. Boys sending unsolicited photos of their penises is a common problem. "We're being caught flat-footed," Crowley said.

The notion of "porn literacy" is still so new that there isn't much evidence about whether and how it shapes the way teen boys and girls think about what they're seeing or about how they're having sex. But we know that teaching critical thinking about the messages embedded in media has been effective at countering other issues, from eating disorders to underage drinking and tobacco use. And there are signs that pornography literacy may help mitigate some of the negative effects of watching porn. A survey of nearly two thousand Dutch teens and young adults found that the more kids watch porn, the more likely they are to see women as sex objects—unless they report that they discussed sexually explicit media in school, in which case the porn effects disappeared.

According to educators and others who work closely with young people (as well as just about every Gen Xer who went through DARE, the ineffective antidrug program founded during the Reagan era), telling kids to just say no doesn't work.

Jennifer Davenport, the IT director at a private school in New York City, said that curious middle school boys have shown themselves to be ingenious at getting around whatever obstacles their parents and teachers try to put up. They've dealt with filters meant to shield them from sexually explicit images by seeking out Japanese porn, erotica, and a certain page on wikiHow that explains how to have sexual intercourse, Davenport said.

The porn literacy approach developed by the Boston trio does not actually involve any porn watching. It's composed of nine lessons, light on lecturing, heavy on discussion and activities. Young people learn about the porn industry and its connection to human trafficking, about the way messages about gender and race and power are embedded in pornography, and about the wide varieties of nonsexual intimacies they can share with other people. And they learn that while everyone has particular desires and proclivities, what is nonnegotiable for every kind of sex is enthusiastic mutual consent.

They also get an overview of research on the effects of pornography on teens, much of which is troubling. Watching porn underage is associated with outcomes that are bound to turn a mother's stomach: starting sex at a younger age, not using condoms, viewing women as sex objects, believing in gender stereotypes, believing in rape myths, and being sexually aggressive. Porn watching is also linked to interest in casual sex and having more sex partners. One study, while not conclusive, found a relationship between porn and academic performance for young adolescent boys. The more pornography a boy used, the worse his grades six months later, even when controlling for other variables.

Violent porn seems to be in a troubling category all its own. One longitudinal study showed that young people aged ten to fifteen who watched violent porn were almost *six times* more likely to be sexually aggressive than those who did not; watching nonviolent porn did not have the same effect. A more recent study on dating violence, published in 2019, found that tenth-grade boys who watched violent porn were three times more likely to sexually abuse a dating partner than those who did not.

In their conversations with teens, though, the Boston team emphasizes that the findings on pornography's impact are not entirely clear-cut. Studies published in 2019 found no connection between watching porn and risky sexual behavior or sexual satisfaction, challenging the findings of earlier research. And while conventional wisdom holds that porn watchers tend to start with vanilla scenes and graduate to ever more extreme hardcore porn in order to get off, that was not the case in another 2019 study that tracked teen boys' viewing habits over two years. Some research even suggests that porn can sometimes be positive, including as a way for LGBTQ youth to understand and explore their sexuality—and to see that their desires are not weird or wrong.

The bottom line is that it is not good for kids to learn how to have sex from porn, and also that porn is not the root of all sexual evil.

In recent years, a growing number of states (and the national Republican Party) have declared porn a "public health crisis." Emily Rothman, the Boston University professor who brings a public health perspective to the porn literacy team, believes that is a distortion and a distraction: use of porn is only one of many factors that shape how we handle sex and relationships. We are missing something when we focus on it to the exclusion of everything else that we know contributes to the problem of sexual violence, from childhood abuse, to the influence of peers and masculine norms, to the messages about sex embedded in the nonexplicit media—movies, music, video games, and Snapchat posts—that our kids are exposed to every day.

If you're worried about porn, you can set up internet filters and check your son's web browser history. But if you're not also talking to him about sexual citizenship, consent, and the pressures that boys often feel to score with girls, then you're not addressing the most important things—his need for guidance, information, and help developing a sense of sexual ethics.

"Sure, porn could be a part of this giant constellations of factors," Rothman told me. "But the idea that it's the biggest and the one that should get the money and the attention as a way to solve sexual violence, at the expense of focus on other risk factors, isn't sound."

Corey, the high school senior who started watching porn in fifth grade, had a chance to take the porn literacy class as a peer leader for Boston's Start Strong program, which employs young people to teach other young people about healthy relationships. The classes were held after school in an unremarkable low-ceilinged room at the Boston Public

Health Commission, and this is where he finally learned about consent. He learned that it means asking what your partner wants and doesn't want, rather than just assuming, and he told me, smiling from beneath the brim of a baseball cap, that he was glad he took the class before he lost his virginity.

He and one of his fellow peer leaders, Jessica, spoke to me in a drafty office down the hall from the room where they took the porn literacy class. Both said that the curriculum helped them understand how porn shapes our ideas about what is normal in sex, and about how men and women should look and behave when they're having sex. Neither of them had ever seen heterosexual porn that showed mutual sex, in which the woman's desires and pleasure seemed to matter as much as the man's.

Jessica—who described herself as a virgin—said she understands now that sex is not a neatly choreographed dance as it is often portrayed, but a messy, special way of knowing another person. "What porn doesn't show is that . . . between the two individuals, sex can be a learning experience— like learning about each other," she said. "If you can't talk about sex, then you're not ready to have it."

After I said goodbye to Jessica and Corey and walked out into a chilly Boston evening, this is what I could not stop thinking about: *If you can't talk about sex, then you're not ready to have it.* Jessica had articulated, better than I had been able to articulate to myself, one of the most important things I want my son (and my daughter) to understand. Communication is an essential part of sex. If you can't talk with your partner about what you want, clearly and directly and sober-mindedly, and if you can't listen to and respect what they want, then you're not ready. If that's the takeaway from pornography literacy class, I'd like to enroll my kids someday.

When the *New York Times* ran its story about porn literacy in 2018, writer Maggie Jones observed that it is so new and so fringe that "few people are optimistic that it will be taught anytime soon in public schools." That's undoubtedly true for the vast majority of public schools—but not all of them. A few have been dipping their toes in, convinced that teaching children about porn is critical for their students' health and safety. The rest of the country should learn from their example, and school districts that find pornography too politically difficult to talk about should consider the price of continuing to say nothing.

Molly Wales, a school nurse from Athens, Ohio, revamped and bulked up her district's sex ed offerings after realizing that some sexually active high school students weren't sure what vaginal intercourse was, or how it was connected to pregnancy and reproduction. Among the changes: Wales decided that she and her colleagues had to start talking to students about pornography—and that they had to start early, in sixth grade.

Wales went before the school board to present the new curriculum publicly, taking pains to underline the fact that pornography literacy was part of the proposal. She didn't want anyone to be surprised. "I said, 'Let's talk about the elephant in the room. Let's talk about how uncomfortable this is, that I am proposing talking to sixth graders about pornography,'" she told me. "'They are being exposed to it, nobody is talking about it, it is shaping what they think sex is, and we need to intervene early.'" The school board, unfazed, voted unanimously and enthusiastically in support of the changes in September 2018.

Sixth-graders in Athens now learn about porn as part of a lesson designed to teach kids how messages about sex and gender are constantly bombarding us, shaping our ideas about how relationships are supposed to work. In the lesson, students look at advertisements that objectify people's bodies and watch movie clips that make coercion and manipulation seem romantic. In a scene from the blockbuster romantic drama *The Notebook*, Noah (played by Ryan Gosling) pursues Allie (Rachel McAdams) by clambering uninvited with her onto a Ferris wheel. She is already sharing her seat with another guy. To pressure her into going out with him, he dangles one-handed from the wheel, several stories above the ground, threatening to let go and fall if she doesn't say yes. Finally, she gives in. (Go watch the clip online—it's unbelievably creepy.)

Jennifer Seifert, the executive director of the Survivor Advocacy Outreach Program of southeastern Ohio, wrote the lesson and now teaches it in Athens classrooms. She explains to students that consuming media is like consuming food, a concrete analogy that works for sixth graders. They talk about how candy bars affect bodies differently than apples, and that though a few candy bars now and then aren't going to wreck an otherwise healthy diet, a steady stream of junk food becomes a problem.

When the lesson turns to porn, Seifert frames it as unhealthy for a sixth-grader's media diet. They talk about how porn paints an unrealistic picture of bodies and sex acts, and how it usually shows men in power over women. And each kid comes up with a plan so if they come across pornography, they have thought ahead of time about what to do and whom they can talk to about it.

With high school students, Seifert extends the conversation from online porn to sexting. Her message is not that sexting is unambiguously terrible but that students should understand the risks and how to minimize them. If you're going to send a picture of a body part, for example, don't include your face. She wants them to be able to make an informed and safe choice when they are confronted with the inevitable decision about whether they're going to send or ask for naked pictures.

Two years after she introduced the new sex ed curriculum, Wales has received exactly zero complaints from parents or students—evidence, perhaps, that many parents are glad for the help teaching about sensitive subjects. When I spoke to Sean Parsons, the school board vice president at the time, he said the same thing—no angry emails, no phone calls, not even any concerns expressed in passing by parents he's run into in the grocery store. He said he was excited for his own children—twins who were at that point headed into fifth grade—to get the sex education his district is now offering. "If we don't talk about it," he said, "they're going to go online and look it up."

CHAPTER FOUR

Shaping Young Minds

How Schools Are Failing Young Children

Detroit: A five-year-old kindergartner, a boy with several disabilities, got off his school bus one day bruised, disheveled, and covered in what appeared to be semen. The bus driver told the boy's mother that he and some other boys on the bus had been "sucking wee-wees," a fact the mother reported to the school district the next day. City police officers found that two other students had assaulted the boy, but school officials never investigated, as they were required to do under federal law, or came up with a plan to make sure that the boy could safely return to school.

Understandably, the mother did not allow her son to go back. Nightmares interrupted his troubled sleep and he didn't want to be around other boys. The school district offered no counseling or other services. Months passed before district officials contacted the family and the boy returned to a different school.

Federal civil rights lawyers dispatched to Detroit in the wake of the mother's complaint discovered no evidence that the school system had responded to any of the 45 instances of criminal sexual conduct by students (or 233 instances of sexual harassment by students) that it had recorded over the previous three years. At the time, the school district did not even have a policy for handling such complaints.

*　　*　　*

Hammond, Indiana: Kids in this district of thirteen thousand spoke plainly when federal civil rights investigators examined sexual misconduct policies in their schools. Sexual harassment was constant, it was everywhere, and no one seemed to care. Students said that they witnessed groping in school regularly, along with cat-calling, whistling, and sexually explicit texts and social media posts. Most said that they didn't bother to tell adults what was going on. "They do not believe a teacher or administrator would take the report seriously," the federal investigators wrote in a letter to the district superintendent. Middle schoolers described "Smack that ass Friday," a tradition for eighth-grade boys to slap sixth-grade girls on the rear end. Everyone knew about it, but adults didn't do anything. Most students didn't know that the school district had a policy against sexual harassment, or what to do if they saw something inappropriate— no one had ever told them.

Chicago: A boy choked a girl when she passed him in the hallway, then pinned her to the floor and grabbed her breasts. He was not disciplined. In another case, a boy grabbed the testicles of one male classmate and exposed his penis to another. In a third case, a boy snatched a girl's belongings and then ran to an out-of-the-way spot in the school building. When she followed him to get her things back, he sexually assaulted her; he received a two-day suspension but no counseling and, two months later, did the same thing to another girl.

For years, Chicago Public Schools utterly failed to respond appropriately to sexual harassment and assault, and abdicated its responsibility to protect students not only from predatory teachers but also from other students, according to a scathing investigative series published by the *Chicago Tribune* in 2018 and an investigation by the U.S. Department of Education. Kids were victimized in hallways, on school buses, during recess, while lining up for the water fountain. But for nearly two decades, from 1999 until shortly after the *Tribune* series, the third-largest school system in the nation did not employ anyone to oversee or manage sexual violence complaints. Its handling of those complaints was "inadequate, unreliable and often conducted by untrained staff," leaving children unsafe in the schools they were required to attend, the Department of Education concluded.

In September 2019, the school system agreed to overhaul its policies and procedures to avoid losing potentially millions of dollars in federal funding. "Over the last several years, Americans have become increasingly aware of sexual violence on college and university campuses," Kenneth Marcus, an assistant secretary of education for civil rights, told reporters. "This case may be a wake-up call that the problem exists on elementary and secondary school grounds as well."

Sexual violence is a problem in schools across the country, in every kind of community. As of November 2019, federal officials were investigating 257 complaints of sexual harassment and sexual violence in K–12 schools in places as far-flung and diverse as rural Custer County, Colorado, on the eastern fringes of the rugged Sangre de Cristo Wilderness, to the affluent suburbs of Grosse Pointe, Michigan, and Fairfax County, Virginia.

In fact, entitlement and privilege may boost a boy's risk for sexual misconduct. In a study published in 2019, nearly one in ten boys between the ages of ten and eighteen admitted to perpetrating sexual harassment, and those from affluent communities were significantly more likely to do so than those from less privileged neighborhoods.

Over the past decade, colleges and universities have cracked down on sexual violence, spurred both by campus activists and by pressure from the Obama administration's Department of Education, which issued new guidelines in 2011 for responding to complaints of sexual harassment and assault.

Sexual assault prevention programs have become ubiquitous, consent has become part of the lexicon, and students disciplined for committing sexual misconduct have fought back in court, claiming that they were treated unfairly by schools under pressure to show the federal government that they took sexual violence seriously. All of this stoked bitter debate: How can we really know what happened between two people in a room?

Who is empowered to decide? What is appropriate punishment? Is redemption possible?

These questions have been conspicuously absent in K–12 schools despite the fact that sexual misconduct is common among children. Nearly half of middle school and high school students are sexually harassed at school, according to the most recent nationally representative survey, conducted during the 2010–11 school year by the American Association of University Women. The survey asked young people about their experiences with unwanted comments, unwanted touching, receiving unsolicited and unwanted nude photos, and being flashed. Girls were more likely to say they'd been targeted, but a lot of boys—40 percent—said they'd been harassed, too, according to the same survey.

These numbers are troubling. But there's been no major public reckoning in our middle and high schools, no national effort to shed light on the sexual harassment and dating violence that our kids witness and experience in hallways, classrooms, and cafeterias. The problem is not just that sex education and other prevention measures are missing, as we saw in Chapter Three. It's also that many K–12 schools are clueless when it comes to responding to the sexual violence that happens to their students and within their buildings.

Scholars and lawyers who work on all sides of the problem, representing victims, accused students, and schools, say that many K–12 schools don't have staff who understand their legal obligations to respond to complaints of sexual misconduct. Some don't even have policies that lay out what *should* happen if a child complains of sexual harassment or assault. The result is that parents send their kids off to schools where sexual misconduct is common and rarely reported—and when it is reported, is too often greeted with nonchalance, dismissal, or outright disbelief.

"It really is like working with the wild, wild West," said Brett Sokolow, a risk management consultant who specializes in helping schools comply with Title IX. Most of Sokolow's clients are colleges and universities, but about 20 percent are K–12 schools, he said. "The level of unawareness and noncompliance is somewhat staggering."

Karen Truszkowski, a Michigan lawyer who works on the other side—representing victims of sexual violence—agreed. She once represented a girl who was sexually assaulted by a boy in a stairwell of their school in the middle of the day; the girl was suspended for ten days under a policy that called for punishing students who engage in "lewd and lascivious" behavior regardless of consent. The school district in that case, in Lansing, ultimately paid $180,000 to settle the case. But there are countless students who are victimized and don't know their rights and don't how to get a lawyer—or can't afford one.

K–12 schools "for the most part have no awareness of Title IX and what the requirements are and what they are supposed to be doing," Truszkowski said. When we spoke, she was representing victims of sexual violence in negotiations or lawsuits with more than two dozen school districts in Michigan. "Not one of them has their shit together," she said.

Stalking and other teen dating abuse are also shockingly common problems that schools struggle to deal with. One in eleven girls—and one in fifteen boys—was hit by a dating partner, hurt by a weapon wielded by a partner, or otherwise physically abused by a partner within the past year, according to a 2017 national survey of high school students by the Centers for Disease Control and Prevention. Nearly one in nine girls and one in thirty-six boys said they'd been sexually abused by a dating partner. Lesbian, gay, and bisexual students were more than twice as likely to be victims as straight students, according to the CDC data. And though little is known about transgender children, the research that does exist suggests that they are at even higher risk.

Other national surveys that include verbal and psychological abuse, like obsessively tracking a partner's whereabouts, isolating them from friends, and other jealous behavior, have found the problem to be even more widespread. And counter to stereotype, it's not always boys who are the aggressors. In fact, these surveys suggest that girls are even more likely than boys to verbally and physically abuse their partners, and that most perpetrators of dating violence are also victims.

We know that this kind of abuse has far-reaching effects on teens' mental and physical health, increasing the risk that they will think about suicide and will be re-victimized by a romantic partner in adulthood. We know that dating abuse has also been linked to academic struggles and poor educational outcomes. We know, too, that when dating violence goes unaddressed, it can be fatal.

A study of 150 teenagers who were killed by an intimate partner or ex-partner between 2003 and 2016 found that 90 percent of the victims were girls, their average age almost seventeen. Ninety percent of the killers were boys and men, average age twenty. Girls were killed most frequently after a breakup or when their partner was jealous, and the most common weapon was a gun.

But even as the public health community has sounded an alarm about teen dating violence as a serious problem, most schools have not made a priority out of addressing it. High school principals across the country are unprepared to handle it. In one study, two-thirds of principals said that they hadn't been trained to deal with dating abuse, and nearly the same number said that they hadn't trained their staff. Three-quarters said that their school had no protocol set up for responding to reports of dating violence among students.

Schools shape student behavior in part by how they respond to misbehavior. And when K–12 schools don't respond to sexual violence and dating abuse proactively, productively, and in accordance with the law, they are missing a chance not only to keep victims safe but to teach young people who make mistakes that what they've done is wrong—so that they can change their behavior in the future.

Nan Stein, a senior research scientist at the Wellesley Centers for Women and one of the nation's foremost experts on K–12 sexual violence, has been arguing for decades that when teachers and administrators ignore sexual harassment, they teach kids that such behavior is unremarkable and unworthy of authorities' attention. They turn schools into a training ground for future domestic and sexual violence.

"In schools, harassment often happens while many people watch," Stein wrote in 1995. "When sexual harassment occurs in public and is not condemned, it becomes, with time, part of the social norm." The boy who calls a girl a slut or a "thot" (short for "that ho over there"), and who is not disciplined or stopped, learns that he can continue to act with impunity. The same is true of the boy who gropes a girl's rear end, and of the boy who rapes a girl in the school bathroom. And other kids—the boys and girls who hear the epithet, see the grope, or learn of the rape—come to regard it as acceptable.

Teachers and principals can't look the other way. But they do, oftentimes because they don't know any better. When I became a teacher, I spent a year apprenticing in high school classrooms and taking graduate-level courses in education. I don't recall that professors or mentor teachers discussed sexual harassment as an issue I would need to confront in my work. When I taught sex education during my first year in my own classroom, in a public middle school, I taught it mostly as a biology unit on reproduction. I don't remember anybody urging me to use that time to teach about conducting healthy relationships, or about consent and dealing with harassment and unwanted touching.

Psychologist Richard Weissbourd, who directs the Making Caring Common project at Harvard University—which studies and encourages the role that educators and parents play in raising moral, empathetic children—believes that this is a critical fuel for sexual harassment in schools: administrators and teachers who are unable or unwilling to confront behavior they witness.

"You walk down a hall, you see a poster about caring and respect—and right in front of the poster, you see some boy harassing a girl or calling a girl a 'bitch' or a 'ho,' and teachers just walking right by," he said. In training sessions at schools, Weissbourd said he's come to learn that teachers aren't equipped with the skills they need in order to be able to intervene successfully when they see or hear something objectionable. They don't know what to say, and they don't know how to stop the behavior without turning themselves into a target. But those are critical skills for teachers to have if they want to create safe schools for kids who are at a vulnerable moment in their lives, just starting to understand their sexuality.

The Problem with Ignoring Sexual Violence in School

Why haven't K–12 schools given sexual violence the same attention that colleges have? Maybe because children who survive sexual assault don't have the same ability as young adults to advocate for themselves, and so their experiences are more likely to remain hidden from public scrutiny. Maybe because many public K–12 schools don't compete for students or alumni donations in quite the same way as universities, and don't feel the same pressure to demonstrate how they are tackling this problem. Maybe because schools are underfunded and overwhelmed.

Or maybe because grown-ups tend to see sexual misconduct among children and teenagers as inevitable, something we shouldn't expect schools to control—something that is, honestly, just not that big a deal.

That view has extended all the way to the Supreme Court, where it defined the contours of the justices' debate over a landmark case that outlined when and how schools can be held liable for failing to deal with student-on-student sexual harassment.

The case was *Davis v. Monroe County Board of Education*, and Davis was LaShonda Davis, a ten-year-old student in a small-town Georgia elementary school. Starting in the winter of 1992 and continuing for five months, she complained over and over to her teachers about a boy in her class who wouldn't leave her alone. He kept telling her that he wanted to have sex with her, and that he wanted to feel her breasts. Then he actually tried to feel her breasts and her crotch—repeatedly. He was always trying to rub his body up against hers in the hallway, and in gym class, she said, he once approached her after putting a door stop inside his pants as if he had an erection. He harassed her almost every day.

Her desk was next to his at school, and even after she complained about the way he was treating her, three months passed before the teachers allowed her to move. LaShonda's mother, Aurelia—frustrated with the school's unwillingness to respond to her daughter's complaints or discipline the boy—ultimately went to the police. The boy pleaded guilty to sexual battery and finally left LaShonda alone. But by that time, her grades had dropped and she had written a suicide note.

Both she and the boy were in the fifth grade. Just kids, but still perfectly capable of meting out aggression and of feeling pain.

By failing to address the harassment more quickly and directly, the school district failed all its students. LaShonda struggled in obvious ways.

But what lessons did the boy learn from his school's apparent tolerance of his misbehavior? And what did their classmates learn as they looked on?

LaShonda's mother sued the school district over its inaction. She argued that school officials had failed to protect her daughter from sex discrimination as required by Title IX. There is no mention of sexual misconduct in the statute, but federal courts had already made clear that school districts could be sued under Title IX for failing to properly address teacher-on-student sexual harassment. Now, LaShonda's mother wanted the court to also recognize that Title IX protected children from harassment by other children, and that school districts could be sued for damages when they failed to act. "They make you send your kids to school, right?" she told the *New York Times*. "So don't you think they should protect them while they're there?"

The case made its way to the Supreme Court in January 1999. In May of that year, by a vote of 5–4, the justices sided with LaShonda and her mother. School districts that didn't live up to their legal obligations to deal with student-on-student sexual harassment could be sued for damages.

Justice Kennedy, famously the court's key swing vote on abortion rights and same-sex marriage, wrote a long, vehement dissent, predicting that the majority decision would unleash a torrent of lawsuits on cash-strapped school districts that were already struggling to do their most important job, teaching the basics of reading, writing, and math. It was ridiculous to put school districts in that situation, he wrote, for a problem that isn't really even a problem so much as a mere fact of teen life, one of the "routine problems of adolescence."

"A teacher's sexual overtures toward a student are always inappropriate; a teenager's romantic overtures to a classmate (even when persistent and unwelcome) are an inescapable part of adolescence," he wrote.

An inescapable part of adolescence. Even when persistent and unwelcome.

Looking through today's lens, two decades later, that sounds to me like a slightly wordier way of saying: boys will be boys. Groping your classmates? Asking them repeatedly for sex? Normal. Inescapable! Something we can't honestly expect schools to handle.

Kennedy's concerns seemed to be on the minds even of the majority. "I'm sure that school children nationwide tease each other, and little boys tease little girls, and so forth throughout their years in school," Justice Sandra Day O'Connor had said, during oral argument, to the lawyer representing Davis. "And is every one of those incidents going to lead to some kind of a lawsuit?"

When O'Connor sat down to write the majority opinion, she set a high bar for victims to hold their schools liable. For a plaintiff to win in court, the sexual harassment had to be really, really bad, and the district had to be really, really negligent. Or, in O'Connor's language, the harassment had to be so "severe, pervasive, and objectively offensive" that it denied the victim access to education. And the plaintiff had to show that the district had been "deliberately indifferent" to the harassment—meaning, specifically, that whatever it did was "clearly unreasonable."

Those parameters have made it difficult for victims to prove Title IX violations in court, leaving room for school districts to prevail even when they do very little to protect students, according to victims' advocates. A school district doesn't have to act reasonably; it only has to act in a way that is *not clearly unreasonable*, a lower threshold. In practice, O'Connor's opinion has meant that school districts facing Title IX lawsuits often have been able to win just by showing they did *something*—even if whatever they did was not effective. "It's a really permissive standard," said Cari Simon, a lawyer who represents K–12 and college student victims of sexual violence. "It's not fair that I as a mother should not be able to expect my school to be reasonable in responding to sexual violence."

In May 2020, the Trump administration announced new rules to govern schools' handling of complaints about sexual harassment and sexual violence. The rules didn't immediately affect the bar the Supreme Court had set under *Davis v. Monroe* for a parent seeking to hold a school financially liable for failing to deal with sexual violence. But they did redefine what schools must do in order to receive federal funding from the U.S. Department of Education. They extended the law's reach in some ways, including by explicitly including dating violence and stalking as forms of sexual harassment. But, adopting the language of the Supreme Court, they also said the harassment had to become extreme—"severe, pervasive and objectively offensive"—before schools were required to address it. Advocates warned that move would make it even easier for schools to look the other way—and even harder for victims to get help.

The Problem with Punishment

Across the country, a generation of teen activists is marching for social change, pressing not just for gun control and for climate change action but also for schools to finally begin taking sexual violence seriously. Counselors and Title IX coordinators at K–12 schools say that girls have become more outspoken about reporting sexual misconduct allegations. These are positive developments for uprooting offensive behavior and keeping schools safe.

But there is some anecdotal evidence that some schools may be swinging from ignoring sexual misconduct to the other extreme, punishing boys harshly for the kind of behavior that was dismissed as normal until very recently. I'm not convinced that's productive, either.

Suspension rates soared when harsh punishment for misbehavior—sometimes called "zero-tolerance" discipline—came into vogue in schools during the 1980s and 1990s. But researchers found scant evidence that principals could punish their way into creating a healthier culture or that suspension and expulsion resulted in safer schools.

On the other hand, they found a lot of evidence that kicking kids out of school can have dramatic long-term effects on their lives and on their prospects for success. Children who are suspended are less likely to graduate from high school and more likely to end up in the juvenile justice system. A ninth-grader who is suspended just one time faces *double* the risk of dropping out before graduation. This is not just because kids who are bound for trouble happen to get suspended as they hurtle along toward their fate; by controlling for socioeconomic class, academic achievement, types of misbehavior, and other factors that could be related to young people's trajectories, researchers have made a strong case for the notion that suspension itself is a factor that knocks children off course.

You know who has borne the brunt of this crackdown in schools? Boys. They make up about half of the U.S. student population but account for close to 70 percent of students who are suspended. The disproportionate treatment starts as early as preschool, and it is even more pronounced for boys of color and boys with disabilities. Black boys are suspended at more than *three times* the rate of white boys. Adults discipline Black boys more frequently not because Black boys misbehave more often, researchers say, but because adults believe that they are troublemakers. More on that in Chapter Six.

In the face of evidence that harsh punishment doesn't work and affects certain kids disproportionately, schools have faced huge pressure over the last decade to find more productive ways to deal with students' misbehavior, and suspension rates have fallen. The pressure to reduce suspensions has been acute in progressive pockets of the country—some of the very same communities where schools are now facing growing pressure to crack down on sexual violence. How schools in those communities will handle that pressure remains to be seen, but there are signs that some of them are now edging toward the kind of hard-line approach to sexual misconduct that they have rejected for other offenses.

Andrew Miltenberg, one of the most prominent lawyers representing college men accused of sexual assault, said that he receives, on average, three to four phone calls per week from distraught parents of high school boys accused of sexual misconduct. Over the past two years, he's gone from representing one or two high school students at a time to now nearly thirty.

Miltenberg said that one of his clients was expelled from a private school after he was accused of sending a text to a friend about a girl whose "tits looked great in that shirt." Miltenberg acknowledged that he would be horrified if a boy had written that text about his own daughter. But he said he still isn't comfortable with such harsh punishment for the kind of behavior that adults have long accepted from teen boys, and even tacitly approved.

We have redefined what is appropriate and inappropriate, he said, without necessarily spending time to make sure that young people—and particularly boys—understand the lines they should not cross. "High schools are definitely cracking down," he said. "These could be teachable moments, and I think that's where high schools are missing the boat."

While it's not surprising to hear that note of caution from a lawyer who is paid to advocate on behalf of boys and men accused of sexual misconduct, I heard the same sentiment from lawyers who represent victims of sexual misconduct and from others who are alarmed about the prevalence of sexual violence in schools. Ignoring sexual misconduct is obviously not the right thing to do. But skipping straight to harsh punishment, for even low-level offenses, is not necessarily the answer, either.

Richard Weissbourd, the Harvard psychologist who trains teachers to effectively confront harassment, said that he has been troubled by stories of boys who have been stiffly punished and shamed for what is, in the scheme of things, relatively minor misbehavior. Ultimately, it just doesn't get us closer to healthier, safer schools. "I'm really worried about sexual harassment and its impact on girls," Weissbourd said. "I also think there are these cases where boys are getting inflated punishments or there's a dramatic reaction that is scaring boys a lot, scaring parents a lot—and is really devaluing and trivializing what real sexual harassment is."

The Case of John Doe 2

The boy known in court papers as John Doe 2 was born in India, adopted from an orphanage as a baby, and raised in Fairfax County, a suburb of Washington, D.C. By the time he turned sixteen, he had established himself as a slightly nerdy straight-A student at Lake Braddock Secondary School. He acted in school plays and rowed for the crew team, and his classmates both teased him—they thought he seemed gay—and leaned on him for help on homework assignments.

He got in trouble for the first and only time of his high school career during his sophomore year, when three of his crew teammates complained to administrators that he had sexually harassed them. His story highlights important, knotty issues about what happens when boys misbehave at a time when schools are under pressure to take sexual harassment seriously. And it underlines questions about the limits of punishment to change school cultures that encourage sexual harassment in the first place.

When John got into trouble, his school had a new interim principal, only a week into the job. The previous principal had retired suddenly midyear, and the athletic director and football coach had been forced out. News stories had claimed that school district officials had failed to respond to girls' complaints about their basketball coach and his alleged habit of making inappropriate sexual comments. Federal civil rights officials had started investigating.

Against that backdrop, John was called down to an assistant principal's office and told that he had been accused of behaving inappropriately.

"You'd cut yourself if you fingered yourself with those nails," he'd said to a girl after she showed him her new fake nails in Spanish class. Another girl said that at crew practice, when one rower asked another if she could borrow a tampon, John had interjected: "Hopefully not a used one." He went on to ask: "Why does a girl not orgasm when they put a tampon in?"

John admitted making these crude statements, but he said he didn't understand why he was being singled out for using language that was common at his school and absolutely unremarkable. He had first heard the masturbation joke when another guy said it to a female coxswain on the crew team. John thought it seemed like she "got a kick out of it." He figured he'd give it a try. Accused of telling girls they were "thick" and otherwise commenting on their bodies, he admitted that he'd talked about girls' butts—but only with other boys. Why? "I guess everybody does it," he had explained under questioning by school officials.

The girls also accused John of inappropriate touching. One said he brushed up against her breast and put his hand on her hip, and another said he grabbed his own crotch through his spandex at crew practice; he said he did neither. The third girl said he grabbed her crotch in the school library when they were horsing around. That was a misunderstanding, he said: they were both poking each other when she lost her balance and fell backward in her chair, and he accidentally touched her below the belly button.

After a brief investigation, John was suspended for ten days. And then, after a hearing, he was removed from Lake Braddock for good. The hearing officers concluded that he had "committed serious repeated offenses . . . by engaging in improper and offensive touching of female students and sexual harassment of female students."

He was sent to an alternative school for troubled kids, which he described as "traumatic" and "horrible." The following semester, he was reassigned to a different neighborhood school. His life was ruptured in a way that must have felt unfixable. He threatened suicide, and his parents were careful never to leave him alone. "I regularly consider harming myself. I feel like it would be easier for my family if I just disappeared," he wrote.

We all want schools to build a culture inside classrooms and hallways where harassment and bullying and unwanted touching are seen by teachers and students as unacceptable. We all want schools to take sexual misconduct seriously. But some may not find the stiff penalty in John's case to be reassuring; they may find it instead to be profoundly unsettling. How can we tell boys that they must be more empathetic, on the one hand, and fail to show them empathy, on the other?

John and his family sued the school district in federal court in an effort to expunge the black mark on his transcript before he applied to college. His argument boiled down to a few key points. The girls had made up some stories about him because one of them had a brother who didn't like John. The school's investigation was biased and incomplete. And the comments John had made were utterly unremarkable, the kind of things boys (and girls) said every day at Lake Braddock. He was being pilloried, his lawyers argued, because he was a boy and the school was under federal investigation for its alleged failure to address sexual harassment on the girls' basketball team.

The school district said that wasn't true. John had himself admitted to using vulgar sexual language and to touching a girl below her belly button, the school district told the court, arguing that administrators had properly disciplined him for violating school rules.

I admit, when I first opened the court filings in John's case, I was prepared to be unsympathetic. I knew that K–12 schools were generally unprepared or unwilling to deal with sexual harassment. And I was predisposed to believe that if John had been kicked out of school, he probably deserved it.

But then I read hundreds of pages of documents, and I sat in a wood-paneled courtroom, watching John watch his lawyer pleading his case. And I came to realize how complicated these issues are.

The judge who heard John's case was Leonie M. Brinkema, a no-nonsense Clinton appointee to the U.S. District Court for the Eastern District of Virginia, which decides a lot of high-profile national security cases. Brinkema presided over the case of 9/11 terrorist Zacarias Moussaoui, and she was one of the federal judges who blocked President Donald Trump's infamous travel ban.

She seemed sympathetic to John's plight. Early on, she called the case "sad" and "troubling." She said she wished the two sides could come to some agreement to save John the burden of carrying his misbehavior into the future in the form of a notation on his high school transcript that might make it more difficult to get into college. In any other kind of case, she said she'd have no trouble finding that John had been illegally denied due process—but students in school discipline cases have far fewer rights than defendants in court.

The district's investigation was flawed, the judge wrote. The administrator in charge of the process, who initially said that she had interviewed the three girls, later said during a sworn deposition that she had only interviewed one, and that girl denied that she was interviewed. School officials never tried to find out who else was in the library on the day of the alleged crotch-grab, and nor did they examine the library sign-in sheet for John's signature.

Had the school district gotten to the bottom of everything that happened? Maybe not. There had been "numerous deficiencies with the investigatory process that were relied upon and compounded at each stage of the disciplinary proceeding," Brinkema wrote.

But in the end, she ruled in the district's favor anyway. John hadn't proved that the way he was treated had anything to do with his gender, she decided, and therefore he hadn't shown that the school district broke the law.

John and his family decided to appeal his case to the Fourth Circuit, and they declined to talk with me while his appeal was pending. The Fairfax County school district didn't answer specific questions about the case, either. In a statement, a spokesman said that the district conducts fair and impartial investigations and doles out fair and impartial consequences. John Doe 2's case "shows that we defend and protect victims of harassment," the school system said. As this book was going to press, the Fourth Circuit Court of Appeals affirmed Brinkema's decision: in disciplining John, the school system had broken no law.

I see John's case through two filters: as the mother of a girl who may someday be subjected to crude comments and unwanted touching at school, and whom I desperately want to protect, and as the mother of a boy who may someday be subject to school disciplinary measures that seem unfair or ill-considered—and whom I desperately want to protect. I want schools to be safe for both my children.

John Doe 2 claimed that some of the allegations against him were false. But even if all of them were true—the alleged touching, the dumb, crude jokes he made about tampons and masturbation, the comments about women's bodies—did the punishment fit the offense? Did the handling of his case help him reflect on what he had done wrong and why it was hurtful? Did it make his school a safer place? Is kicking out the Johns of the world really what's needed to create the kind of safety that students deserve?

A parent involved in volunteering with the Lake Braddock crew team that John was a member of, and where he allegedly said and did some of the things for which he was disciplined, told me that raunchy talk and inappropriate sexualized behavior were startlingly common among rowers—both boys and girls. John's removal didn't change that, this parent said.

But it did take an emotional and financial toll on John and his family. They hired three teams of lawyers for different portions of the administrative and legal appeals; just one of those teams billed $176,000, according to court documents. John was diagnosed with anxiety and depression and struggled with thoughts of hurting himself.

The picture of his case is surely incomplete, as the court record is nearly silent on the impact of John's misconduct on the girls who complained about it. But thousands of pages of documents paint a picture of a dorky kid who said and did foolish, rude things in an effort to be cool and fit in. It seems like behavior that could be unlearned or reshaped.

After he was suspended, his parents hired a therapist to help him understand consent and appropriate boundaries. Yet there had been no room within the school district's disciplinary approach for this kind of teaching, no attempt to help John understand why his actions were wrong before he was kicked out. "No one ever sat John down and told him to stop this behavior, or to discuss how to interact with the girls in his class more maturely," one of his lawyers wrote in an unsuccessful appeal to the school board to overturn his reassignment to the alternative school.

That teachable moment is long gone. John now sees himself, not the girls who complained about his behavior, as the victim. In his sworn statements, he comes across as angry and depressed and focused on the behavior of the school officials who wronged him. He flatly denies that he is guilty of sexual misconduct, and declares it unfair that making "a couple juvenile comments . . . should destroy the rest of my life."

"I'm not going to get accepted into a good college because of what has happened here, and it's, it's not fair," John said, when he was asked to reflect on his experience. "I deserve to go to a good college. . . . I had built such a good foundation and it was just, achieve achieve achieve. And it was like everything just came tumbling down in my face."

John's case has pushed me to think about the purpose of punishment. Punishing a boy's misbehavior is not the same thing as keeping a school safe, persuading him he did wrong, or helping him see his actions through the eyes of the people he hurt. Punishing sexual misconduct harshly is not the same thing as taking the problem seriously, doing the work necessary to prevent it, and creating a culture where it's not accepted. If schools aren't doing that deeper and more sustained work, then punishment is just a fig leaf. And it can be counterproductive, alienating boys who might otherwise be recruited as allies in the effort to make change.

The Potential for Another Way: Restorative Justice

It feels sometimes that we have a terrible and impossible choice, both in schools and in society at large. Punish sexual violence harshly to send a message that it will not be tolerated. Or let it go unpunished and send the message that sexual violence is normal, acceptable, no big deal.

But maybe that's a false choice. Maybe there is another way: restorative justice.

Rooted in traditions of the Maori people in New Zealand and other indigenous groups around the world, restorative justice asks the person who's harmed another to acknowledge that harm, and then to come to an agreement about how to repair that harm. Sometimes that happens face-to-face, in a restorative circle—a meeting between the victim and the offender, their close supporters, and a trained facilitator. Sometimes it happens by letter, with the victim writing down what they want the offender to hear, and the offender responding in kind.

Restorative justice is built on the belief that a person who accepts that he has hurt another person, and who takes responsibility for that hurt, is more likely than a person who goes through the traditional court system to actually understand the impact of his behavior and behave differently in the future.

Using restorative justice in response to sexual harm has long been a controversial idea. Skeptics fear it is just a way to let rapists off easy. Others doubt whether it is wise or fair to ask a survivor to face down the person who violated them. But advocates for restorative justice argue that we could do better by victims and offenders alike if we stepped back and rethought our whole approach to redressing harm—including sexual harm—by focusing not on how we punish boys but on how we help them learn to take responsibility and make amends. Supporters of restorative justice say this is much more likely than a criminal prosecution to yield the outcomes that so many survivors of sexual violence say they want: acknowledgment, explanation, apology, and a promise not to hurt anyone else in the same way.

This is a revolutionary idea. The traditional school discipline system— as well as the traditional criminal court system and the punishing court of public opinion—encourages a person accused of doing something wrong to deny responsibility and evade accountability. Parents of boys who do wrong may also encourage their sons to deny responsibility, fearing for the repercussions if he is found guilty, especially of a sexual offense. But when boys hurt someone, accountability is exactly what they need if we want them to learn and change. What if we redesigned our school discipline and criminal court systems to encourage more of it?

A growing number of schools have embraced restorative justice as a way to address misbehavior without resorting to suspension or arrest, but it remains rare in cases of sexual misconduct, according to experts in the field. It takes a real commitment—and money—to hire skilled staff and give them the time they need to do the job right. Many—most?—schools are not equipped to do that. Counselors who use restorative justice told me that the combination of scarce resources and mounting pressure on school districts over the last decade to reduce suspensions can and does distort the process, turning what is a theoretically powerful tool into a box-checking exercise. Misbehavior is neither punished nor fully addressed.

Even California's Oakland Unified School District, which has led the nation in bringing a restorative justice approach to K–12 schools, does not recommend restorative justice in cases involving sexual harm. David Yusem, the district's restorative justice program coordinator, told me that while he believes that restorative justice can be transformative in those cases, he also knows that success requires a facilitator with considerable time, skill, and sensitivity. Absent such a skilled guide, he said, the experience of sitting in a circle with a person who's hurt you—whether through sexual harassment or assault—could end up being much more harmful than healing.

But if schools are not equipped to do this kind of work, that doesn't mean it cannot be done. In Washington, D.C., an experiment is underway to use a restorative justice approach with teenagers accused of crimes, including some sexual crimes. On a sweltering day in July, I hopped on my bike and rode three miles to a hulking city government building downtown, a few long blocks from the U.S. Capitol. I wanted to meet Seema Gajwani, the lawyer who was behind this experiment.

Gajwani worked for D.C.'s top elected prosecutor, Attorney General Karl Racine. But she was no dyed-in-the-wool prosecutor, bent on locking up bad guys. On the contrary, she had spent her early career working as a public defender, and, now in her early forties, she was looking for a way to reform a prosecutorial culture that she worried undermined justice, serving neither victims nor offenders very well. When she observed a restorative justice circle at Ballou High, one of D.C.'s most troubled schools, in 2015, she felt like she'd found a path toward that goal.

No one was more surprised than she was. She had been skeptical of restorative justice, describing herself in a 2019 speech to advocates working on juvenile justice reform as "the worst kind of critic." She added, "I both didn't really know what restorative justice was, and I was also pretty sure that it would never work."

The case that turned her into a convert involved a big kid who beat up a much smaller boy, mercilessly, inside a classroom. Gajwani had been spending time at the high school, trying to figure out what could be done to help school staff solve more disciplinary problems on their own, without calling the police who would arrest kids and send them into the criminal justice system. A few days after the fight, a restorative justice facilitator—an outside expert hired to train Ballou's faculty—asked Gajwani if she wanted to observe the boys' conference. She said yes.

She watched as the smaller boy, Darren, arrived with his mom and his aunt, the white of his eye still bloody from the beating. She watched the big kid, Malik, arrive with his mom and her fiancé. And then she saw something she had never seen before: a ninety-minute conversation that got to the root of what had happened, and that seemed to lay the groundwork for change.

The boys each had a chance to tell what happened. Malik, who was painfully shy and spoke so softly he could barely be heard, explained that Darren and his friends had been teasing him for a long time, making fun of his name. Darren wouldn't say much, and his mom had walked in angry at the other boy and his family. But in that moment she held her own son accountable in the way that only parents can. She told the group that her son was a joker, someone who was always trying to get a laugh, and that he didn't understand how he hurt people.

Malik's mom spoke. She said that she worked two jobs to keep her family afloat, that she had missed work on the day of the fight and then again for this meeting, and that the situation between the boys was stressing her out. Both mothers told the group that they hadn't raised their sons to be violent. Both moms cried, and apologized, and then the boys apologized to each other.

Darren's aunt asked him to practice what he would say if his friends wanted to make fun of Malik again. Malik's mom's fiancé offered to take the boys to the boxing gym where he worked out, so they could let off steam. Two families that might have gone to war against each other were instead drawn closer.

"It was totally transformative," Gajwani told me. She could envision what would have happened to Malik in the regular criminal justice system. Arrested, locked up, encouraged by a public defender—someone just like her, in her old job—to plead not guilty for the crime. In pleading not guilty, he'd be relieved of the obligation to accept responsibility, and he'd lose perhaps his best chance to reckon with what he'd done and change his behavior. Eventually he'd come back to school, and everyone would be angry and looking for vengeance. Gajwani could so clearly see the way one fight would lead to the next. Instead, three years after their fight, the two boys had gone to the boxing gym together a couple of times—and they hadn't fought again.

Gajwani brought what she had seen with Malik and Darren back to her boss, the D.C. attorney general, who was interested in exploring new ways to get at the root of crime. He authorized a restorative justice pilot program starting in 2016. Instead of charging juveniles for certain crimes, prosecutors would send them to a conference. If the young person went through the process and lived up to the agreement with the victim, they would avoid prosecution.

By late 2019, six full-time employees (plus Gajwani) had facilitated 124 conferences, and only 8 of those had failed—meaning the offender refused to show up for the circle or follow through with the agreement and the case was sent back for traditional prosecution. In surveys, 94 percent of conference participants—including offenders, victims, and their supporters—said that they would recommend restorative justice to others.

At first, Gajwani's team dealt only with low-level offenses like robbery and assault. And they had a rule: no crimes involving guns, intimate partner violence, or sexual violence. But as prosecutors came to understand and trust the process, they sent more serious cases. A few months before I met Gajwani, she and her team had decided to start taking referrals for some cases of sexual harassment and assault.

The attorney general's office had been pursuing a lot of low-level assaults in court—grabbing and groping cases, mostly—because they wanted to drive home a point about the seriousness of sexual violence. But Christina Jones, who supervised juvenile prosecutors at the time, became concerned that in doing so, they were also sucking a lot of young men—particularly young men of color—into the vortex of the criminal justice system, setting them on a path toward more serious offenses. She wanted a way to hold them accountable without unleashing that chain of events. She went to Gajwani, who agreed to take some of these cases on. Since then, her team has taken cases involving increasingly serious crimes—up to and including rape, in instances when victims request restorative justice.

In one case, the boy facing charges had a crush on a girl. He was always approaching her to talk, to flirt, and to tell her that she looked good. She didn't have the heart to tell him that she wasn't interested in him, and so on he went, believing they had a relationship. He was always hugging her, his hands always drifting to her butt. He thought it was cool—but she had been sexually assaulted before and felt deeply violated by his touching.

"They had totally different stories in their heads about what was happening," Gajwani said.

The different stories became clear during the restorative conference, when each had a chance to share. The girl did not want to have to deal with seeing the boy, so she didn't go; instead, she sent a letter that the facilitator read aloud, detailing her depression and the panic that overtook her when he touched her. She also wrote down what she wanted from the boy: for him never to speak to her again, to stay away from her, and to apologize to her in writing. He agreed.

In another case, a boy took a girl's hand and tried to get her to touch his penis. During the restorative process, the girl wrote a letter explaining how his behavior had affected her and what she wanted from him. She wanted to stay friends, but she wanted him to apologize to her in person. She also wanted him to tell his friends what had happened—and admit that it was his fault.

Gajwani said that during these conferences and the handful of others involving sexual harm, boys have invariably learned that their mothers—and/or the mothers of the girls involved, and/or other women in the room—have also been victims of sexual violence. The boys have learned that women move through the world feeling vulnerable. When they hear people they know and love talking about how it feels to be violated, what it is like to feel unsafe, it changes the way they think about their behavior, Gajwani said. They feel bad about what they've done, and they want to do better.

"Our sexual harm cases are some of the most transformational we've seen," she told me. "There's no doubt in any of these conferences that I've sat in on that this child, typically the boy, is never going to do this again. It really feels like it's a course correction for these young people."

Restorative justice won't work for every crime, for every victim or every offender. It can't work without trained facilitators and a commitment of time and resources. It might not work as well inside some schools as it does outside of them. But in the messy and painful work of trying to hold boys accountable for sexual harassment and sexual assault and other forms of harm inflicted, in trying to create a lasting and positive transformation, I think it can offer the closest thing to fairness, accountability, and change—the closest thing to hope.

As a mother, I realize I cannot control the consequences my son may face for hurting another person. But I can control how I talk with him about his behavior, and whether I encourage him to take responsibility for his actions or shirk it. It starts now, with how I react to the news that he bit a classmate at school in a feud over a toy. I know it will get more complicated as he grows up and his potential to do harm grows with him. I hope I can remember that my job is not to protect him from the consequences of the mistakes he makes but to help him learn how to take responsibility for them.

CHAPTER FIVE

The Problem with "Consent"

Lessons from Grace, Aziz Ansari's Accuser

In October 2018, President Trump told reporters at the White House that it was a "very scary time for young men in America." Brett Kavanaugh was on the verge of losing his dream job after Christine Blasey Ford accused him of sexual assault, and Trump was arguing that young men could not feel safe in an America where a woman's story carried such power. His claim drew eye-rolling and derision from critics who accused him of using fear and division to appeal to aggrieved white men. But in my conversations with boys and their parents and their teachers, I found many—including many who believed Ford, and who considered themselves fierce opponents of virtually everything Trump stands for—who agreed with the president on this point.

Anxiety about keeping boys out of trouble, and concern about protecting girls from sexual assault, has crystallized in a new urgency to teach young people about consent. In homes and schools all over the country, adults are now beginning to have more explicit conversations with children and teenagers about the importance of respecting boundaries. As we saw in Chapter Three, that's a welcome development, given how rare these conversations have been to date. But when I traveled to schools to learn how we are talking to young people about consent today, I learned that complicated questions are boiled down into oversimplified slogans for handling the heat of the moment: *no means no* and *yes means yes.*

In health class, children watch videos that narrate these rules. Some schools bring in cops or prosecutors to lecture on the statutory definition of sexual assault. How drunk does a person have to be to qualify as too drunk to legally consent? This question and others are parsed at school assemblies. It's easier to talk about the law, after all, than it is to talk about sex.

The problem with the rule-of-law approach to sexual consent is that it ignores the dynamics that lead to assault and to uncomfortable, unwanted sexual experiences. It doesn't take into account the social pressures that make boys feel as if sex is something they must get from girls. A student at Wabash College, in Crawfordsville, Indiana, one of the few remaining all-male colleges in the country, put it succinctly during a discussion about consent in his Gender Studies 101 class.

"We're taught no means no," he said, "so that teaches boys we need to get her to say yes."

Get her to say yes.

A yes given under pressure, of course, is not consent at all. But things get distorted when we talk about consent as if it's something that girls give and boys get.

In one extreme case, a mother told me she had advised her son, a high school senior, that if he chose to have sex—she hoped he wouldn't, but if he did—he needed to get the girl to consent in writing. She said she could easily imagine that a girl might get carried away in the moment and regret it later and claim it was nonconsensual when she faced the prospect of confessing to her parents.

This mother and I were talking on the phone, so I couldn't see her facial expressions, and we sat in silence together while I tried to figure out whether she was speaking literally. I wasn't sure, so I asked: Are you serious? Do you really think your son should get consent for sex in writing?

"If I were an eighteen-year-old boy going off to college? Hell yeah."

She was hardly unusual in her thinking. During Harvey Weinstein's sexual assault trial in New York, his criminal defense lawyer, who argued in court that all of Weinstein's sexual encounters were consensual, told the *New York Times* that if she were a man today, she would protect herself by getting consent in writing before having any kind of sexual contact with a woman. The same impulse has given rise to cell phone apps, by such names as LegalFling and Consent Amour that provide contracts for two people to sign, affirming their willingness to have sex.

On one level, I get it. We all want to protect our kids. But on so many other levels, this is a deeply messed-up way to talk to boys about sex.

It is meaningless for two people to sign some sort of ostensible contract when both parties could conceivably change their minds, at any point, about what they are comfortable with and willing to do. It is cynical and sad to teach our sons that they can't trust women. And I think it completely misidentifies the problem. Among the biggest challenges boys face are not deceitful girls but low expectations and lack of guidance from adults.

When we fall back on repeating the catchphrases of consent instead of digging into deeper conversations about sex and communication, and when we focus on blaming girls for being unclear about their intentions instead of on making sure boys understand their responsibility to listen, we are not protecting our sons. We're endangering them, leaving them without the skills and information they need to navigate their sexual lives safely and respectfully.

One high school senior from San Rafael, California, told me he knows the rules. They've been drummed into him. But he doesn't know how they're supposed to work in the real world. As a heterosexual guy, he feels like it's still his job to ask girls out, but he's confused about how to find the line between showing sincere interest and being creepy.

"I think it's tougher to court these days, know what I mean? If you want to date someone, if you want to pursue somebody . . . if you ask repeatedly, persistence is one thing that people look for," he said. "But also, if you do that, it could be perceived as sexual harassment. So that makes it difficult."

I empathize with him. Ideas about consent are tangled up with an old and powerful narrative: boys pursue while girls play coy. This narrative tells boys that real men get sex, and that a girl's no is just a precursor to her yes, myths that put our sons at risk of assaulting their partners or coercing them into doing something they're uncomfortable with. It tells girls that they don't have to worry about getting consent because boys always want sex, an assumption that raises our sons' risk of having sex they don't want.

Some young people are challenging this narrative, but so many of them are still buying into it. Rape survivor Abby Honold, who regularly speaks to middle and high school students, told me that when she explains that sex is only consensual when both people truly want it, some young people are so shocked that their jaws go slack. They've learned from movies and music and their parents that sex is something that boys want and girls put up with. The idea that a girl can want sex—can enjoy it, can find it pleasurable—blows their minds.

"The response I get from boys is, well, girls never want to. They have this mind-set that girls always need to be convinced," she said.

If we want to protect our sons from being accused of sexual assault, we have to go beyond *no means no* to the more difficult job of dismantling this old narrative about how men and women approach sex differently. Boys must hear the clear message that girls can like sex, too, and that a person—a girl or a boy—should be believed the first time they say no, whether they say it verbally or with body language. If we don't make that clear, if we leave our sons unsure whether persistence is cute or creepy, then we're setting them up to overstep another person's boundaries.

There's some use in zooming in on that moment where one person is trying to figure out whether another wants to go further or not. We can help boys understand how real people communicate in awkward situations (spoiler alert: rarely does a person scream no at their date, a person they usually like or at least don't want to offend). But we also need to zoom out to everything that leads up to that one moment, and everything that comes afterward.

Our sons need to understand how alcohol clouds their judgment, tricking them into thinking other people are more interested in sex than they really are. They need practice handling rejection gracefully, so they can hear and accept another person's no.

And perhaps most important, they need to hear from us parents that consent is a low bar. We don't want our sons to merely avoid sexual assault, after all. We want them to have sex that is mutually satisfying for both them and their partners.

The truly scary reality in America today is that a lot of boys are not hearing much about any of that.

"No" Is Not Always Spelled "N-O"

I cannot think of a better tool for helping boys think beyond *no means no* than the story of alleged sexual misconduct by comedian and actor Aziz Ansari. Ansari was not accused of rape or of using physical force. Instead, he was accused of something less violent and more common: pushing so persistently past a younger woman's no that she gave him oral sex. In a story that went viral in January 2018, she described the encounter as dehumanizing and coercive, and she called it sexual assault.

Ansari said he was shocked. As far as he understood, he said, their encounter had been "completely consensual."

Of all the stories of sexual misconduct that have been told in recent years, this has been among the most unsettling to the parents of boys. In conversations with me, they brought it up unbidden as an example of a righteous movement gone awry, swung too far toward indicting men for women's failure to clearly communicate and stand up for themselves. Even mothers who had marched in pink pussy hats—progressive women who believed women but who could also imagine their sons in Ansari's position—struggled to come to terms with what this meant for men and the future of sex. What were we all supposed to learn from this episode?

I would have loved to have had a conversation with Aziz Ansari about that, but his publicist politely declined my request for an interview and pointed me instead to what Ansari said about the whole thing during his comeback to public life, a standup comedy tour in 2019. (However embarrassing this has all been for him, it has not ended his career.) Sitting alone onstage on a stool, speaking in hushed tones, Ansari said that he had felt humiliated and scared, but that the episode had ultimately made him a better, more thoughtful person. He barely mentioned the woman at the center of the story, and she had not spoken since her story lit up the internet in early 2018. I wanted to know what she had made of her own experience, and what lessons she thought we might all take away.

I tracked her down, and, to my surprise, she was willing to talk. She had spent two years second-guessing herself, enduring waves of regret over calling Ansari's behavior sexual assault and sometimes over telling the story at all. She hoped that sharing her experience, and what she had learned from it—not just from that night but in the aftermath—might be in some way useful, especially to parents trying to raise sons.

"I think it's important that I do somehow contribute what I can to this conversation that I in some ways started," she said.

An abridged version of her story, which was originally written about in a piece on the website Babe.net, goes like this: The two of them met at a party where they connected over their shared interest in old-fashioned film cameras. She was twenty-two, just out of college. He was a thirty-four-year-old celebrity, the star of his own Netflix series. After some flirtatious texting, he asked her to dinner, and she was thrilled. They went to a nice restaurant on a boat on the Hudson River, ordered lobster rolls and wine.

But after dinner, back at his apartment, he came on to her boorishly and aggressively, and her excitement shifted to discomfort. When she complimented his marble countertop, he asked that she climb up. Within minutes, he had undressed them both and was saying he was going to get a condom. She asked him to slow down.

He kept pushing, first giving her oral sex and then asking her to do the same for him. She kept sending what she thought were clear signals of discomfort. When he moved her hand toward his penis, she moved it away. He followed her around his apartment, she said, repeatedly sticking his fingers into her mouth and then into her vagina. He kept asking her where she wanted him to fuck her, and she kept demurring. "Next time," she said. He asked if she meant on a second date. "Sure," she said. If he poured her another glass of wine, he wanted to know, would it count as a second date?

At one point, she left the room and, upon returning, told him that she didn't want to feel forced to do anything. He asked her to sit with him on the couch, and she thought he seemed to understand. But within a few minutes, he "sat back and pointed to his penis and motioned for me to go down on him," she told Babe. Surprised he was still pushing, unsure how to get out of the situation, she gave him what he asked for. Then he bent her over in front of a mirror. "Where do you want me to fuck you?" he asked, thrusting against her backside. "Do you want me to fuck you right here?"

Actually, she did not want to fuck at all. She had not wanted to give him the blow job, either. She left, and she cried on the way home. When she texted him to tell him how uneasy she had been and how violated she felt, he apologized to her, saying he had clearly "misread things in the moment."

A few months passed before she agreed to tell her story to the Babe reporter. She had seen Ansari wearing a Time's Up pin when he accepted a Golden Globe for his performance in the Netflix series *Master of None*, and she had been disgusted. The pin was supposed to be a sign of support for the fight against sexual harassment and assault, but she saw it as a sign of fake empathy and deep hypocrisy. She wanted people to see that Aziz Ansari—a self-described feminist who had written a whole book about modern romance—was not the man he claimed to be. Hoping to stay anonymous, she went by the pseudonym Grace.

The story was published online on January 13, 2018, a Saturday. Grace was working that day, photographing a birthday party in a basement without cell service. She put her phone down, and when she picked it up four hours later, her world had changed. Everyone had a take on how she had handled herself and what it meant. Some people were coming to her defense, arguing that she was pushing conversation about sexual misconduct in a necessary direction, past sexual predators and toward everyday sexual entitlement. But broad swaths of the internet were condemning her. Trolls had figured out her identity and posted her name and image. Some of her fiercest critics were feminists who accused her of cheapening the #MeToo movement with a breathless tale about plain old bad sex that she could have avoided, if only she'd had the strength to walk away.

"What you have done is appalling," television host Ashleigh Banfield said on-air, reading aloud a blistering open letter she had written to Grace.

"You had an unpleasant date, and you didn't leave. That's on you." Bari Weiss, then a *New York Times* opinion writer, accused Grace of transforming "what ought to be a movement for women's empowerment into an emblem for female helplessness." In the *Atlantic*, Caitlin Flanagan decried what she described as Aziz Ansari's professional assassination by an anonymous woman who apparently didn't know how to call herself a cab.

Even Grace's parents, with whom she had a close and supportive relationship, didn't understand why—if she was so upset by Ansari's advances—she hadn't done more to make her discomfort clear. Her father had asked: *Why didn't you just leave?* He had asked the question lovingly, but still it stung.

The backlash to Grace's story sent her reeling. She knew that what had happened to her was different from what had happened to women who accused their bosses of rape. But she had been sure that people would see that Ansari's behavior was, as she put it, "shitty." Instead, she was being inundated with messages telling her that *she* was the shitty one. The questions she had hoped to raise about a man's behavior were drowned out by the mushrooming criticism of her own behavior. "I've never experienced so many people telling me, 'You're really wrong,'" she said.

By late 2019, she was still digging out of deep shame. But she had come to this: It was a mistake to call what happened to her sexual assault. It was not a mistake to call it out as wrong. When she looks back to that night, she can't imagine how she could have more clearly communicated her discomfort. Ansari didn't miss her signs, she concluded. He just ignored them.

This is what Grace hopes parents of boys will take from her story: we should worry less about whether our sons can pick up on subtle signals and more about whether they know to heed them. She hopes parents of girls, meanwhile, can see in her story how important it is to make sure their daughters know they have no obligation to be polite when they're feeling uncomfortable in a sexual situation. They should feel empowered to say how they feel, even if it isn't "nice."

Grace had refused Ansari's advances repeatedly, according to the Babe story. Her resistance started when he announced he was going to get a condom, a few minutes after they arrived at his apartment after dinner. "Whoa, let's relax for a sec, let's chill," she had said.

She resisted with nonverbal signals. "Most of my discomfort was expressed in me pulling away and mumbling. I know that my hand stopped moving at some points," she told Katie Way, the Babe reporter. "I stopped moving my lips and turned cold."

She resisted when she said no nicely. "Next time," she had said, before he tried to joke his way into "next time" by pouring that second glass of wine.

She resisted by retreating to the bathroom to gather herself, and then by declaring, when she returned: "I don't want to feel forced because then I'll hate you, and I'd rather not hate you."

In her New York Times column criticizing Grace for failing to stand up for herself, Bari Weiss declared that Aziz Ansari was guilty only of "not being a mind reader," as if there was no way Grace could have expected him to understand what she was feeling. But did he need to be a mind reader to understand that the young woman in his apartment—the person more than a decade younger, working to establish a career in the same New York where he was known as a star—was feeling uncomfortable?

No, said Charlene Senn, a psychology professor at the University of Windsor in Ontario. Senn has studied sexual violence for decades. "All he had to do is be a regular human being who pays attention," she said.

Some researchers argue that sexual assault is often caused by miscommunication: men tend to overestimate their partners' sexual interest, while women are too timid to say how they truly feel. Senn's work is part of a body of research that challenges this theory. Men are not somehow broken when it comes to reading their sexual partners, Senn argues. They are as capable as women are of using and interpreting verbal and nonverbal cues, and a man who repeatedly ignores those cues is sending signs not that he can't understand but that he doesn't want to listen—perhaps because he's so driven by the pressure to initiate sexual activity, and to accomplish what he initiates.

Senn developed one of the only antirape interventions proven effective— a self-defense and empowerment curriculum, aimed at college women, that is shown to reduce rape by an impressive 50 percent. No intervention for college men has been nearly so effective. She believes our sons need and deserve a clear message: in a sexual encounter, any indication that one person is uncomfortable should prompt the other person to stop and not start up again until the person who expressed discomfort chooses to initiate.

Senn says we should make clear to our sons (and daughters) that there is space for being completely self-centered and thinking only about their own needs. It's called masturbation. But sex with another person is a mutual give-and-take that involves listening to and caring about what your partner is communicating, including via nonverbal signals.

Despite their skill in reading those signals, when it comes to discussing rape and sexual assault, boys and men tend to insist that a woman has not been clear about her intentions unless she says no verbally. "If she says no you gotta respect it, that's when rape comes up," one teen told researchers at Brown University and Rhode Island Hospital, in a study of adolescents' concepts of consent. When boys don't hear a no, they interpret its absence to mean consent. That's a problem, because even though girls agree that silence can sometimes mean consent, the Brown team found, girls also say that it can be a way of saying no. When girls refuse sex, they often do so nonverbally (as Grace did initially with Ansari), by pushing a guy's hands away or making a face of disgust. Often, boys don't respond to these refusals.

As parents, then, our most important job is not to train boys to interpret signals from their sexual partner; they're already pretty good at that. Our job is to make sure they understand that a subtle signal of discomfort or resistance is the same thing as a flashing neon sign that says NO, and that they should not persist past either one. And our job is to teach them that if they're not sure what their partner wants, they should assume the answer is no. If they're not sure whether the other person is too drunk to consent, the answer is no. If they have any niggling uncertainty at all, the answer is no.

A Blow Job Is Not Consent

So why, if Grace was so troubled, did she give Ansari a blow job? Why didn't she walk out of his apartment earlier? When her father asked her that question, she wasn't able to give him much of an answer. But looking back at that night, she says she didn't leave earlier because—as shocked and disoriented as she felt—to do so seemed unthinkable. And not necessarily because Ansari was a celebrity who, she acknowledged, lived a lifestyle she found exciting and alluring. She'd found herself stuck in similar situations with regular guys—"Brooklyn losers," she called them. She actually felt she'd been more straightforward and verbal with Ansari than she usually was with guys, and yet he acted like he didn't understand what she was saying. The blow job was a concession, a way to change the trajectory of the evening and avoid having intercourse. It was not a sign of consent.

At least if she was giving him oral sex, she would retain some control. "I didn't want him to touch me," she said.

She thought about what her critics would have wanted her to do differently. Scream? Yell? March out in a huff? Those were extreme and unrealistic options in a situation where she was dealing not with a stranger groping her at a bar but with someone who had just bought her a meal. "It's hard to walk out of anybody's room when they take you out to dinner. No matter who they are," she said. "I can't be rude in those situations."

I was surprised to hear this frank admission. It seemed to me, at first, awfully old-fashioned to believe that a man who buys dinner is owed a degree of sweetness, or that it is rude for a woman to speak up clearly about what she wants and doesn't want. But this is not unusual; this is what many girls (and many boys) are learning from their parents, from their friends, and from the media as they grow up.

As part of the SHIFT study on sexual violence at Columbia University, which I described in Chapter Three, female students told researchers that they knew the concept of affirmative consent cold. They *knew* that consent requires both people to say yes, but they actually lived by a very different set of rules. In real life, these educated young women—talented students who had made it to the Ivy League—were not sure whether it was okay for them to firmly reject a man's advances.

"It would have been rude" to say no, one young woman told the Columbia team about a sexual encounter. Another, like Grace, said she gave a guy oral sex as a way of escaping from his room. They had started kissing, and she didn't want to have sex. The blow job was the path of least resistance to an exit. "I just wanted to get it over with," she said.

Young men also feel pressure not to offend their partners. Recall what one college student told me in Chapter One about why he didn't resist unwanted advances from a woman: "You don't want to be rude. You don't want to be weird," he said.

Other research shows that most of us don't want to be rude, so we try to express how we feel gently. By analyzing conversational patterns, psychologists have shown that people use indirect tactics to turn down all sorts of social invitations, sexual and otherwise, because rejecting someone—no matter the context—is awkward and hard. It is normal for all of us to look for ways to let others down easy, to look for ways to let them save face, to make the rejection feel less personal by arguing it is out of our control. "Sorry I can't stay over tonight, I have an exam to study for," you might say. Or you might leave open the possibility of having intercourse later. "Next time," as Grace put it. Both men and women are able to interpret these excuses as the refusals they are, the research shows.

So while Grace was skewered for not standing up more forcefully for herself in an uncomfortable situation, in many ways her behavior was more rule than exception. We raise children—especially girls—to prioritize social harmony over self-advocacy. We need to teach our sons how hard it is for most people to say no, and how it only becomes more difficult in unbalanced relationships, when one person in the room holds more power than the other.

We also need to do a better job teaching our sons and daughters that being clear about what you do and don't want in a sexual encounter is not rude at all. It is the right thing to do, and a person who persistently ignores your clear messages about what you do and don't want is not someone you want to hang around with.

This is something Grace is trying to learn now, in her mid-twenties. She doesn't think she's to blame for Ansari's behavior. But in the future, she doesn't want to leave room for anyone else to claim misunderstanding or confusion. She has resolved to be more forceful about speaking up and to get comfortable saying uncomfortable things—like no, or "let's not do that right now," or "it's time for me to take off."

She has been practicing in daily life, hoping that it will eventually become easier and more natural to risk awkward honesty during intimate moments. She has forced herself to interject in meetings with bosses to steer conversations toward her priorities, and to interject in doctor's appointments to make sure her questions get answered. "I've just learned how to be louder," she said. "Once you get comfortable with actually saying what you're thinking and feeling, everything changes, and that goes for both males and females."

Learning to Handle Rejection

What had Grace dreamed might happen when she decided to go public? What had she wanted? When I asked, she laughed a little sardonically. "I wish someone had asked me that before I talked," she said.

She has spent a lot of energy wishing that she had stayed quiet. But at times she has also felt a creeping hope that her decision came with an upside, that she hadn't undermined the #MeToo movement but forced it to expand to consider everyday, unremarkable, and yet unacceptable sexual disregard. She has noticed how her allegations against Aziz Ansari have become a bookend, on the other end of the spectrum from Harvey Weinstein. That is okay with her. "If we don't understand all the kinds of assault and abuse and issues," she said, "then how are we going to solve it?"

She hopes that her experience might be particularly meaningful to guys who consider themselves good guys, who might be moved to rethink their past encounters and think about ways in which they might not have listened very well, or might have disregarded what their partner was trying to tell them. And she hopes that younger boys and their parents might see more clearly how a sexual experience can be harmful even when it is not a sexual assault, even when it is not rape.

In fact, it was the utter normalcy of the interaction between Ansari and Grace that was so unsettling—and so unforgettable. "The behavior of a Harvey Weinstein is simple to condemn," physician James Hamblin wrote in the *Atlantic*, explaining why Grace's story mattered. "The harder work is ahead, in the more common and less clear-cut moments that leave people feeling somewhere between uncomfortable and trapped. . . . These are exactly the stories that people, particularly men, need to hear."

The vast majority of boys are obviously not rapists, and will not grow up to be rapists. A review of dozens of surveys of more than twenty-five thousand college men over the past two decades found that an average of 6.5 percent have admitted to behavior that meets the legal definition of rape. Many boys, knowing they would never forcefully rape someone, shrug off earnest discussion of consent and sexual violence, reasoning that it has nothing to do with them.

But a lot of men—an average of about one-third, and in some studies considerably more—admit to a broader range of sexually aggressive behavior, including nonconsensual fondling (touching without permission) and sexual coercion (pressuring or threatening another person into oral, anal, or vaginal sex). When you consider how common sexual misconduct is, how truly unremarkable it is, it's harder to hold onto the idea that "good" guys don't sometimes do harm—especially when they are young, navigating their first sexual encounters.

Those men, according to veteran sex assault researcher Mary Koss, often lack experience with sex and sexual communication—a problem she believes is exacerbated by poor sex education and the rise of internet porn. They make the kind of mistakes that new drivers make when they first get behind the wheel—they didn't mean to hurt someone, they just didn't know what they were doing. "When you're learning to drive your penis," Koss told me, "you can really hurt people by mistakes you make due to inexperience."

We could help keep a lot of those good guys from doing harm if we did a better job of teaching them that consent is more than getting a woman to say yes. One young man, a senior at Wabash College, told me that in high school, he coerced his girlfriend into losing her virginity with him, badgering her about it until she finally gave in. "I don't think I ever thought about her saying no," he said. "I just really liked her, and I guess I felt ready." He hadn't thought about whether *she* was ready, and he hadn't realized at the time that his badgering was wrong. After all, he had never physically forced her to do anything. He had gotten her to say yes. He had followed the rules, as he understood them.

"I do regret it," he told me. "Not regret having sex with her, but regret making her do it, when it was not mutual."

The challenge, I think, is to ask boys to think beyond what they have to do to stay out of trouble and to think instead about what they have to do to make sure they're only having sex with someone who truly wants to have sex with them.

This is the frame that Hanna Stotland brings to her conversations with college men. A lawyer, Stotland now works as a consultant in "educational crisis management," which means she helps students, including many who have been kicked out of college for sexual misconduct, get back into school somewhere else. She's worked with dozens of clients across the country, most of them middle-class white men.

She tries to get these young men—who almost universally believe they were wrongly accused and unfairly disciplined—to see that even if they don't think they committed a punishable offense, they have to face the fact that they hurt someone.

She tells them that if they want to persuade another college to admit them, they need to show that whatever happened before isn't going to happen again. That means they have to acknowledge having had a sexual encounter that left someone feeling disgusted or disrespected or violated, and they have to explain how they're going to avoid doing so in the future. "You had some kind of physical encounter with someone, and that person looking back is like, 'Yech, God, I hope that never happens again,'" Stotland said.

Even if Stotland's clients don't think they committed sexual assault, she asks them to admit to themselves that they don't want someone they were intimate with to feel disgusted by their shared experience. "What are you going to do so that people aren't ever going to leave your bed ever again—or the broom closet in the frat house—saying, 'Ew.'"

This is the standard I want to set for my son. The goal is not just to stay out of trouble but to treat your partner with respect and dignity and avoid making them feel gross, used, manipulated, or violated. I want my son to know that his job is not to get another person to say yes, but to listen to what that person is saying about what he or she wants and doesn't want. Then he has to accept that person's wishes, which means he needs to learn how to handle rejection.

This is not a conversation I'm going to start when he's fifteen, or even twelve. I am starting now, as he tries to persuade me to let him eat applesauce for every meal or needles his sister to play with him. *You don't always get what you want,* I tell him. *It's hard, I know.* Sometimes he collapses in tears.

Truth is, his disappointment is not just hard for him. It's hard for me, too. I want tell to his sister to give in, to placate him—but I fight that urge, figuring I do him no favors by protecting him from rejection and disappointment. (I do the same when the roles are reversed, and it's my daughter who is upset that her brother doesn't want to play.) I figure as he grows older, and his rejections and disappointments feel bigger, my desire to swoop in and rescue him will only grow stronger. But I hope that instead of protecting him from those experiences and feelings, I have the strength to help him through them. And I hope by the time he starts thinking about sex, he's had enough practice that he can hear and respect another person's no.

What We Can (and Can't) Blame on Alcohol

Overall, half of all sexual assaults on college campuses involve alcohol, meaning that one or both people were drinking beforehand. For a long time, that stat has been used to urge girls to beware of drinking too much, lest they become victims. It's time we did a better job explaining that drinking also puts young people—especially boys—at risk of hurting other people.

Drinking messes with self-control, with decision making, and with perception, making it harder for anyone to accurately read the person with whom they're trying to be intimate. Drunk people suffer from what researchers call "alcohol myopia"—their ability to notice their environment narrows to the most attention-grabbing thing before them. They aren't good at reading subtleties, and they aren't good at taking in information that doesn't jibe with the way they see things. A drunk guy who is focused on having sex with a woman—and who believes that she wants to have sex with him—is apt to ignore her resistance or lack of interest, even her outright refusal. "Alcohol makes you see what you want to see," Antonia Abbey, one of the nation's foremost researchers studying sexual assault and alcohol, told me.

Beyond the pharmacological effects of alcohol on the brain, introducing liquor into a social situation seems to shift men's perceptions. Studies have shown that men are more likely to see women who have been drinking as sexually available—no surprise in a culture where beer and liquor companies have long used scantily clad women, in-your-face cleavage, and not-so-veiled references to sex to sell their products. "The perfect beer for removing 'no' from your vocabulary for the night" may sound as if it is straight out of the 1950s, but is actually a Bud Light tagline from 2015.

Easy access to alcohol may be one lever that colleges and communities can use to deal with sexual violence. Some research has suggested a relationship between the density of liquor stores and the prevalence of domestic violence. Now, Laura Salazar—the same Georgia State professor whose research, discussed in Chapter Three, revealed that one in five men was sexually violent before college—told me that such violence is significantly less common on dry campuses than on those where alcohol is allowed. Her findings come from a study of sexual violence at thirty colleges across Georgia with varying policies on campus drinking.

But we have to be careful in turning alcohol into a scapegoat for problems of sexual entitlement and poor sexual citizenship. What alcohol does not do is fundamentally change a person. Instead, it frees you of your inhibitions. If you feel like you're supposed to always be dominant in sex, or you tend to misread women's platonic smiles as an indicator of their desire to have sex, or you consistently hang out with guys who talk about forced sex as if it's no big deal, you are simply more likely to show your true colors when you're drinking. The same basic thing is true of regular old aggression—drinking doesn't turn you into a bar brawler, but if you're predisposed to be aggressive, a few drinks can unleash your desire to fight.

"Alcohol makes whatever you'd kind of like to do easier to do," Abbey said. "It can impel you to do something you want to do anyway, but it's not likely to make you do something you didn't want to do anyway."

In one study, college men listened to a 6.5-minute audiotape of a sexual encounter between a man and a woman who have returned home after a date. The man becomes increasingly coercive as he tries to persuade her to have sex, using verbal threats and physical force before he finally rapes the woman.

As they listened to the tape, the college men were told they should press stop at the point where they thought the man in the scenario should cease pressuring the woman. The men who had a history of being sexually aggressive toward women allowed the tape to roll longer than nonaggressive men, and were *six times* as likely to allow the tape to roll to the point of verbal threats. If they were told that the couple on the tape had been drinking together, sexually aggressive men allowed the tape to roll even longer, while nonaggressive men stopped the tape just as quickly as they had before. Alcohol seemed to be an excuse for reading the woman's refusals as insincere attempts to stop the man's advances.

Some scholars and activists argue that it's unrealistic for adults to tell young people that they should swear off mixing alcohol and sex. But when we fail to make sure our sons understand how drinking raises the risk that they will either violate someone else's boundaries or be violated themselves, we are setting them up for harm. I have interviewed dozens of people who say they were assaulted. And I have read dozens of lawsuits filed by young men challenging the disciplinary consequences doled out by their universities after they were accused of sexual assault. Some of the most troubling cases are those in which both people claim that they were blackout drunk, and both claim that the other took advantage of them. Besides the knotty problem of how to assign blame in such cases, this is just not what I want for my son— intoxicated sex that can't quite be remembered, but that leaves everyone feeling wronged.

Signs of Change

Parties and bar crawls aren't going away anytime soon, and neither are drunken one-night stands. But I did find signs that some young men are being careful not to mix alcohol and casual sex. Many are motivated by sincere anxiety about unintentionally hurting a partner. Others are interested in self-preservation at a time of less tolerance for violating sexual boundaries.

A recent college graduate working in D.C. told me that public debate about sexual assault had made him think back to sex he'd had with a fellow student when he was nineteen. They had both been drunk, and he wasn't sure now whether she had been sober enough to consent. He also wasn't sure if today, she would consider their encounter something she had actually wanted or, instead, something she had merely endured. He'd been troubled by the anxiety of not knowing, not only because of the stakes for himself—in the anxious wee hours of the morning, he feared she could accuse him of assault, and what would he say?—but also because of the stakes for her. He genuinely hadn't meant to hurt her, he said.

He said he's not taking risks like that anymore. He is saving intimacy for people he knows and trusts and cares about. Part of it is that he wants to protect himself against accusations of assault ("One poor decision can be your downfall," he told me). But that's not the only thing—he also feels like sex is something special that he wants to experience sober, and as part of a meaningful emotional connection with a woman. Research studies and psychologists who work with men tell us that many men want more emotional intimacy in their romantic relationships; maybe, in the cultural upheaval over sexual misconduct, they have more space to admit it out loud.

Angel Duran, whom I met through his Los Angeles high school English teacher, told me much the same thing. Now a student at Humboldt State University in Northern California, he has decided on no one-night stands, no sex with anyone who's been drinking. It's too risky. He's Mexican American, and said that he feels young men of color like him have more pressure to be careful because they have less room for missteps than white men. We don't have comprehensive data on the race and ethnicity of men accused of rape on college campuses, but some young men and professors have raised concerns that racial bias puts men of color at greater risk of being investigated and disciplined for campus sexual misconduct. "I'd rather not do it and be sure that I'm not getting accused than do it and wake up to someone saying they accused me of rape," Angel told me.

One night recently, a friend of his—a girl he'd hooked up with before—came to his room drunk, saying she needed a place to sleep. She wanted to cuddle, but Angel refused. He was pretty sure she wanted to have sex, but she seemed too wasted to consent. He told her he'd sleep on the floor, and she could have the bed. His roommate said even that was too risky, and they ended up asking her to leave. Angel walked her to her dorm.

Angel said for him to feel comfortable having sex with someone, he has to know and trust the person. "When you talk to a person, when you start talking to a stranger, the more you talk to them, the more you feel the person is trustworthy or not. For me, I've got to talk to them more than one day," he said. "I can't go to a party then bring back a chick from the party. I just can't."

Young Black men from Chicago and Washington, D.C., told me that they cannot ignore the racial dimensions of their encounters with women, given the long American history of Black men facing false accusations of sexual misconduct—from Emmett Till, fourteen, lynched after he was falsely accused of flirting with a twenty-one-year-old white woman in Mississippi in 1955, to Dhameer Bradley and Malik St. Hilaire, two Black football players at Sacred Heart University whose academic and athletic lives were derailed after a white woman falsely accused them both of rape in 2016. (She later admitted to lying to win the sympathy of another man, and in 2018 was sentenced to three years in prison, with the final two suspended.)

Christian Champagne, a twenty-three-year-old Chicago native, told me that he protects himself and the women he's interested in with a hard-and-fast rule. If he's at all unsure about whether she wants sex, or whether she's too drunk to consent, he takes a rain check. "If it's two o'clock in the morning and you're with someone and you're not sure if you have consent . . . leave it alone, try again in the morning, and then you'll have your answer," he said. "It's not a dangerous time to be a man. It's only a dangerous time if you're a predator, because people will call you on your B.S. now."

He said he and his friends watch out for each other to make sure that no one is doing anything questionable with a woman that could land him in trouble for sexual assault. "You don't want to be in jail, because we all got futures, we all trying to do something for our community, shift the narrative on how Black men are perceived," he said. "We don't need that bad press."

We don't know how many men are making decisions like this, abstaining from one-night stands or refraining from mixing sex with alcohol because of their desire to reserve sex for people they feel connected to or because of concerns about making sure they have consent. We do know that young American men are having less sex, as we saw in Chapter Three, and while that's given rise to lots of hand-wringing about the rise of porn and the postponement of marriage, it also may be that people are having less sex in part because they're trying harder to have good sex—sex that everyone involved actually wants.

That's what Debby Herbenick, a sex researcher at Indiana University who teaches courses in human sexuality, has seen among her male students. Each year, she asks students to write sexual autobiographies. Usually, a few men describe themselves as wanting to take things slow, but in 2018 she noticed that almost all the young men described an impulse to delay having intercourse until they could find a partner they really liked and could see having a relationship with. Men who had already lost their virginity said they wanted to put off their next sexual experience until it was with someone special. They hadn't confessed their real feelings about sex to their friends; they worried that their desire for emotional connection with a sexual partner was weird.

"I found myself over and over again having to write responses back to them saying, 'A lot of people feel like you feel, a lot of people want meaningful connection,'" Herbenick told me. She hadn't launched a formal study to investigate of this phenomenon, but she said she had a hunch that the shift she has noticed can be traced in part to concern about sexual assault accusations and in part to a greater freedom—at a time when more and more young people are identifying as transgender and nonbinary—to think critically about gender norms.

Maybe young men are starting to feel more comfortable resisting cultural ideas about how they're supposed to behave sexually in favor of developing their own ideas about how they actually want to behave. I am heartened by this prospect, and so is Herbenick—not because she's a puritan, but because it's healthy for people to seek the kind of sexual encounters they desire. "I've been hearing forever, and I see in the data," she said, "that most people want connection and intimacy. What I think is great is when they go for what they want."

CHAPTER SIX

Racism, Violence, Trauma

How Close Relationships Can Help Boys Cope

In a small room inside a Chicago public middle school on the city's South Side, a group of ten seventh-grade boys gathered in a circle. They were boys of color, almost all of them Black, all here for their weekly meeting of Becoming a Man, a group therapy and mentoring program with a record of success in some of the city's most distressed neighborhoods. They stole glances at me as Jarvis Burks, their twenty-seven-year-old counselor, kicked off a discussion about one of BAM's six core values: respect for womanhood.

Burks asked each of the boys to name a woman he loved and explain why he appreciated her, and so around the room they went, naming their mothers and grandmothers and aunts. Dressed in their maroon school uniform shirts and gray pants, the boys kept their eyes on Burks as he pulled out giant pieces of yellow paper. The week before, on these pieces of paper, they had listed adjectives used to describe women (sensitive, irritating, gossipy, nags) and men (harmful, aggressive, gangbangers, strong). Burks talked about the choice that they faced, to be oppressors or liberators, and how that basic decision started with choices about the language they used.

"I've seen a woman I love and respect be oppressed, and I couldn't or didn't do anything about it," said Burks, wearing jeans and a t-shirt and his hair in chin-length locks. "And I've been that person as well, I've oppressed women. But it's not about staying in this place. It's about what do we do—about getting back into integrity with ourselves."

This is part of what makes BAM what it is, the willingness of the young men who serve as counselors, many of whom grew up in neighborhoods like this one, to be frank about their failings and feelings. Alumni tell me that it helps everyone else open up, too, and creates the tight bond that makes the program work. It does seem to work. Participating in BAM boosts boys' high school graduation rate by 19 percent and reduces their arrests for violent behavior by an astonishing 50 percent. The program's results have piqued interest in cities around the country that are struggling to figure out how to help young men change the trajectory of their lives.

On this day, in the circle at Burnham Mathematics & Science Academy, Burks's vulnerability was not enough to crack things open. The seventh-graders were polite and clearly eager to please. But they were also mostly silent. Whether because the topic was too awkward or too abstract, or because I was there in the room, the conversation that Burks wanted to start about gender hung in the air, going nowhere.

But the boys became animated when the discussion zigzagged toward race. I asked them how they thought people saw them, as Black boys. One talked about the people "living in high-up neighborhoods who think Black boys grow up to be robbers," and another said that girls' fathers seemed to believe that all young Black men have only sex on their minds. A short, bespectacled boy brought up Emmett Till—a Chicago native. Till was lynched, he said, because it was so easy for white people to believe that a Black boy had behaved inappropriately toward a white girl. "Lots of people are still racist," he said. "That's what they think all Black boys do."

The boys' Blackness and their maleness did not just affect the way that the world saw them. It also affected the way they saw themselves, and that became clear when another BAM counselor in the room, Kenneth Orr, asked them why they thought white kids always seem to score higher than Black kids on standardized tests. "Do you think other nationalities or cultures are smarter than you?" Orr asked.

"Sorry," the Black boy sitting next to me said warily. "I'm not being racist. I just feel like some kids who are not colored, they really listen well. Black kids act a certain type of way. They don't listen to their teachers." He had soft cheeks, a baby face, and later he would tell me that he had spent part of the previous year in a group home for troubled kids after he was kicked out of school. He was doing better now, he said. He'd learned to control his behavior, and he was getting pretty good grades, and he wanted to be an FBI agent. But he was carrying around this idea of himself as a person hobbled by his race, an idea that had been given to him by the world he lived in. "People who aren't colored, they're more mature," he said matter-of-factly.

Other boys explained the test-score discrepancy by pointing not to their own bodies or skin but to forces outside themselves. One, who spoke so quietly I could barely hear him, said that their school had to use old books, while schools for white kids had newer materials. Another brought up the ever-present threat of violence that forced him and his friends to stay indoors, playing *Fortnite* for hours instead of going out and playing basketball.

This boy had no doubt why white kids score higher on reading and math tests. "They haven't grown up in the neighborhood like we have. They haven't been through what we been through. That's why the statistics are higher," he said. "Yesterday eighteen shots went off right outside my cousin's house. In the suburbs, I don't think these shootings happen like this."

Race, Racism, and Black Boys in America

The children I met at Burnham understood that they were not just boys, they were Black boys, and not just Black boys, but Black boys from a poor and violent part of town. The impact of that identity on their lives—the way in which they could see the power they didn't have—was pressing and clear to them in a way that the discussion about gender was not.

And that makes sense. They know Black boys and other boys of color face a rising tide of explicit racism and hatred spread by increasingly vocal and visible white nationalists. But they also face something less obvious and more pervasive, something the rest of us, who are not Black, have learned to the steady thrum of Black boys and men killed by police—George Floyd, Eric Garner and Michael Brown, Walter Scott and Philando Castile, seventeen-year-old Laquan McDonald and twelve-year-old Tamir Rice. They know from experience what a growing body of research on implicit bias has pressed the rest of us to acknowledge: the particular weight that Black males bear because of assumptions that they are aggressive and dangerous. These are assumptions that people like me often don't even realize we are making as our brains do what brains do: recognize patterns and create categories.

Even if we believe deeply in racial equality, we are inundated with messages that Black is inferior to white—whether from news reporting that echoes stereotypes of Black men as threatening and criminal, or from television and movies that portray Black characters as suspicious. Those messages shape the way we see and treat Black boys and men in our day-to-day lives.

It starts as early as preschool, when Black children are 3.6 times more likely to be suspended from school than white children. How could it be so uneven? Researchers at Yale University tried to answer that question by asking teachers to watch video clips of preschoolers and flag evidence of "challenging behavior." The kids in the clips were actors and there was no challenging behavior to be found, but teachers—who didn't know that—spent more time looking at Black children than white children, and even longer looking at Black boys.

Yale child psychology professor Walter S. Gilliam said that the teachers were watching Black boys because they expected them to make trouble. And we all tend to find trouble where we look for it, not where we don't. "Implicit biases do not begin with Black men and police. They begin with Black preschoolers and their teachers, if not earlier," Gilliam told me, when I first wrote about the study for the *Washington Post* in 2016, amid national protests over the killings of unarmed Black men by police officers. "Implicit bias is like the wind: you can't see it, but you can sure see its effects."

Black boys, regardless of socioeconomic class or family status, contend not just with the assumptions that they're troublemakers but also with stereotypes that they're irresponsible, violent, and hypersexual. For Montez McNeil, a student at D.C.'s Georgetown Day School, that means being constantly aware of how his race and his size—he's six foot five—puts him at risk of being misperceived. "There's literally not a day where I cannot keep my head on a swivel or not be cautious of every action that I take," he told me in a windowless office at school. He sat across from me, his tall frame folded into a chair. He has to think twice before he wears a hoodie, for example, and as he's grown older he's choosing less and less to go to parties where underage kids are drinking or where he might find himself alone with a girl he doesn't know well. "I don't even want to get close to being accused of doing something that I had no intention of doing," he said. "Just hearing about or knowing about false accusations of Black men raping white women, or women in general, has had me more aware of how I treat the women around me and what women I allow in my circle."

Like the rest of us, Black boys are more likely to see Black men celebrated as elite professional athletes or hip-hop artists than as successful professionals and intellectuals. Montez is weary of feeling as if he is seen as a basketball player and nothing more. "You know, people see me walking down the street and they don't see me as an educated Black man or a young Black man who's trying to go to college," he said. "A lot of people don't take time to recognize and understand that I have other passions, too—they won't assume me being an artist or writing poetry and stories. . . . Walking around in this world, you know, I'm always constructed in everyone else's opinions about me."

His mother, Marlo Thomas, an administrator at Georgetown Day, said she talks with her son often about how his Blackness and his maleness shape the way people see him and treat him. She also told him about her own experience surviving a rape when she was his age. As a single mom, she said, "it was the way I could connect, woman to man, being able to say that I as your mother need to teach you about what healthy manhood looks like. A way for him to understand that you're not that far removed, this isn't just something that happens on television." She wants him to understand how racism affects his life, and at the same time needs him to grapple with something that may be harder for him to see—the power and responsibility he has as a man.

How Trauma Is Linked to Violence

The stereotype of Black men as dangerous looms large, but there is no similarly strong narrative about Black men as victims—even though they are disproportionately victims of violent crime. More Black boys and men aged fifteen to thirty-four die of homicide than any other cause, according to the CDC. In 2016, Black boys and men between the ages of ten and twenty-four were murdered at nearly fifteen times the rate of white boys and men. That year, 1,768 Black boys and men were killed, 94 percent of them by guns.

This reality was not lost on the boys I met in BAM, who were keenly aware of the risk they faced as Black boys living in a violent neighborhood. "You have to watch people who you hang around," one boy said. "You have to watch your surroundings. You never know what can happen."

I grew up in a safe neighborhood, and I cannot imagine living with this kind of anxiety. Every day. All the time. Yet this is reality for so many children, of all races and classes. The anxiety can come from living in a neighborhood wracked by violence or struggling against the uncertainties and deprivations of poverty. It can come from growing up in an abusive home, or with parents who misuse drugs or alcohol. It can come from experiencing the effects of racism.

If we care about helping boys build healthy lives and strong relationships, we have to care about this anxiety. The chronic toxic stress that kids develop in response to violence in their homes and communities—violence that they witness and violence that they experience directly—can alter the architecture of their brains and have long-lasting effects on their health. And it can increase the likelihood that they might use violence in their own lives.

In the late 1990s, a landmark study by the CDC and Kaiser Permanente examined the following ten kinds of childhood adversity, including: being neglected or abused physically, emotionally, or sexually; watching a man threaten or beat your mother; having parents who are separated or divorced; having a household member go to jail; and being exposed to substance abuse or mental illness at home.

The study found that the more of these "adverse childhood experiences" a person has, the more likely they are to struggle with poor health, including heart disease, cancer, and substance abuse. They are more likely to take risks, to want a lot of sexual partners, and to contract a sexually transmitted infection. They are more likely to become depressed and die by suicide. The accumulation of childhood stress literally shortens lives. A person with six adverse childhood experiences has a life expectancy twenty years shorter than a person with zero.

And the initial list of adverse experiences in the Kaiser study doesn't even capture the full range of a child's vulnerabilities. A decade after that study, the National Scientific Council on the Developing Child—a coalition of universities working to apply science to early development—recognized a range of outside-the-home adversities that were just as toxic, including community violence, racism, and poverty.

Pediatrician Nadine Burke Harris has been a leader in the push to address childhood trauma as a serious health risk. She often asks audiences to imagine what happens to you if you come upon a bear while walking in a forest. Your heart beats faster, you take rapid breaths, and your body is flooded with the hormone cortisol as it prepares to fight or run. Children who experience chronic trauma are essentially always running into bears in the forest.

When a child's body is constantly responding to stress, constantly on high alert, it gets run down. The chronic state of overdrive takes a toll on the immune system. It also affects hormones and the wiring inside children's brains—especially the parts that determine how they learn, store memories, control their impulses, and deal with fear. The bodies of children suffering from chronic toxic stress are primed to react strongly to even low-level threats and disturbances.

Long term, those changes affect not only a child's physical health but also his mental health, his ability to learn in school, and his propensity for violence. The more adversity and violence a boy experiences when he's young, the more likely he is to be violent to others as he grows up; this includes committing sexual violence, intimate partner violence, and physical assault. Mass public shootings may also have roots in toxic stress. The vast majority of the (overwhelmingly young, white) men who have committed such shootings experienced childhood trauma, according to an analysis of shootings since 1966.

This science suggests that we could prevent some violence in the world—including sexual violence—if we did a better job protecting children from the violence they witness and experience in their homes and communities.

In the avalanche of think pieces that have been published since the advent of the #MeToo movement, discussing what we need to do differently with boys, it is easy to find arguments that we need to help them revise their ideas about masculinity. It is harder to find arguments that we need to protect boys from violence. But it is clear that allowing our boys to be subjected to violence as children, allowing them to witness violence and believe that it is normal, not only endangers their own bodies but puts the bodies of their sexual and intimate partners at risk as well.

It's important to know that toxic stress does not doom boys to ill-health or a life of violence. To the contrary, many people endure great adversity and do fine. Scientists are still working to understand why some people are more resilient to childhood adversity than others, but they know that feeling connected to a caring adult can buffer kids from the worst effects of stress, giving them tools and safe places to allow their bodies to calm down and recover. Research suggests that just as adverse experiences cumulatively increase a child's risk for poor mental and physical health, an accretion of positive experiences at home and at school lends protection against toxic stress. The greater the number of good relationships and the greater the sense of belonging, the better the outcome.

Schools are beginning to learn how to help kids who have been traumatized, but mental health services are often lacking. Three-quarters of U.S. public schools say they don't have enough money to provide the services that their students need.

Adverse childhood experiences are an epidemic across social and demographic groups. The Kaiser/CDC study conducted in the 1990s surveyed seventeen thousand mostly white and well-educated Californians. It found that two-thirds of subjects reported having had at least one adverse experience, and 12.6 percent reported having had four or more. But Black children accumulate significantly more adverse experiences than white children—not because of the color of their skin, but because of the social realities they live in, realities shaped by discrimination and racism that have historically fenced their families off from economic and educational opportunities.

John Rich, a physician and MacArthur Foundation "genius" grant winner, interviewed young male victims of violence in Boston in an effort to better understand how to help them heal. Some had been caught in random crossfire, while others had been living aggressive lives as a form of survival in neighborhoods where shrinking from a fight just puts a bigger target on your back.

One seventeen-year-old gunshot victim, Jimmy, explained that in his community, young men shoot and fight to build reputations as men to be feared. Jimmy said that's what he had done, and that's why other guys usually didn't mess with him. They knew who he was. "Violence worked in his world to accomplish something that all of us wanted—to be somebody—but that Jimmy could not find any other way to do," Rich wrote, in *Wrong Place, Wrong Time* (2011).

Jimmy and each of the other victims Rich interviewed were grappling with the trauma of their injuries on top of unaddressed childhood trauma that they had been carrying for years. Yet they did not have words for the symptoms they experienced—the jumpiness, the sleeplessness, the tendency toward rage. Rich came to believe that the trauma they experienced was particularly harmful in combination with the social norms that told them that, as men, they could not cry or show weakness or vulnerability. All of their feelings were channeled into the narrow groove of rage, which too often had nowhere to spill out except in acts of aggression against other people—against other men in the street or against lovers at home.

Rich told me his critics sometimes argue that he uses men's trauma to try to justify violent behavior that can't be justified. What he is offering, though, is not an excuse but an explanation for why violence is so hard to uproot. And that explanation has led him to help develop efforts to steer young male victims of gun violence toward a different life. Now a professor at Drexel University in Philadelphia, Rich helps run Healing Hurt People, an effort to reach young men before they leave the hospital to reduce their risk of further violence. Social workers help them connect with therapy to deal with their trauma and get the help they need—whether housing, job training, or treatment for alcohol or drug addiction—to navigate a constructive path forward.

"Ultimately, I believe that if we want to make ourselves safe, if we want to end the high levels of violence affecting young Black men, we must focus on their safety: the very people we have blamed for making the community unsafe," Rich wrote in his book. "We are only as safe as they are."

"We Can't Police Our Way Out of This"

When Arne Duncan left his job as President Obama's education secretary at the end of 2015, he chose to give his farewell address not in Washington, whose politicians he had grown weary of, but before a small crowd in the basement of Saint Sabina, a Catholic church on the South Side of Chicago that he said felt like home. And he chose to focus not on the controversial education issues that defined his seven years in the nation's capital, like Common Core math and literacy standards and teacher evaluations, but on what he said was the "greatest frustration" of his tenure: the scourge of gun violence in America.

His voice cracking with emotion, Duncan spoke of the sixteen thousand children who were shot and killed during the Obama administration's first six years, of gridlock on Capitol Hill that stymied meaningful gun control legislation, and—in the aftermath of so many police shootings of Black men—of the broken trust between law enforcement officers and the people they swear to protect. He argued for a new "new deal" that would not only improve the education of children in the most impoverished and violent neighborhoods but would help transform those neighborhoods altogether with more mentors and more jobs.

"If we were to fix every police department today in need of help, in need of change, if we were able to do that, that'd be great," Duncan said that day. "But if we don't fix the communities where so many of our children are dying, if we don't address the underlying causes of why so many children are dying and so many children are dropping out, then we cannot begin to declare victory."

The speech led to whispers that Duncan, a Chicago native who had announced he was moving back home, was contemplating a bid to replace his former Obama administration colleague Rahm Emanuel as the city's mayor. Instead, in the months after his speech at Saint Sabina, Duncan witnessed the beginning of a spike in murders that left 769 people dead, making 2016 the city's deadliest year in recent memory. And Duncan—who had grown up working for the after-school tutoring program his mother ran on Chicago's South Side—decided to answer his own call to transform the city's most violent neighborhoods by trying to create a safety net for the young men most likely to actually pull a trigger. Like John Rich, he believed these men—the ones who had shot someone or been shot themselves—were the foundation for creating safer communities.

With the backing of the Emerson Collective—a California-based social-impact firm headed by Laurene Powell Jobs, the widow of Apple cofounder Steve Jobs—Duncan has brought together community partners who recruit the young men most at risk of gun violence into a web of support meant to launch them into a different kind of life. Activists working in the streets had been calling for an approach like this for a long time, and Duncan brought the connections—and the private dollars—to make it happen.

"We can't police our way out of this, and we can't arrest our way out of this. We have to provide opportunities," Duncan told me in 2016 when he announced his effort, which would later be called Chicago CRED, or Creating Real Economic Destiny. "The thesis is, if we can help young men and women get real skills that will lead to real jobs and pay them to gain those skills, then you give them a reason to not sell drugs and not get caught in the violence."

When I met him a few months later at his office in downtown Chicago, he said he had been talking with incarcerated young men at the Cook County Jail, asking how they had become involved in selling drugs and what it would take to persuade them to get out of that business. A steady job, they told him. Paying $12 or $13 an hour. They were in the drug trade not because they particularly wanted to be but because it was the only job they could see in their neighborhoods. It provided the most obvious path to support themselves and their families.

Chicago CRED started in the fall of 2016 with thirty guys who were paid to help demolish abandoned homes while they got some job skills training, therapy, and other support. But the program has evolved as Chicago CRED has focused more exclusively on gang members and has learned more about the depth of their struggles. About one-third are homeless and half don't have high school diplomas, according to Paul Robinson, Chicago CRED's director of service strategy. Almost all of them suffer from post-traumatic stress disorder.

"The basic premise was, if guys have jobs, they won't have to participate in the illegal economy and that will make them safe. What we discovered was how much more they needed," Robinson told me one rainy day in April 2019, on the second floor of the Cook County Courthouse. We were standing in an empty echoing hallway waiting for Jamon Lynch, a twenty-four-year-old man Robinson had been mentoring for more than two years. Lynch was due to appear for a hearing.

Now, Robinson told me, the men's first job with Chicago CRED is to start building the skills they need to divorce themselves from the street. They are paid to spend five days a week at one of several community centers on the south and west sides of town, where they get help with housing, access to high school diploma programs, and therapy. They also get matched with a one-on-one life coach who often has survived violence and incarceration himself and can serve as a mentor and guide.

Once a man's life has stabilized and he's separated from his gang, Chicago CRED hooks him up with a transitional job meant to teach and reinforce skills like reporting for work consistently and on time. The salary for those jobs—many of which are in manual labor like maintenance and construction—is paid by Chicago CRED until the young man can secure a job on his own.

Ideally, that transitional job would last just a few months, and then off he would go, ready for a new life as a taxpaying citizen in the legal economy, and as a role model and force for stability for the children—his own and others'—who are growing up in violent neighborhoods.

That's not always how it went, but CRED was making a difference in a growing number of lives. Between 2016 and 2019, the organization reached nearly 350 young men. More than 50 earned high school diplomas, and 97 were placed in jobs. The organization also ran basketball tournaments and sponsored summer jobs for thousands of Chicago youth, and it played a key role in coordinating a massive block-by-block effort to reach out to gang members and quell disputes in the city's fifteen most violent neighborhoods. Homicides in Chicago fell 15 percent between 2016 and 2017, and then another 15 percent between 2017 and 2018, and 13 percent in 2019.

"The numbers are real, but I always check it. I'm in schools all the time talking to kids, and I always ask, 'Do you feel safer yet?' And nobody feels safer," Duncan told me in late 2019. "The numbers are real but we're not at a tipping point yet."

Chicago CRED's role in the declining violence was not clear, but Duncan said he believed that the organization and its partners were on the right track to fundamental change in the city. Before the COVID-19 pandemic changed everything, they had set a goal of reducing murders by 20 percent in 2020—a decline that would put Chicago below four hundred homicides in one year for the first time in more than half a century. Duncan was pressing city and state officials to help fight violence by investing tax dollars in the highest-risk men, arguing that it was not only the moral decision but also the fiscally responsible one. The Boston Consulting Group estimated that gun violence cost the city of Chicago about $3.5 billion in 2018, or up to $1.5 million per homicide and $976,000 per non-fatal shooting.

But helping a man untangle his life from the violence surrounding it takes time. It takes failure. It also takes commitment, something like love. That's what I learned from Jamon Lynch, Paul Robinson's mentee, a gunshot victim who was one of Chicago CRED's earliest recruits. I met Jamon when he was two and a half years into the program, still working at a CRED-funded job, still working every day to build a future he could be proud of. "I hate half the things I did in my life, but I can't go back and change them," he told me over coffee. "The only thing I can do is be different."

"I Still Deal with the Pain Every Day"

Jamon was the middle of five kids in his family, and nothing about his growing up was easy. His father was absent, sometimes locked up and other times kept at a distance by Jamon's mother. Jamon never got along well with his mom, and he couldn't understand why she dated abusive men. He hated watching her boyfriends hit her. Once, after one of those boyfriends punched her in the eye, Jamon said he and his brother confronted him and beat him, Jamon with a broomstick, his brother with a mop. Jamon was eleven.

At thirteen, he and a couple of other boys—bored and looking for something to do—headed to a golf course on the south side of town. "We took three golf carts and were driving down the street with them. The owner pulled up behind us," he said. They got a warning, but they didn't heed it. Instead, they circled back to take the golf carts again. This time, the police were waiting, and Jamon was arrested. "Hardheaded little boys," Jamon recalls now.

He was seventeen when he was charged with his first felony. The way he tells it, he and three of his friends were bored, looking for something to do. They broke into the stables at the South Shore Cultural Center, a grand former country club on Lake Michigan where police horses were housed. Jamon said he and his friends stole fire extinguishers and used them to spray cars up and down South Seventy-First Street. But someone also let twenty-seven of the thirty horses out of their stables and sprayed them, too, burning at least one horse's eyes. Jamon said that he had nothing to do with hurting the horses—he's afraid of horses, he said, and wouldn't get near them. But he admitted that he was there that night. He was charged with burglary and cruelty to police animals, and he spent 157 days in jail. That same year, he was kicked out of school for fighting. He never returned.

When he looks back on his childhood now, Jamon said that he never felt he could completely trust another person. The person he felt closest to was an older man who lived on his block and enlisted Jamon to sell drugs. "I did it for a month or so, then I stopped," he said. "That's not something for me."

His best friend was his dog, a black-and-white pitbull named Tyson. "He never left my side," Jamon said. A neighbor asked if he could buy Tyson. Jamon refused, and then that same neighbor killed the dog, he said, running over his head with a car.

Jamon was livid. He went looking for the guy.

"I ain't gonna lie. I wanted to fight him. I wanted to beat his head in," Jamon said. He didn't find the guy who killed his dog. Instead, Jamon got shot. Six times. He thinks the shooter was acting on his neighbor's directions, seeking initiation into a gang. Growing up may have left Jamon with scars, but this was something new. Three years later, he still hurts. He can't sit for long periods because of discomfort in his back and his left leg, where a metal rod runs from hip to knee. Besides physical problems, the shooting left him feeling raw and useless. He couldn't sleep, and when he did sleep, he had nightmares. "I still deal with the pain every day," he told me.

*   *   *

In 2016, Chicago CRED set Jamon up with a job ripping out the walls of abandoned homes for a few months. He wasn't thrilled about it, but it was better than sitting home. He also started studying online for his high school diploma, which he found tedious. Paul Robinson, his life coach through CRED, wouldn't let him quit.

"Paul is like a hungry shark. You can't hide from Paul, he's always going to find you," Jamon said, half grinning. "If I woulda met Paul in middle school, I woulda never been locked up, ever. He wants better for me. I feel like he saw something in me that I didn't see in myself."

Over the course of our conversation that day, and later on the telephone, Jamon kept coming back to the difference that Paul had made in his life. The word he used to describe Paul, over and over, was "committed." He called Paul almost every day and Paul always answered. Paul was always there to try to help him think through and navigate the latest obstacle, whether it was family drama or financial trouble or a terrible boss. "Every day is something new, and every day I call Paul," Jamon said. He seemed bowled over by the notion that someone would commit to him when he, in his own telling, had never committed to anything himself. Not to a job, or an ambition, or a woman.

"How Paul committed himself to me and making sure I'm staying out of trouble, making sure he can help me any way he can, that's how I want to be," he said. "I want to be a positive role model."

Unlike many of the mentors and life coaches who are working with the young men in Chicago CRED to build these kinds of relationships, Robinson did not come from similar neighborhoods or face similar challenges as a child. He grew up west of Boston in Wayland, Massachusetts, an affluent town of gently rolling hills, verdant lawns, and houses with circular driveways.

As a teenager, Robinson got into trouble for knuckleheaded decisions, just like Jamon, he said. But his status as a well-to-do white boy protected him from the consequences Jamon faced—dropping out of school, going to jail. "I had a much more forgiving environment," Robinson, now in his late thirties, told me. "Jamon had none of the stuff I did. I don't know where I would be if I grew up in his situation."

The relationship Jamon shares with Robinson is no small thing, according to Donald Tyler, a psychologist who serves as Jamon's therapist and as director of clinical services for CRED. Just as a close, caring relationship with an adult can shield a child from the effects of toxic stress, Tyler said, close, caring relationships are also important for grown-ups who are grappling with accumulated traumas, which condition the body to respond to any perceived threat by fleeing or fighting.

"These young men grow up in circumstances where being afraid is not acceptable, so to flee is not acceptable, and that leaves you with fighting," Tyler said. A close friend or mentor offers another option: someone to talk to, a refuge for calming down and recovering. And yet many of the men who are at greatest risk of doing violence do not have these critical supportive relationships with their parents, who are themselves struggling with the weight of generations of racism, mass incarceration, segregation, poor education, and lack of quality health care. "I'm not blaming the families," Tyler said. "The families are overburdened by generation after generation of trauma and stress."

Chicago CRED is experimenting with working with younger people—teenagers from thirteen to seventeen—as well as their parents. They are offering therapy and case management. Many of the parents are single moms or grandmothers who are dealing with their own unaddressed trauma, including the chronic stress of a lifetime in poverty. Tyler believes that ultimately this is what's needed to end the cycle of violence: helping not just individual boys and men but their entire families, so that parents and guardians have more tools to give their kids stable lives. But families are complicated, and so is figuring out how to help them. "It's challenging work," Tyler said. "These parents face a lot of longstanding problems."

How Gun Violence and
Domestic Violence Are Intertwined

In 2018, Arne Duncan and Paul Robinson and Donald Tyler—and everyone at Chicago CRED—learned that they couldn't fight gun violence without also paying attention to domestic violence.

That lesson was delivered painfully, through the deaths of two CRED alumni. One was stabbed to death by his girlfriend, a woman with whom he had two children and a longtime tumultuous relationship. The other—one of CRED's earliest recruits, a star of the program who was among the first to land a full-time job—apparently killed his girlfriend and then killed himself, according to a police report.

His crime stunned the staff at Chicago CRED—he was charming and bright, he didn't do drugs or abuse alcohol, and when he messed up, he was quick to apologize and make amends.

But after he died, they saw the roots of his violence in an autobiography he had written when he was in CRED, warning signs they had previously missed. He described a harrowing, traumatic childhood—abandoned by his mother, who was addicted to drugs, surviving on the street, selling drugs, contemplating suicide. "I felt like putting a gun to my head and just ending all this," he wrote. His girlfriend had saved him, showing him a kind of love he'd never felt before: "The hole that lived in me has been filled with love. And it's all because of you."

It's impossible to completely understand anyone else's relationship, to know why it goes sour or becomes violent. But the people at CRED who knew this man, including Tyler, the psychologist, believe that he snapped when his girlfriend threatened to leave him. They believe he couldn't bear another abandonment.

The deaths in 2018 were not the first sign that the young men in CRED struggled with relationship violence. Therapists and life coaches had noticed it was a common theme in their lives. Many of the men had witnessed domestic violence as children and were neglected or physically or sexually abused, said Tyler. They were primed by experience to lash out, including at the women in their lives.

"I think it's pretty naive to think that somehow guys can be violent on the street and then come home and have a normal healthy relationship," Duncan told me. "I don't even use the term 'domestic violence' anymore. It's just violence."

The killings in 2018 persuaded CRED that its young men needed more education on healthy relationships and healthy masculinity. Now, as part of their training, they go through workshops led by Chicago Alliance of Local Service Organizations (ALSO), an organization that has spent years examining and understanding the connections between domestic and community violence—a rarity in a world where street violence is often treated as if it's a problem distinct from family violence that unfolds in private. One in eight neighborhood conflicts, including homicides and shootings, was rooted in intimate relationships, according to the organization's analysis.

A young man affiliated with a gang who is abusing his girlfriend, for example, may be at risk of retaliation by her father or uncle in a rival gang. Or a woman might have a baby with a man in one gang, then break up with him and start dating a man in another gang—if she tries to coparent with her child's father, she is seen as someone who can't be trusted and is at greater risk of gun violence. "People don't live their lives in silos. All these things are connected," said Chicago ALSO's executive director, Lori Crowder.

Domestic violence is not just something men do to women, of course— often, men are also victims, subjected to abuse by girlfriends who have themselves grown up surrounded by violence, and who have learned to use violence to deal with conflict and dispute. This is how Jamon described his relationship with his on-again, off-again girlfriend, who he said had a drinking problem and a habit of trying to provoke him into physical fights when she was drunk. They argued frequently, but he said he fought her physically just once—before he learned to control his anger. "I felt so bad, because I used to watch my mama get beat," he said.

Jamon's story is not simple, and it's not finished. He's still writing it, still deciding every day who and how he wants to be. Giant change doesn't just happen. It comes from the ritual of going to a job every day, even if you don't love it; going to therapy every week, even when you don't feel like it;

choosing consciously, moment by moment, to control your anger instead of allowing it to control you.

Jamon had cycled quickly through jobs, first at the Pullman Sugar plant and then pulling weeds for a conservation nonprofit. When I met him, he'd been employed with the same construction company for six months, making $12.50 an hour, the most stable employment of his life. Jamon said he'd only been able to keep the job because Tyler had helped him learn to manage his anger, which had been overwhelming in the wake of the shooting. "I don't get mad over the littlest things," Jamon said. "He helped me out so I don't lose my mind."

Every time they met, Jamon would unload about his anger, and every time, Tyler would ask him the same question: What's the most important thing in your life? Jamon always gave the same answer: his kids. He wanted to be a good dad to them, and Tyler's determination to pull him back to that bigger picture gave him a strategy for managing the frustrations and disappointments of everyday life. "If you do something dumb, how would that impact the most important thing in your life? Now when I look at things, I think of that," Jamon said.

He hated the construction job he was working, but Paul had persuaded him to start saving money from every paycheck, and he liked the feeling of being able to take care of his children. He had two young sons with his girlfriend in Chicago and a daughter with another woman who now lived in Texas. He wanted to be a role model for his kids.

In this way, Jamon was trying to rebuild his life. But then he was arrested again. After he was shot, he had been deeply wary of being shot again. Determined not to be a target, he had bought a gun for protection and peace of mind. That decision landed him in handcuffs again, with a felony charge for illegal firearm possession in April 2018, a year and a half after he started CRED.

He had been afraid, he told me, because being a tall, strong Black man makes him feel paradoxically vulnerable in Chicago's toughest neighborhoods. Guys who see him are afraid he'll jump them, so they pull out a gun to protect themselves. Everyone is afraid, and the fear that pinballs around the neighborhood puts everyone in danger. "People say I have a mean look, they feel intimidated. They feel they have to prove something about themselves," he said. "There's a lot to deal with living out here. There's a lot to deal with, being a male."

He paused. "I hope my son is not tall," he said, thinking of the danger that his own size attracts. "I just don't want to have to get that phone call about my son."

By the time we met, Jamon had been on home monitoring for thirteen months for the gun charge, essentially confined to his bedroom when he wasn't at his job or in therapy. He was waiting for a judge to decide whether he had to go to jail. Every month, he reported to court, and every month, the decision was postponed.

He watched television and played video games and went to work and called Paul. He kept working on his new life, even as he remained weighed down by his old one. He said the gun charge was a wake-up call. He knew he had to do better. He wanted to leave Chicago and move to Hawaii. It felt more realistic, though, to dream of Missouri. It was far enough away and he'd never been there, either. "Some people say I'll never be successful. Some people say I'll die," he said. "I want to be something that people never thought I would be."

Sitting across a table from Jamon, watching him stand and stretch to ease the lingering pain from his injuries, listening to him narrate the story of his life, I thought about the enormous obstacles he faced. Poverty, violent and segregated neighborhoods, racism: he was a Black man with a criminal record and an interrupted education. What place would the nation's economy be willing to make for him? I thought of the history that the author Ta-Nehisi Coates laid out in "The Case for Reparations," a history that began with the enslavement of Black people and continued through many decades of racist laws and policies, which not only diminished opportunities for Black Americans but also stole their wealth.

CRED cannot remove those obstacles or rewrite that history. No program could. They are systemic problems, and fixing them will require systemic change in schools, in communities, in the wages and benefits available to workers, in the support afforded to struggling families. But CRED was helping to keep Jamon safe, out of the path of bullets. And his relationships with Paul Robinson and Donald Tyler were giving him tools to navigate the challenges he faced.

Seven months after Jamon and I first met in Chicago, a few days before Thanksgiving, Paul texted me with good news. A judge had decided that Jamon would not go to jail. He had already served his time, 609 days of electronic monitoring and home detention. Now he could finally move forward.

"It Makes You Feel Like You Have Someone"

If CRED aims to reshape the lives of young men who have fallen into patterns likely to get them killed, then BAM aims to catch boys earlier on and give them the tools they need to thrive.

Jamon never knew his dad until he was an adult. Many of the boys in BAM, too, don't have fathers in their lives. One twelve-year-old who had never met his dad told me that his guardian—an uncle—kept his absent father's photograph in the car, so they could keep their eye out for him as they drove around town. Another twelve-year-old said that his father had been incarcerated the previous year, but that he hadn't told anyone in BAM yet. It was still a secret. "It can mess a kid up knowing that their father is not there," the twelve-year-old told me.

Anthony Ramirez-Di Vittorio created the BAM curriculum out of years of trial and error working with boys in Chicago. Ramirez-Di Vittorio also grew up mostly without his dad, after his mother fled their abusive relationship, taking Anthony with her. He was a skateboarder who loved nothing more than the White Sox and his friends on the block. He modeled BAM after the work that he himself had undertaken in an effort to heal from the grief and rage he felt over his father's absence. An outgrowth of the men's movement of the 1990s, the work consisted of participating in intensive gatherings with people who were in the same position and who challenged each other to dig up and deal with their emotional wounds.

"I got into this work to break the cycle of fatherlessness. That's why I'm here. That's my mission in this world," said Ramirez-Di Vittorio, a muscled fiftysomething Mexican Italian known affectionately in the BAM world as "Tony D" and "the Bamfather." Insisting on introducing me to the best of Chicago while I was in town, he told me BAM's origin story over a couple of gut-busting breaded steak sandwiches at Ricobene's, a pizza parlor next to an interstate overpass in Bridgeport, the South Side neighborhood where he grew up.

In designing a program to help fill the holes that boys with absent fathers feel, and to teach them the skills they would need to be good fathers themselves someday, Tony D also created a program that made a measurable impact on the problem of youth violence. The University of Chicago Crime Lab conducted two randomized controlled trials—the gold standard for rigorous research—showing jaw-dropping results. Boys who participated in BAM were arrested for violent crimes at *half* the rate of their peers who did not participate.

BAM's success earned the attention of President Obama, who joined a BAM circle at Hyde Park Academy in 2013 and then, in 2014, cited it as an inspiration for My Brother's Keeper, his administration's initiative to empower boys and young men of color.

The program also won attention from Microsoft founder and philanthropist Bill Gates, who after sitting in on a circle in 2018 declared the boys' intimacy with one another—and their ability to deal with their anger in the face of so much personal tragedy—"inspiring." Now, BAM is in more than 130 schools in Chicago, serving more than seven thousand students. It has expanded to Boston, Los Angeles, and the suburbs of Seattle, and across the Atlantic to London.

It's not yet clear whether the formula that Tony D developed for his hometown will work as well in other places—in part because it's not entirely clear what makes BAM work in Chicago.

Tony D started developing the BAM curriculum in 2001, when he was working in schools for Youth Guidance, the nonprofit organization that runs the program and has fueled its growth. For years, he was the only BAM counselor in Chicago. He was supposed to be working with boys on their résumés, but the men's movement retreats had lit a fire in him, and he wanted to share it with students. So he ignored the résumés and started bringing the boys together in circles to talk about their lives. The circles became confidential, safe places for boys to open up about their struggles and practice being vulnerable.

"That's why I think BAM works," he told me. "We embrace our softness. It's not embracing a feminine skill—it's a masculine skill, to be soft."

Each meeting starts with check-ins, where boys share whatever is on their mind. Then they do group activities that require problem-solving and cooperation. Later, they debrief, talking about how each of them confronted the challenge and either sabotaged or supported the group's success. The discussions are arranged around six core values: integrity, accountability, self-determination, goal-setting, positive anger expression, and respect for womanhood.

BAM counselors purposely do not lecture boys about what choices they should be making—or not making. Tony D figured they have already been told a thousand times that they should obey their teachers and do their homework, and should not skip class or do drugs or join gangs. Instead, he adopted something of a Socratic approach, asking boys to reflect on what they were doing well or not so well. Why are you getting into trouble with your teacher—what's that about? Why are you fighting—is that who you are? Are you being the kind of person you really want to be?

Boys won praise when they opened up about whatever pain or struggle was beneath the day-to-day. "I'd go, 'This is real men's work. You're looking at who you are,'" Tony D said.

He wanted to help them build an internal compass so that when they made a decision that didn't jibe with their idea of themselves, they would feel an ache in their guts—the same ache that Tony D said he felt in high school, when he started stealing spray paint to get high and skateboarding more than going to class. It didn't feel good, making those choices. It didn't feel right. Eventually, it was that ache that caused him to change course.

"What I care most about is that you've learned the skill of vulnerability and self-reflection and to go deep, and to have these basic values as barometers for decisions," he said.

The researchers at the University of Chicago who have studied BAM's impact believe that the program's refusal to tell boys how they should act, and its emphasis instead on honing boys' skill at thinking about how they're thinking, is responsible for its success.

This kind of reflection happens during check-ins, when a counselor might push a boy who laughs at one of his fellow BAM brothers to explain what was going on for him when he made the decision to laugh. It also happens during group games, when counselors ask boys to reflect on why they made the decisions they made.

All of this practice helps boys develop what the Nobel Prize–winning psychologist Daniel Kahneman called "slow thinking." We all have automatic responses to certain situations, shortcuts that help us operate more efficiently in the world—or "fast" thinking. BAM appears to help boys take a moment to consider their options and avoid reacting impulsively, behavioral scientist Anuj Shah told me. It's a skill that is particularly useful for young people who are constantly switching between environments with very different codes of behavior. Fighting back on the block might make sense, but it's not the appropriate response to a teacher in the classroom who asks you to be quiet.

In one BAM activity, boys are given thirty seconds to get a ball from their partner. Almost invariably, they try to physically wrest the ball out of the other boy's hands. In the debrief, counselors ask questions that lead the boys to realize that they could have simply asked for the ball instead of assuming they needed to use force. "This exercise, like many in the program, teaches youth to think more carefully about the situations they are in," Shah and his colleagues wrote.

To test the "slow thinking" hypothesis, the researchers had BAM and non-BAM boys play a game that required making decisions in the face of conflict. BAM students took 80 percent longer to make their decisions. They literally took more time to think. We tend to assume that people who commit crimes are making intentional choices to do wrong, so prevention efforts tend to focus on trying to persuade people to make different choices, Shah said. But many of those efforts have failed—perhaps because people's choices are not actually all that purposeful. The research on BAM shows that there may be promise instead in helping people slow down so that they can make a constructive decision that might otherwise be overridden by automatic impulse.

"There's often not as much intentionality as we think there is," Shah said. "People might not be thinking very much at all."

But while Shah's slow thinking and Tony D's core values may be necessary for changing boys' lives, the boys themselves identify another ingredient that comes only with time and sincerity and is therefore hard to take to scale: relationships.

The brotherhood among BAM boys and their counselors is unlike anything else, said Christian Champagne, a BAM alum who spent three years in the program at Hyde Park Academy, and who introduced President Obama at the White House at the My Brother's Keeper launch in 2014.

The boys and men involved in BAM see you and the challenges you're facing—whether it's not having enough to eat, or mourning a gunned-down friend—in ways that teachers do not, Christian said. And that creates a sense of responsibility to live up to the values that the program makes sacred.

"It makes you more aware of what you are doing. It makes you feel like you have someone, and you don't want to let them down," he told me as we shared a plate of calamari at an Italian restaurant on the north side of Jackson Park, not far from where Obama plans to build his presidential library. "Picture you don't want to disappoint anyone, and you're trying, you're really trying."

Christian, twenty-three when we met, told me how shocking it had been the first time he sat in a circle during his sophomore year at Hyde Park. He had come to the group because his friend had told him they sometimes got free tickets to Chicago Bulls games, but he was hooked when he saw the boys around him—guys he'd only passed in the hallways, guys who seemed tough—letting down their guard and being emotional with one another.

They held him accountable when it came to his grades, he said, but also when it came to the women in his life. Christian is magnetic, with a wide smile and long, curly hair. Girls had always been interested in him, but he never understood what a healthy relationship was. The youngest of six children, he grew up with no father and a mother who had been in abusive relationships.

When he admitted being unfaithful to his girlfriend, the BAM guys told him she didn't deserve that. She deserved respect. "I was bogus for that. I was treating her wrong," Christian told me. "You get so comfortable in those BAM meetings that you just ramble off and tell everything, and then people will understand, point out where you are wrong and where you should fix that, looking at you like you crazy. And that's exactly how you learn."

It was also in BAM that he learned he was being verbally abusive to his girlfriend; he had thought he was just acting as men act. "Getting into arguments and saying some real messed-up stuff to people is not really a positive way to let our anger or frustrations out," he said. "BAM taught me to talk about my feelings, how to articulate what I'm feeling in the moment, instead of cussing someone out."

Christian graduated from Hyde Park and then went off to Morehouse, the all-male historically Black college in Atlanta. He was stressed about paying the tuition bill. He was homesick. And then he was hospitalized, struggling with symptoms of the sickle cell disease that had troubled him on and off his whole life. BAM couldn't fix these enormous problems for Christian. But he needed people to talk to about what he was going through, and he felt the absence of BAM intensely.

He left Morehouse and went home to Chicago, where he worked briefly for Youth Guidance—the nonprofit that runs BAM—and then enrolled at Western Illinois University. When I met him, he only had a few more classes to finish before graduation. He was still in touch with his BAM counselor, Marshaun Bacon, and in the absence of BAM circles, he had learned to deal with his emotions and his challenges through journaling.

"There's an art form to helping young men find their resiliency," Bacon said when I called him up to ask about Christian. "We see that spark in these young men. We see that brilliance and we want to cultivate it."

The seventh graders I met at Burnham agreed with Christian. What was special about BAM, they said, was the counselor, Jarvis Burks, and how he created a space where boys could be honest about whatever was on their minds without worrying about being teased, where they could talk about difficult, private things without fearing those secrets would be leaked.

Burks was a father figure, one boy told me unprompted. He was always there to help, but he didn't let BAM boys off the hook when they messed up. Instead, he expected more from them. And that felt like something a father would do.

BAM and CRED are hopeful, and it is tempting to believe that they and programs like them are solutions to the problems that so many boys and young men face in Chicago and nationwide. But of course, they are not. The relationships they help boys forge with older mentors, and the skills they teach, are necessary—but they are nowhere near sufficient. They cannot alone erase or reverse the giant toxic forces that shape so many boys' lives: racism, economic desperation, underfunded and sometimes dysfunctional schools, community violence, and family strife.

The COVID-19 pandemic drove that home in Chicago. As the new coronavirus spread and economies shut down, unemployment rose and violence spiked.

Arne Duncan and Chicago CRED had hoped that murders would decline 20 percent in 2020; instead, by the end of June 2020, shootings were surging and the city had recorded 329 murders—34 percent more than the number at the same time in 2019.

Among those killed were far too many children. One of them was a BAM student, a boy from Burnham. He was shot in July, one of sixty-four people shot that weekend, one of eleven killed.

Also in July, Jamon Lynch called me from the Cook County Jail. He said he had been arrested and jailed on a domestic battery charge. He insisted that he hadn't laid his hands on her, his on-again, off-again girlfriend, but she had called the cops and made up a story because he wasn't giving her enough attention. He said the charge had been dismissed, but he remained locked up on a parole violation. He didn't know how long he'd have to stay.

I asked his girlfriend what happened. She said she didn't want to talk about it. Paul Robinson, Jamon's mentor, said he was trying to help her find a job. He wanted to do what he could to help her take care of her two little boys—the sons she shared with Jamon.

CHAPTER SEVEN

Why Harry Needs Sally

How All-Boys Schools Are Trying to Stay Relevant

De La Salle High School is a Catholic boys' school with a nationally recognized football team and, in the months before #MeToo became a viral hashtag, a couple of high-profile sexual assaults. In 2016 and again in 2017, two different De La Salle football players raped two different girls, both students at a sister high school across the street. The boys were both found guilty.

The media descended on the school, nestled in the hills thirty miles northeast of San Francisco. Television vans parked outside, and reporters approached students on their way to class. Students, parents, and administrators suspected that the press was taking particular glee in the story: a famous football program with a rape problem. The De La Salle Spartans owned the national record for longest winning streak in U.S. high school football history—151 games between 1991 and 2004. It had been hailed in the pages of *Sports Illustrated* and memorialized in a 2014 Hollywood film, *When the Game Stands Tall*. Now the legend was tarnished, giving outsiders what seemed, to the boys at De La Salle, a degree of satisfaction.

The boys felt attacked, as if they were all considered guilty by association, and singled out, as if this never happened at any other school. "You can't judge all of us by just one bad action," said Gunnar Rask, a football player who graduated in 2019.

But even as the reaction to the rapes pricked the boys' feelings of defensiveness and pride, the crimes also forced the school to reexamine the lessons that its boys were learning about sex, gender, and consent—and to attempt to do better. "We needed to use it as a lightning rod to try and make as much change as we possibly could," said Justin Alumbaugh, a social studies teacher and the head coach of the varsity football team.

Ever since Christine Blasey Ford's allegations against Brett Kavanaugh trained the media's klieg lights on Kavanaugh's all-male alma mater, Georgetown Prep, boys' schools across the country have faced sharp questions about whether they nurture old-fashioned gender stereotypes, encourage male entitlement, and numb young men to the basic humanity of girls and women.

Though boys' schools educate only a small fraction of the children in this country, arguably we all have a stake in how they do their job, because so many graduates of venerable single-sex institutions end up in positions of power in government, business, and civil society. The Supreme Court is a good example. Of the nine justices, six are men, and four of those men are graduates of all-male high schools.

The questions all-male schools have faced in the aftermath of Kavanaugh's nomination have forced many of them not only to spend more energy figuring out how to better teach students about sex and relationships, but also to examine—often for the first time—the fundamental question of what it means for their boys to be in school all day without any girls.

"It's just the greatest irony that these schools focused around single-sex education, and focused around gender, themselves don't really talk about gender," said Kristin Ross Cully, who has worked with Jesuit boys' schools for more than fifteen years. Ross Cully wrote her doctoral dissertation on the experiences of female faculty members in boys' schools. In the year after Kavanaugh's confirmation fight, she said, a growing number of boys' schools sought guidance on how to discuss gender and sexism. "This is no longer on the minds of a few people," she said. "It's of interest to everyone."

Indeed, principals of boys' schools rate "healthy concepts of masculinity" as the most important challenge they face, according to a confidential survey of administrators at more than 330 schools conducted by the International Boys' Schools Coalition in June 2019.

At St. Albans, a prestigious all-male school for fourth- through twelfth-graders in Washington, D.C., where students wear blazers and ties to class and many aspire to the Ivy League, headmaster Jason Robinson believes that this is an existential moment for boys' schools. Survival, he says, will require embracing the national debate about how we teach boys to be men. Robinson, who has two daughters and has worked at both coed and single-sex schools, believes that boys' schools should be arguing that they are well-equipped to chip away at rather than reinforce old-fashioned tropes about men. "We have an opportunity to confound people's stereotypes," he said.

But to confound stereotypes about boys and boys' schools, Robinson will have to do the hard work of making real change at an institution steeped in tradition. Like other boys' schools, and many coed schools, St. Albans has struggled with deeply rooted sexism.

Robinson became headmaster in summer 2018. Soon after, the Kavanaugh confirmation fight rattled the elite boys' school world in Washington and drew new attention to what they were teaching young men who aspired to the nation's halls of power. As the nation studied vulgarities in Kavanaugh's 1983 Georgetown Prep yearbook, news surfaced that the St. Albans yearbook had also featured sexist slurs and not-so-veiled references to sex and girls' bodies. It had happened just three years earlier, during the same school year in which girls from St. Albans's sister school had circulated a Google document describing sexual misconduct by St. Albans boys. "Truly reprehensible," Robinson said at the time, pledging to build a culture of respect and dignity.

A few months later, in a speech to parents, Robinson laid out his case for boys' schools as places uniquely positioned to challenge masculine stereotypes. He described listening to a high school student deliver the first chapel talk of the school year, and then watching as the boy's classmates congratulated him afterward with handshakes and hugs and unselfconscious expressions of pride and affection. "I love you," they said. The boy looked his friends in the eye and said, "I love you, too."

Speaking with me in his wood-paneled office at St. Albans, whose Gothic campus on the grounds of the Washington National Cathedral evokes Harry Potter's Hogwarts, Robinson described boys' schools as among the few institutions in America that don't equate maleness with toxicity, that see and cultivate boys' full emotional selves, and that consciously push boys to explore pursuits that might once have been considered less than masculine at coed high schools, like acting and singing.

I heard this same argument at De La Salle and other boys' schools I visited. They framed themselves as rare places that both celebrate boys and intentionally create space for boys to challenge conventions of masculinity. "They need to love being a man, and interrogate it," said Jason Baeten, who cofounded the East Bay School for Boys in 2009 in Berkeley, California. The students I met there, in a church a block from the UC Berkeley campus, spoke easily about the boxes that the world tries to put them in, and joyfully about their efforts to defy stereotype and expectation. When I asked a dozen students if they wanted to stay home to take care of their kids someday, almost every single one raised his hand. They told me proudly that their school embraces their boy energy, offering an elective wrestling course and a traditional shop class with power tools and a blacksmith's forge at the same time that it gives them space to be themselves.

"You know that term 'boys will be boys'? That's true here, but it means boys can be whoever they want," a sixth-grader told me. "You can be creative. You can be compassionate. You don't have to be held back by the stereotypes in everyday social life."

At a Jesuit boys' high school in St. Louis, juniors gushed about a recent retreat that had given them four days together without their cell phones. It had been a bubble where they hugged and cried and told each other "I love you." It was one of the best things about their school, they told me—the chance to take off their masks and be at once vulnerable and safe. Such retreats are also a tradition at De La Salle. They are organized by Roger Hassett, the director of campus ministry, who was wearing a Pride t-shirt when I met him—not what I expected at a Catholic school. Hassett uses the retreats to ask boys to consider and challenge the notion that men must never show weakness. Every retreat, he shares his story about becoming an alcoholic and getting sober. And every retreat, he cries. "You are one of the most emotional people I have ever met and that makes me a stronger person," one boy wrote to him after a retreat. "Seeing you, it helps me feel not alone when I feel like crying, hugging or telling somebody I love them."

Advocates for girls' schools have long argued that in the absence of boys, girls can be more unapologetically powerful and smart, more fully themselves. Boys' schools are making a parallel argument about the unique space that exists in the absence of girls, a space where boys can access parts of themselves that are otherwise uncool and off-limits.

I found myself wishing, in my conversations with boys at these schools, that the goal was to help them be more fully themselves in mixed company—and to give them the skills, experience, and understanding they need to resist sexism. Wouldn't it be transformative for boys to learn to let down their guard with girls, instead of saving that vulnerability for a segregated space? And wouldn't it be powerful for boys to see girls, too, being fully themselves—fully human?

David Armstrong, the executive director of the International Boys' Schools Coalition, told me that headmasters are increasingly coming to see the lack of day-to-day experience with girls as the Achilles' heel of their institutions. To run an excellent boys' school, they are realizing—to truly prepare students for life in college and beyond—boys need to interact with girls. I was surprised to hear Armstrong say this out loud. Boys' schools are by definition places without girls—that is what they sell to prospective students and their parents. And now they are recognizing that what they need is . . . girls.

At St. Albans, Jason Robinson said that one of his priorities as a new headmaster is building a closer partnership with the all-girls National Cathedral School, whose campus is just a short walk away, so that his students have more chances to interact with girls outside of parties and dances. Some students want the same thing. In 2018, after the Kavanaugh hearings, Jack Tongour, a St. Albans senior, partnered with National Cathedral student Isabella Houle to form a coed group to fight sexism and sexual violence. Jack, a self-effacing cross-country runner with curly red hair, said he was motivated by a friend who told him that she had been sexually assaulted by a St. Albans student. Her story turned sexual assault into an issue that felt personal to Jack, and he wanted to do something about it. "I thought, this shouldn't happen here. We should do whatever we can to stop this from happening here," he told me.

The group he formed ended up being a place where boys were able to share their earnest questions and uncertainties about how to show interest in a girl without crossing a line. One boy told the group that he had kissed a girl who kissed him back, but then she pulled away, and he didn't know how to handle it. Had he done something wrong? ("We said, it's always okay to be like, oh, can I kiss you?" Houle said. "Our motto is it's always better to endure a little bit of awkwardness in asking than being wrong on the tail end and hurt someone.")

The group also became a place where boys considered, some for the first time, what it was like to be a girl. Liam Chalk, a friend of Jack's and a fellow member of the Class of 2019, said he learned how much energy girls devote to avoiding sexual violence and navigating the pressures they feel to be sexual without being promiscuous—"Things boys never think about," he said.

I appreciated the boys' interest in understanding how the other half lives and feels and experiences the world. But if the antidote to sexism at boys' schools is more contact with girls, then do we need all-boys schools at all?

"I Lost Out on the Ability to Relate to Girls": Single-Sex Ed and Social Skills

Boys' schools have enjoyed something of a renaissance in the United States since George W. Bush's Education Department wrote new regulations in 2006 that gave public school districts more latitude to offer some single-sex classes—or even open entirely single-sex schools—without running afoul of federal law. At the same time, concern about a "boy crisis" was building amid evidence that boys were lagging behind girls in school, and particularly in reading. Between 2004 and 2014, the number of single-sex public schools and classrooms grew, according to the *New York Times*, as evangelists—notably author Michael Gurian and physician Leonard Sax, whose books are mainstays among boys' school administrators—sold the idea that boys and their brains are so fundamentally different from girls' that they need different teaching techniques. Boys' schools also gained traction as a strategy to improve outcomes for low-income boys of color in some of the nation's largest cities.

Even as arguments in favor of boys' and girls' schools took hold in American schools, they met with fierce criticism from the American Civil Liberties Union, the Feminist Majority Foundation, and a group of feminist scholars who disputed the supposedly scientific basis for single-sex schools. Separating girls and boys is no more ethical, effective, or necessary than separating kids by race, they argued, and it only gives rise to schools that reinforce outdated sex stereotypes. (The ACLU pointed to writings by Gurian and Sax, including a 2003 "action guide for teachers" in which Gurian wrote that girls have trouble in math "for biological reasons." Boys' spatial skills are boosted by multiple testosterone surges a day, he wrote, whereas estrogen levels in girls are elevated only during their menstrual periods, and therefore they perform well on tests—including math tests—"a few days per month." He also wrote that girls "often cannot master physics or calculus in high school, with everything written on the board and the boys and the teacher going so fast.")

With the dispute over gender and learning at the fore, most research on single-sex education has focused on its impact on academics and careers. Despite the fierce arguments for and against single-sex education, once you control for socioeconomic and demographic differences between the kids at your average coed school and your average girls' or boys' school, it turns out there isn't much difference at all.

But what does going to an all-girls or all-boys school means for kids' social lives, including their impressions of and friendships with members of the opposite sex? Scholars have arrived at very few clear answers; the subject just hasn't been well studied. As a group of British researchers from the University of London put it drily in 2012: "This is an area where strong opinions thrive in the absence of much evidence."

Common sense suggests that, for a boy, spending your days with other boys would have an effect on how you deal with girls. And that is supported by a few studies. A group of psychologists from the University of Hong Kong found in 2018 that high school students who go to single-sex schools have fewer mixed-gender friendships and more anxiety in mixed-gender groups. Those differences persisted even after kids went off to college. The results suggest that boys who go to single-sex schools may struggle to connect with women in the workplace and in heterosexual romantic relationships, said Wang Ivy Wong, the lead author of the study. And in fact, the University of London researchers, who studied the life experiences of British children born in 1958, found that by the time they hit middle age, graduates of all-boys schools were more likely to have been divorced than their counterparts who graduated from coed schools.

There are of course plenty of graduates of single-sex schools who are happily married and employed productively in coed workplaces. But some students and alumni told me that their experiences left them feeling handicapped when it came to understanding girls and women. They couldn't fathom being friends with girls because—as Billy Crystal put it in the classic 1989 romantic comedy *When Harry Met Sally*, "the sex part always gets in the way."

One man in his late thirties told me that after his initial resistance to his all-boys high school—his mother made him go—he grew to love it. He was an only child, and playing football helped him make friends and come out of his shell. But spending his adolescence almost solely in the company of boys left him feeling as if he had a "developmental delay" when it came to interacting with girls, he said. He had girlfriends, but never many female friends. "I guess I lost out on the ability to relate to girls without wanting to date them," he said.

This rethinking of the boys' school experience is not uncommon among graduates who see the single-sex environment differently after spending time in the adult coed world. Liam Mather loved his middle and high school years at St. Michael's College School, a venerable Catholic boys' school in Toronto with a reputation for producing hockey stars. He was not a sports guy, but he loved the challenging academics, the debate team, the student government, and the close friendships with other boys. He thrived. But after he graduated in 2013 and went to McGill, a coed university in Montreal, he came to question the all-boys world he had inhabited for six years.

At St. Michael's, boys only saw girls at parties and at dances, where sex was a tangible undercurrent. In classrooms and in hallways, it was normal for boys to speak about girls in crude terms, as objects of desire instead of as people with ideas and brilliance and interests of their own. The way the boys spoke about girls became the way they thought about them, and the language they used—and attitudes they held—went mostly unchallenged, Liam said. But at McGill, he realized how harmful to women those words and ideas were. "It was a little bit of a shock," he told me, speaking over Skype from his apartment in Beijing, where he lives and works now.

His misgivings intensified in the wake of the Kavanaugh hearings, as the media painted an unflattering portrait of Georgetown Prep that Mather thought sounded a lot like St. Michael's. Then, in November 2018, two months after Kavanaugh's confirmation, a sickening video was posted to social media showing St. Michael's boys holding down a classmate and sexually assaulting him with a broomstick. Then came reports of other attacks; altogether, police were told of eight alleged incidents of physical and sexual abuse, which led to criminal charges against seven students and the expulsion of eight.

Some in the school community argued that the assault was isolated, the result of a few bad apples. Others said it was a sign of a rotten culture. One alumnus, ultramarathoner Jean-Paul Bédard, alleged that the sexual attacks among athletes at the school stretched back decades; it had happened to him when he played football there in the 1980s, he told Canadian media.

To Liam, who had never witnessed anything like this, the allegations were horrifying, but somehow not surprising. St. Michael's had dropped insecure teenage boys into a hypercompetitive, hypermasculine environment without much adult guidance or supervision. It had re-created *Lord of the Flies*, he said. On Facebook, he urged his fellow alumni to stop reflexively defending the school and consider the possibility that it might be time for real, meaningful change. The assaults reflected a "cultural failure" at St. Michael's, an unwillingness of adults to challenge the impulses of boys, he wrote. "The notions that define manhood are changing. Society used to demand that men be physically strong, emotionless, and chauvinistic. But increasingly, empathy and intelligence are valued. What version of manhood is St. Michael's imparting onto its boys?"

I asked Liam whether St. Michael's could change, whether there was something it could do to make up for the problems he saw. He said he'd been struggling with this question for a while. St. Michael's had helped him learn to be open with other boys, and he had developed tight friendships there. But do boys really need all-boys spaces to learn how to be emotionally authentic? Liam didn't think so. He thought boys could learn to be real in the presence of girls, and that boys and girls could also do academics together at the highest levels. Arguing otherwise, he said, "feels like it's a bit of an excuse not to change."

He questioned whether anyone in charge really wanted cultural change. When the principal resigned in the midst of the scandal, Liam hoped that he would be replaced by the school's first female principal as a sign of a new direction; instead, the school chose a man with a long career in Catholic education, including as an athletic director.

The school has professed that it does want to change. It established an independent committee to examine its culture, which found that bullying was widespread, affecting one in five students. It recommended that the school hire more women teachers (only 20 percent of the faculty were female); redefine what it means to be a "St. Michael's Man"; and more directly confront racism and homophobia. There was no discussion of going coed or of looking for ways to give St. Michael's students more exposure to female students. To Liam, the recommendations seemed necessary but not nearly sufficient.

"I'm not really sure of the purpose of having an all-boys school in society anymore," he said. "I don't really know if it serves a positive value to society, to incubate privilege and a lot of masculine tropes that we should be stamping out."

Changing Culture at All-Boys Schools

Ideally, we would raise children to be real with one another regardless of gender. In the world we currently inhabit, though, the pressure teenagers feel to impress the opposite sex can be overwhelming. For all the drawbacks of boys' schools, I understand the impulse to shield kids from that pressure. So what does it take to maintain the best parts of boys' schools and shed the worst—to build brotherhood without misogyny? How do you teach boys and about gender and sexual violence in a way that opens them up instead of shuts them down?

Because of its football players' crimes, De La Salle arrived at these questions in 2016, two years before Kavanaugh's nomination. Since then, key school leaders have been trying to figure out how to teach boys about preventing and standing up against sexual violence without making them feel guilty about being male. It's a fine line, and they don't know if they've figured it out. They don't know if instruction can overcome the destructive messages about gender, violence, and sexual consent that are beamed at young people from every direction—and that can be particularly intense at a boys' school. But they're trying. "There is no guidebook," De La Salle president Mark DeMarco said. "I don't have all the answers, but we just can't sit back and do nothing."

The first rape happened in an out-of-the way spot near some portable classrooms on the De La Salle campus, according to the events described to me by Jean Skilling, the Contra Costa County district attorney who prosecuted the case. The boy was a freshman football player on the De La Salle team. The girl was a student at an all-girls school just across a narrow two-lane street, Carondelet High.

The boy's lawyers argued that the two teenagers had consensual sex. Video surveillance footage showed the two of them together but did not show evidence that the girl tried to protest, they said. Skilling agreed that the video was ambiguous. But on the stand, the girl testified that the encounter was not consensual. The boy had ignored her protests, including her efforts to physically push him away. When the boy testified, Skilling asked him why he thought the sex was consensual, given the girl's resistance and struggle.

"That's just what virgins do," he said, according to Skilling. It was a shocking moment in the courtroom. "We all went, 'Oh my God,'" she said. "I did not even have the appropriate comeback to that, I was so shocked."

Clearly, he hadn't learned about consent or respectful, mutual agreed-upon sex. "He didn't have anybody in the back of his brain saying, 'She said no, Dad told me to stop when she starts doing this, I'm going to step back and look at the situation,'" Skilling told me. "There was nothing in his world that told him to stop."

His father—a registered sex offender who was convicted of molesting a child under the age of fourteen—believed that his son was not to blame. "He's tall, dark and handsome, he plays for De La Salle, there's a lot of girls that want to be with my son," he told the *East Bay Times*. "When young, fast girls see something they like, they go after it."

The judge believed the girl, found the rape and forced oral copulation charges against the De La Salle player to be true, and sent him to a group home for sex offenders.

Nick Brdar, who was a junior at the time, said students got the message from De La Salle teachers and administrators that they were not to talk about the rape. He understood the need to respect the privacy of the two students involved, but he thought it sent the wrong message. "As an all-boys school, we had a responsibility to at least be talking about this," he said. "I think we spent a little too much time trying to separate ourselves and not realizing that we had a role in this."

It was the second rape, less than a year later, that prompted De La Salle officials to act, Nick said. Another football player was accused of raping a Carondelet student inside a car at a house party after the homecoming dance, and of forcing her to give him oral sex. The girl managed to record her refusal in a ten-second Snapchat file that was introduced as evidence at the boy's trial. "No, please stop!" she could be heard saying in the audio recording.

He, too, was found guilty.

"We had the second one and it was devastating," DeMarco, the school president, told me. "It was like: What do kids need today? Something is wrong."

Terry Leoni, a lawyer for the first victim, said that her client had faced bullying and disbelief from many members of the De La Salle community. Leoni was frustrated that the school had not acted more quickly in response to her client's rape, and she was skeptical that it would make meaningful change. "Are they really trying to educate their students about consent and sexual assault and change that 'boys will be boys' mentality?" she said.

A year after the verdict in the second case, De La Salle decided to let me in to see how they were responding to this crisis. I don't know why, but I suspect that decision had a lot to do with Heather Alumbaugh.

Alumbaugh has chin-length blond hair. She talks fast, smiles a lot, and curses frequently. She is an unapologetic feminist with a doctorate in English from New York University, a penchant for talking about the patriarchy, and no patience for bullshit. In 2016—a few months before the first rape—she had become the first woman to head academics at De La Salle. She believed that the school and its students were more than the media had made them out to be, and she wanted the world outside to see that. She hoped that De La Salle could figure out how an all-boys school might deal with misogyny and sexual violence.

She is also a Bay Area native and a graduate of Carondelet. Justin Alumbaugh, De La Salle's head varsity coach, is her brother. At once an outsider and an insider, she can see the need for change at De La Salle, and she can persuade those around her that her push for change is not about disdain or disapproval but love. And so she is uniquely equipped to do what she is trying to do now: nudge these boys and their parents past their defensiveness and their protectiveness and their pride in De La Salle to see how they can and must learn a different way of being, for their own sake and for the sake of the girls in their lives.

She said that Nick Brdar's impression was correct. De La Salle hadn't known how to respond after the first rape. But in the months after that first incident, the school put together a plan to handle crises, and Alumbaugh proposed a "respectful masculinity" initiative, including a plan to train coaches, teachers, and students to recognize sexual violence and intervene to stop it.

How to Talk to Boys

When it comes to preparing its boys to live in a world with girls, De La Salle has an advantage: its proximity to Carondelet. Though students are separated by sex for their first two years of high school, they share many classes as juniors and seniors. Unlike students at so many boys' schools, students at De La Salle therefore do get practice learning alongside and working with girls.

Like most girls' schools, Carondelet pitches itself as a school designed to champion girls by giving them a break from stereotypes that limit what they think they should be interested in and who they think they can be. Students from Carondelet have pushed De La Salle to spend more time teaching boys about sexual violence so that girls aren't alone in bearing the burden of prevention. When local prosecutor Devon Bell gave a presentation at Carondelet about sexual consent, she told the girls that she would soon be giving the same presentation at De La Salle—and the girls cheered. The girls "want to know the same conversations we are having over here, they are having over there," Sarah Alpert, a counselor at Carondelet, told me.

Even before the two rapes, and before Heather Alumbaugh's arrival, De La Salle teacher and wrestling coach Mike Aquino was teaching about sexual violence. Two girls in his criminal justice class told him that they thought he should be talking to boys about recognizing and challenging rape culture. "'We're often taught how not to get raped or sexually assaulted, but what are you guys talking about?'" Aquino, recalled they had said. "And I was like, I think that's a great question."

It was that question that spurred Aquino to push at De La Salle for more education and conversation about gender, masculinity, and sexual violence. His internet searches for a curriculum to help structure those conversations led him to Mentors in Violence Prevention, or MVP, which was developed at Northeastern University in the early 1990s and has been widely used with college and professional sports teams and in the military. MVP was one of the earliest and most influential efforts to prevent gender-based violence and bullying by focusing on the role of bystanders. Instead of lecturing men on how to avoid being a predator, or instructing women in how to defend themselves, bystander intervention programs like MVP address their audiences as if they are all people who can—and should—interrupt bad behavior ranging from misogynist language to sexual harassment and assault. You may not be the creepy, handsy guy at the kegger, but you can stop that guy from feeling up the obviously uncomfortable girl he's cornered on the dance floor.

As Aquino looked for opportunities to talk with De La Salle boys about sexual violence, he started using pieces of MVP in his classes. When Alumbaugh arrived at De La Salle and wanted to figure out a more comprehensive way to educate boys about gender and sexual violence, she decided to keep going with what Aquino had started.

MVP was cofounded by Jackson Katz, a fast-talking and fiery former high school football star and self-described progressive feminist who is much in demand on the college speaking circuit. He left Northeastern two decades ago to strike out on his own, offering training and consultation on MVP's bystander approach. His company's clients include a long list of professional basketball, baseball, and football teams and the Marine Corps, army, navy, and air force.

In his strong Boston accent, Katz argues that though we talk about gender-based violence as a women's issue, it is in fact a men's issue, related to traditions of men's dominance, power, and privilege. "What's going on with men? Why do so many men rape women in our society and around the world? Why do so many men rape other men?" he asks, in a Ted Talk that has been watched by more than 2 million people. "We need more men with the guts, with the courage, with the strength, with the moral integrity to break our complicit silence and challenge each other and stand with women."

MVP directly challenges gender norms and stereotypes. It is built on Katz's conviction that we can't prevent sexual violence without examining the ways we teach boys to be men, and that we won't stop sexual assault and rape without confronting misogynistic language and sexist jokes— the lower-level, everyday stuff that lays a foundation for treating women poorly. This approach tends to trigger eye-rolling among high school boys. After Katz spoke to De La Salle students as one part of their introduction to MVP, they retreated to their lunch tables and complained that he was attacking them.

"He came on as blaming us," one De La Salle student told me.

"You know, once you feel like you're getting attacked as being a man, then you just shut down and don't listen," said another.

"He had a good message and he spoke really well, but just the way it was received with a thousand and fifty high school boys was very defensive," said a third.

Katz expects young men to resist his message. He likens it to the defensiveness that white people feel in discussions about racism. "When you occupy the dominant social position and somebody challenges you to think critically about how you're helping to perpetuate injustice or inequality, it's totally predictable that a lot of people are going to react defensively," he told me. But he believes that MVP can get beyond that defensiveness by appealing to boys' desire to be strong, courageous leaders who want to do good in the world, and then giving them the tools to actually do that good.

"A fifteen-year old boy who turns to his friend who just told a rape joke and says, 'Hey, dude, that's not funny'—that fifteen-year-old boy has just executed a leadership protocol. It takes more guts to be a guy who speaks out in the face of abuse rather than staying silent. Being one of the guys takes nothing special," he said. He worries that progressives and feminists do not articulate a vision for how young men—especially young white men—are and can be part of positive change.

"What a lot of young men hear is that they should feel guilty for being men, that they should feel guilty for being white," he said. He wants them to hear a message not that they should feel guilty for being men, but that they should feel responsible—responsible for noticing and challenging sexism, heterosexism, and racism.

There is some evidence that helping boys interrogate gender norms can change their attitudes and behavior toward women. And MVP has been used successfully in some schools, but it has never been rigorously evaluated on a large scale. Katz said that he's never been able to get the large grants required to fund such studies. So he is arguing for MVP's approach without the benefit of data from randomized controlled trials showing that it works.

Another widely popular bystander intervention program, called Green Dot, *has* been shown through such randomized controlled trials to be effective at reducing sexual violence (more on that in Chapter Eight). But Green Dot doesn't ask or expect young men to deal with deeper questions about gender norms and manhood, the way MVP does. Alumbaugh wasn't bothered by the scarce scientific evidence of MVP's effectiveness. She thought it was De La Salle's responsibility to help its boys rethink their masculinity—both for the sake of the girls and women in their lives and for their own sakes. She thought it was De La Salle's responsibility to teach about sexism and sexual violence as systemic, deeply rooted problems. And she wanted the boys to hear Katz's fierceness, even if it turned them off. "Jackson is in their face, and that was a choice," she said. "I wanted that so that they understood that we meant business."

What to Look for in a Boys' School

Alumbaugh believed that the school wouldn't succeed in persuading boys to rethink masculinity, or see and address everyday misogyny, without first training teachers and coaches to do the same. When I visited De La Salle, she had hired substitutes for more than a dozen teachers so they could attend a workshop with two MVP trainers, the third time the school had offered such training. Coffee cups in hand, they gathered at circular tables in the school library.

"Some folks are like, 'I could never rape anyone, so I guess this doesn't apply to me,'" said La Shonda Coleman, who works as a trainer for MVP Strategies, Katz's company, and serves as Title IX coordinator at Pepperdine University. "But you may be in that locker room overhearing conversation. You're in the schoolyard with a picture being passed around. Our program is saying, when you hear it, what can you do in that moment?"

Coleman asked the teachers to stand up and move to different sides of the room depending on whether they agreed with, disagreed with, or were unsure about the following statement: "If I'm aware that my coworker is being abused or is abusive in a relationship, it is none of my business." Most people clustered in the "disagree" zone. The "agree" zone was empty. A few people were caught in the middle.

"It's not okay, but at what point would you step up and say something? I'm not sure," one young male teacher said. Through questions and discussion, Coleman guides them to the understanding that the abuse *is* their business, but what they choose to do about it may depend on how much they know about it and how well they know the people involved.

These kinds of group discussions about real-life scenarios are the centerpiece of MVP. Is it okay to call a girl a bitch if you're joking around? What do you do if you're sitting outside on the steps with some guys who start hooting at a girl who walks by in a miniskirt? Join in? Say knock it off? Or stay quiet in the moment, and tell your friends later that you don't like it?

De La Salle football players who had already been through MVP training repeatedly told me about one activity that made an impression on them. Everyone had to share what they do on a daily basis to stop themselves from being sexually assaulted, and inevitably, boys and men couldn't think of a single thing, while girls and women rattled off a long list.

The football players had simply never considered the very different ways in which boys and girls move through the world. "That really hit me," Gunnar Rask said. "I went back home to my mom and asked her, do you do anything like that? She's like, 'Oh, yeah, I walk with my keys in my hand, always make sure I have a phone with me'. . . . I never really thought about my own mother doing something like that."

Alumbaugh planned that starting in spring 2020, every De La Salle sophomore would be trained in MVP in religion class. Sports coaches were expected to reinforce the program's teachings.

One mother, whose son was a De La Salle freshman when the first rape happened, said she appreciates the bystander approach. "It's, 'Look, you might not be a jerk, but if you're not calling the jerk out at the party that's behaving inappropriately, you have a shared responsibility in a bad outcome,'" she said. She said she wouldn't have let her son stay at the school "if he was going to be told day after day that they're all rapists."

Aquino said he hopes that the conversations that the program is starting in classrooms and on athletic teams and among faculty will make a difference—if not immediately, then over time, as boys navigate their own sexual relationships. "I have to believe that some of this stuff will stick," he told me. "I'm hoping that they'll be able to engage with it when they're ready in a way that makes them the type of young man that we want them to be in the world."

It's asking a lot of anyone, including an adult, to do the uncomfortable and sometimes split-second work of stepping in to shift or challenge the behavior of another person—especially another person in your social sphere. But De La Salle faculty are trying to turn intervention into an expectation. While I was visiting, one of the young men I met who had already been through MVP training—and who earnestly, and I believe honestly, decried the sexist language he hears from his classmates—stood by and said nothing as his friend called another boy a whore. An assistant football coach, Terry Eidson, called him out for his silence. "You've got to try to get those words out of their vernacular," Eidson told me. "You have to have your ears open. You can't let things go."

These days at De La Salle, the faculty uses terms like "rape culture" and "toxic masculinity," but that doesn't mean everyone is completely comfortable with the lessons the school is teaching about masculinity. "I mean the workshop's great, but it's going to take me a year or two or three to really own what it means," one English teacher said after the MVP training. He said he worries that the push to get boys to see beyond gender stereotypes may bleed over into trying to strip them of some essential maleness. "You know, do we end up emasculating a generation where we didn't have to go that far?"

Culture change is hard for any institution, including at boys' schools that cherish tradition and history. And pushing to rethink gender norms and sexist language and behavior is even more complex and difficult at schools associated with a faith in which only men may ascend to the highest levels of power. Teachers and students at De La Salle and other Catholic boys' schools told me that speaking frankly about sexuality and sexual consent can be fraught given the church's disapproval of premarital sex—and of masturbation and sexual activity between people of the same sex. If you can't acknowledge that boys are engaging in sexual exploration and, sometimes, penetrative sex, how do you help boys navigate the puzzles of consent and contraception and closeness and respect and dignity?

Many teachers and coaches and administrators are trying to walk a fine line between the teachings of their faith and the needs of their students—and it might be impossible. "You have to be able to live in the real world a little bit," said Justin Alumbaugh, the football coach. "I can't say, 'You should never attempt to have sex.' I'm immediately closing the dialogue. I want them to be able to speak to us."

But even when individual teachers or administrators are willing to push the envelope, faith and inertia and tradition can all be real obstacles to change, I learned from teachers and families at multiple schools. I spoke to LGBTQ students who said their schools made them feel a little less than legitimate, with rules prohibiting gay-straight alliance clubs or same-sex dates at school dances. I spoke to female teachers who said students treated them differently than their male colleagues, with less automatic respect and more sexual jokes. I spoke to one parent who had repeatedly emailed her son's principal asking how the school planned to educate boys about issues like school culture, sexual assault, and consent. She never got a reply.

Boys' schools are not doomed to toxicity, nor are coed schools immune from it. But in the absence of female students, boys' schools do have to be strategic and intentional about how they plan to prepare their sons for a coed world. Parents considering all-male schools for their sons would do well to listen carefully to schools' sales pitches, looking for signs that they aim to reinvent rather than reinforce old-fashioned ideas about who boys are and can be—and looking for signs that the school is pushing beyond making room for boys to be fully themselves and into the more uncomfortable space of challenging boys to see and resist sexism.

If I ever consider an all-boys school for my son, I will ask female teachers what their experiences have been. I will find out about opportunities for boys to interact with girls outside of dances and parties, in the realms of academics, leadership, service, arts, and sports. And I will look for administrators who don't wait for parents' inquiries to explain how their school teaches about gender, masculinity, sex, relationships, and consent—and why those lessons are necessary.

CHAPTER EIGHT

Boy-Friends

The Power of Male Friendship to Create a New Culture

Julian Avenilla didn't like the talk he heard every day as a member of the football team at Richard Montgomery High in suburban Maryland. He didn't like the way his teammates tried to get him to spill intimate details about his girlfriend. And he didn't like the feeling of swimming upstream, seemingly always alone, against a current of misogyny and sexual harassment.

So before his senior year started, he went to his football coach, Josh Klotz, with a suggestion. He asked Klotz if he'd be willing to try Coaching Boys into Men, a program that asks high school coaches to spend fifteen minutes a week talking with their athletes about respect, sexual consent, and healthy relationships.

Coaching Boys into Men is a rare sexual violence prevention program that actually succeeds in changing behavior, according to rigorous studies that have shown a significant impact on both middle and high school boys. Boys who go through it are less likely than other athletes to abuse their dating partners physically, emotionally, or sexually. They are also less likely to stand by silently or laugh when they witness abusive behavior.

Klotz, an English teacher with two young daughters, was game to try this new thing. And to Julian's surprise, other players were, too. Over the next few months, as the conversations unfolded, he said, the boys were positive and attentive. The locker room talk—the bragging about sexual conquest—mostly dried up. And something changed between the players, too: the time they spent in small groups talking about sensitive topics seemed to create a new sense of closeness. Upperclassmen started talking to freshmen instead of ignoring them. And the team, which had been accustomed to losing, improved mightily and made the playoffs for the first time in years.

"During that season, I saw a lot more respect around the team, which is awesome because it resulted in a really good football season," Julian told me at a Starbucks in a strip mall near the University of Maryland, where he was a senior majoring in American Studies.

Coaching Boys into Men is built on the idea that coaches can use their influence with boys to reshape their ideas about gender stereotypes and change the kind of language and behavior that players consider normal. If they can change what boys consider to be normal, then they can make it easier for the vast majority of guys who want to do the right thing to do the right thing. And they can make it less acceptable for other guys, guys who might have more aggressive or violent tendencies, to do the wrong thing.

Researchers have found that middle school and high school boys sexually harass girls mostly because they want to fit in with other boys, and that they tease other boys about being insufficiently "masculine" for the same reason. In college, the friend groups a young man chooses can either encourage him to be sexually aggressive—or can serve as a brake on that behavior.

This chapter is about the small but growing efforts around the country to harness the power of peer culture to help boys forge stronger and healthier relationships with themselves, with other boys, and with girls. While boys' parents undeniably play a critical role in shaping their attitudes and beliefs and behaviors, so do the boys around them—the teammates and classmates and upperclassmen who define what is cool and decide who belongs. Raising boys differently means thinking beyond how we are raising our individual sons to how we are giving boys collective space to create a different kind of boyhood.

There is a narrative, often repeated by parents and teachers, that boys—handicapped by a slow-maturing prefrontal cortex—just can't control their impulses, and somehow that inborn deficit contributes to sexual impropriety. But of course there are many boys who do control their impulses, who do not sexually harass, and who are not sexually aggressive.

A boy's ability to control impulses depends in part on the company he keeps, according to Laurence Steinberg, a psychology professor at Temple University who has studied adolescents and their brain development for decades. It's true, Steinberg explained, that the brains of teen boys are more susceptible to impulse than those of either adult men or teen girls. That's not only because their still-developing brains struggle with regulation, but also because puberty (a flood of testosterone, a rush of dopamine) leaves them feeling particularly strong urges to seek sensation, pleasure, and reward. But teen brains, and especially teen boys' brains, are keenly attuned to the rewards they get from friends—and so their behavior, too, is especially influenced by their friends.

In one study, Steinberg and his team had teenagers and adults play a video game called *Chicken* in which the goal was to win points by driving as far as possible along a course. They had to decide, when faced with a yellow stoplight, whether to stop (and forgo the opportunity to drive farther and get more points) or to continue (and risk a crash and the loss of all the points they had built up). When they played alone, thirteen- to sixteen-year-olds drove just like adults. But when they played in front of friends, they took twice as many risks. The presence of peers seemed to encourage and reward risky behavior, eroding the driver's ability to control his impulses.

In another study involving a game called *Stoplight*, eighteen- and nineteen-year-olds were told to drive across town through multiple intersections as quickly as possible. Confronted with yellow stoplights at those intersections, they had to make split-second decisions about whether to hit the brakes or keep going. Again, they were less likely to play it safe and more likely to try to make it through the intersection—risking an accident—when they played in front of two other teenagers than when they played alone.

When boys are surrounded by friends and peers who reward sexual harassment with laughter and approval, they are offering a powerful incentive to a brain that isn't as well equipped as an adult brain to resist it.

The question is, how do we encourage peer pressure that pushes boys toward kindness and empathy? How do we make consent culture cool? How do we make it easier for boys, who have a human desire to fit in, to do the right thing? From football coaches to psychologists and epidemiologists, a lot of people are trying to figure that out—and while there is still a lot of work left to do, they have started finding answers.

The Roots of Sexual Harassment

Why do boys say rude and intimidating things to girls, slap their rear ends, grab their breasts? It's not about the girls at all. It's not even about sex. It's about boys proving themselves to other boys.

Will Powers grew up in a conservative small town in the Appalachians of southern Kentucky, a place where it was not okay to be anything other than straight. Once, after play-wrestling during Sunday school, two boys sat down and one put his arm around the other, Will recalled. The Sunday school teacher looked at the pair of them and said, "Get your arm off him. What are you, gay?"

I spoke to Will when he was a senior in high school, preparing to go off to college in California. He had only recently come to terms with the fact that he was gay, and he had not yet come out to his family. He had fought his sexual orientation for a long time, hoping he would be what everyone else seemed to want him to be: straight. To prove it—to protect himself—he had dated a lot of girls. And he had said hateful things, cultivating a homophobic bravado to shield himself from accusations that he was anything other than straight.

"We were sitting on a bench before soccer, and somebody asked me, 'Are you gay?'" Will told me. "I was so appalled. I said I would burn every gay if I could. Because I just did not want anyone to think that of me." Another soccer player—a boy Will knew was not straight and was in the closet—proclaimed that if he had a gay kid, he'd hang him.

Will said that he knows things are better now for LGBTQ people than they used to be. Homosexuality is not a crime. Marriage equality is the law of the land. But it's still really hard to realize you don't measure up to your community's definition of a successful, respectable, worthy boy. It was more socially acceptable in his hometown to wear a Confederate flag, he said, than to cuff your jeans. "It feels like not much has changed when there are so many different things that you feel you can't be or you can't do or you will be labeled less than," he said.

Will is not alone. Many boys, including straight boys, feel that in order to be accepted, they have to prove that they are not gay and not feminine. This impulse is so strong that it can push boys into saying and doing things that they otherwise know are wrong.

Sociologist C. J. Pascoe spent a year and a half inside a California high school, where she documented how boys' harassment—of girls and of other boys—is a part of normal everyday life, tolerated by teachers, administrators, and students. In her 2007 book *Dude, You're a Fag*, Pascoe documents the fierce bullying of a flamboyantly gay boy named Ricky, who told Pascoe that he carried a rock in his hand to protect himself and had become accustomed to being called a "fucking fag." The taunting and violence eventually drove Ricky to drop out of school.

But Ricky was not the only boy called "faggot." In fact, Pascoe noticed that the slur was hurled at any boy who showed emotion or affection or otherwise edged toward qualities considered girly. Boys lobbed homophobic barbs to attack behavior that they considered insufficiently manly as a way of proving their own manliness. Just as they constantly policed each other's behavior, they knew that they were always being watched and judged. "To call someone gay or fag is like the lowest thing you can call someone. Because that's like saying that you're nothing," one boy told Pascoe.

Boys' sense that they must always prove their manhood shows up in the way they treat girls. They boast to other boys about their (often mythical) sexual conquests—"I did her so hard, when I was done she was bleeding," one boy told his friends in Pascoe's presence—and they sexually harass girls in the hallways, a way to show in a public place that they are straight and manly. Pascoe watched a boy poke a girl in the crotch and yell, "Get raped! Get raped!" Another pushed his crotch up against a girl, grinding into her backside as she tried to make her way to lunch.

Many boys I interviewed were aware of this dynamic and articulated it. The homophobic slurs that are so common in their day-to-day lives are not really about accusing someone else of same-sex attraction. They are about proving one's own masculinity. "No homo" is what you say after you admit that you appreciate your friend, and that you even love him. And bragging about sexual exploits, grabbing girls and harassing girls, is not so much about pursuing someone as it is about making a statement and showing off in front of friends.

This isn't just my impression—or Pascoe's. It's also what psychologist Dorothy Espelage, one of the nation's foremost experts in bullying and sexual harassment, saw in data she collected from thousands of middle school students she tracked as they grew up and went to high school.

Espelage believes that boys who sexually harass tend to buy into stereotypical ideas about masculinity and are trying to shield themselves from any suspicion that they might be attracted to other boys or be insufficiently "manly." As she puts it: "Grab the nearest set of tits, and that will calm any perception that you're gay."

The data she has collected over the years support her theory: boys who report that they believe in a stereotypical, restrictive version of masculinity are at higher risk than other boys for committing sexual harassment.

In tracking boys over time, Espelage also found that middle school bullies who use slurs like "fag" and "gay" and "homo" are significantly more likely than other students to later sexually harass their classmates by making sexual comments, spreading sexual rumors, sharing sexual images without consent, and forcing sexual contact. These boys are also more likely, as they grow up, to be sexually coercive and physically abusive in a dating relationship. One of her studies shows that middle school bullies are *seven times* more likely to physically abuse a dating partner later on.

Homophobia doesn't just prod boys to be sexually aggressive to prove their masculinity. It can also be a weapon that girls use to coerce boys into sex. Christina Jones, a prosecutor in D.C. who speaks to teens about sexual violence and consent, told me it's not unusual for boys to tell her that they've been pressured into doing something sexual by girls who say boys only refuse when they're gay. Sometimes a girl threatens to tell everyone at school that a boy is gay. "Your masculinity is defined by you, not by anybody else," Jones said she tells these boys. She tells them what the rest of society so often hasn't: boys can be coerced into sex they don't want, and it's as wrong when it happens to boys as it is when it happens to girls. "If you have sex with her because she's manipulating you, because she's spreading rumors about you, that's sexual assault."

Countless antibullying programs have sprung up in K–12 schools over the last two decades since two teen boys opened fire on their classmates at Columbine High School. Initial (and, as it turned out, incorrect) media reports that the shooters had been motivated by a desire for revenge against bullies led to a national movement to reframe bullying from a childhood rite of passage into a serious school safety issue. But according to Espelage, many anti-bullying efforts have failed to explicitly confront homophobic teasing, gender norms, or gender-based harassment—which means they've ignored a big part of the problem.

And even effective programs only appear to have an impact up until seventh grade. By eighth grade, it's too late—kids are apparently set in their ways, and prevention programs have little to no effect.

It may seem hopeless. Don't boys everywhere laugh at furtive ass-grabs? Aren't all middle schools dens of homophobia? Aren't all locker rooms filled with sexist talk and bragging about recent conquests? No. In some school communities, adults have used their time and their authority to make sure that sexual harassment and demeaning talk about other people, including girls and women, are considered unacceptable.

One boy, a junior in high school, told me that he had bragged to his basketball teammates about how many girls he'd slept with. It was a lie, but he had wanted so badly to fit in, and at the all-boys school he had gone to as a freshman, that meant a lot of big talk about sexual conquest. "Somebody might say, you know, 'I've been with three girls,' and the other guy's, 'Oh, I've been with five.' Now you're sitting there not saying nothing and you feel this urge. 'Well, I've been with six,' when really you've only been with one. I feel like it's a pretty crazy dynamic," he said.

At the time, his parents were splitting up, and he felt lost. He was coming to terms with the fact that his father, whom he'd thought of as his best friend, had also physically abused him and carried on extramarital affairs. "I just wanted to be accepted. I really wanted to, you know, feel cool. I wanted to have friends. I was just looking for some sense of comfort," he said. "I didn't get that sense of comfort, but at the time, in the moment, it felt good. Like knowing that I had a couple of people who accepted me, yeah, which I really think drove me to make those decisions."

Then he transferred to a coed school in D.C. and found a completely different culture, where it was unacceptable for boys to talk about girls that way—even when girls weren't around. While I was visiting, I happened to see a promposal (involving carrots) unfold outside on the athletic fields. A girl was asking a boy to be her date to the prom, a refreshing update on the traditional boy-chases-girl script. At this school, there was more pressure to figure out who you are than there was to figure out how to be like everyone else. Stereotypes about gender, race, and sexual orientation were a matter of frequent discussion among students, inside and outside of class. Homophobic slurs would bring reproach, not reward.

This new school was a relief. He didn't feel like he had to violate his own ideas of right and wrong to be able to exist happily here. "Everyone is comfortable with everyone," he said. "You're able to be yourself."

This is what I want for my son as he grows up: the ability to be himself without paying a social penalty. It's what I want for both my kids.

Harnessing the Power of Sports

A couple of months after Julian Avenilla told me about the transformation of his high school football team's culture, I went to visit his alma mater. Five years after the team first introduced Coaching Boys into Men, the Richard Montgomery Rockets were still using it, still working to redefine what is normal and acceptable for teen boys.

It was mid-August, the first day of football practice—a windy, humid day that definitely felt like the end of summer, with freshly painted yard lines on the field, administrators buzzing around inside preparing for the impending arrival of students, and dark clouds outside threatening to unleash a downpour.

Dozens of players clad in black practice jerseys and flip-flops gathered in the air-conditioned auditorium, taking great swigs from water bottles and finishing the last bits of lunch as they listened to Coach Klotz, a compact man with an easy smile and sunglasses perched atop his visor. The goal of their team was not just to win, he told them, but to build young men of integrity while winning. He promised he would push them to consider how they treated one another, their families, their teachers, and their peers as rigorously as he would push them to improve plays on the field.

"You'll be challenged to think . . . what's the right thing to do to have mutual respect, and to create that culture of respect?" Klotz said.

The players split up into small groups so that upperclassmen could explain to freshmen what they had learned from the program in past years. I sat with the guards and centers. The older guys talked about how they had learned to stop and think before they did something stupid, and how it felt good to know that if they stepped in to challenge someone else's inappropriate behavior, they had the backing of a hundred other football players. The younger guys listened silently.

"I've willingly been trying to change," said senior Daniel Baiyeshea. People always talk to boys like they're bad, he said, but these conversations made him feel like they could choose to be a force for good. "We're trying to break that stereotype and be a new generation of men," he said.

The next day, I sat with quarterbacks and fullbacks in the school's empty dance studio, whose floor was buffed to a shine. An upperclassman reminded everyone that last year, the team had lost a key player for a key game because he had decided to "forget everything we were taught." He had grabbed a girl's rear end at school, and so he wasn't allowed to play. "It can really affect us as a whole team, not just you, if you make a decision like that," the boy said.

On this team, the coaches didn't just say that sexual harassment was not acceptable. They meant it, and the players could tell.

Created by the nonprofit Futures Without Violence, Coaching Boys into Men is rooted to varying degrees in about twenty communities nationwide, from places where one fired-up coach is leading a charge in San Francisco Unified School District, which has offered training to staff at each of its high schools. It doesn't require much in the way of time or money. Lesson guides, free to download, outline discussions for coaches to lead with their teams fifteen minutes a week for twelve weeks. Coaches ask boys to think about the pressures they face to brag about their sexual conquests, to plan how they'd intervene if they saw someone disrespecting women with their language or with their behavior, and to recognize that the aggression that serves them well on the field is not appropriate off the field.

Klotz told me that Coaching Boys into Men had created a new kind of positive peer pressure among his players. He said he'd heard boys subtly remind each other to give a young woman space, or to stop using derogatory language, with a quick, half-ironic phrase—"boys to men"—uttered under his breath. It was easier than getting involved in a whole embarrassing, finger-wagging conversation. "It at least makes the guy in question think about his actions and what he's saying," Klotz said.

"That's so gay," "don't be a fag," and "don't be a girl" are almost excised from players' vocabularies, he said. "Pussy" has been a harder habit to end, maybe because it's a word that's everywhere in our culture—including in the music kids listen to, but also famously in the *Access Hollywood* tape featuring President Donald Trump. "Our players hear so much from pop culture, and from our president, with messages contrary to Coaching Boys into Men," Klotz said. "I think the more that we can reinforce the same message consistently, the more effective it is."

Not everyone has an appetite for this kind of work. A spokesman for a domestic violence agency in Virginia's rural Northern Neck region told me that he had trained eleven local coaches in Coaching Boys into Men—and they all eventually decided not to use the lessons with their players, saying it seemed too time-consuming.

Certainly, there are endless competing demands for the time of teachers, coaches, and parents. But if we know that there is something coaches can do once a week—something that in just fifteen minutes will reduce the chances that boys will behave abusively, and will give them the confidence to make kind, respectful choices—why would we not demand that they find the time?

The Promise of Social-Emotional Learning in School

The work of preparing boys for healthy relationships often has nothing to do with sex at all. Often it is about helping kids navigate some of the trickiest parts of being human—balancing what you want against what others need, taking responsibility when you mess up, rafting emotions without being swamped by them.

I have never seen these skills taught more deftly than by the fourth-grade teachers at Maury Elementary in Washington, D.C., a school I've reported on for years. On one visit, on a windy morning under blue skies, students learned how they had fared in the lottery that determined where they would go to school the following fall. In a city where public school choice means many kids scatter after fourth grade, it was intense. Some students were nearly vibrating with excitement, having gotten into their first choice; others had been disappointed, and were crumpled and teary.

One boy with freckles and a chapped upper lip was so upset that he had to go outside and breathe. When he came back inside, he gave his teacher, VanNessa Duckett, a hug and slipped into the classroom. What I was seeing was evidence of a transformation, Duckett told me. A few months earlier, the boy's feelings regularly boiled over into angry outbursts. Now, he knew how to recognize those feelings and deal with them.

The boy told me that what changed for him was his teachers' focus on social-emotional learning, or SEL. In some conversations, SEL can be one of those abstract educational acronyms that no one can quite define. It encompasses a huge range of programs meant to foster children's sense of determination and responsibility, as well as their ability to manage emotions, relate to others, and solve problems.

But to the boy at Maury, it had a very specific meaning: the concrete skills he had learned to deal with the storm of feelings and interpersonal drama that come with being a nine-year-old (and, more generally, a human being). He had learned not only to breathe when he got upset but to use "positive self-talk," he told me, and to talk to a friend.

"I've learned how to manage my feelings," he said.

If we care about preparing our boys for healthy relationships, this may be one way to do it—making time and space in school, where so much of their social world exists, to teach them how to name and handle their emotions and solve problems that crop up among friends. Creating a classroom culture where students are expected to think about how other people feel and notice what they need, and to be as earnest about kindness and empathy as they are about academics. Helping them see that while it takes practice to learn how to navigate our inner lives and our social lives, it is something we all can—and should—learn to do.

For most of the last two decades, public schools had little incentive to focus on these human skills because they were judged and sanctioned almost solely according to students' performance on standardized reading and math tests. A new federal education law, passed in 2015, has broadened the definition of school success, making more room in the curriculum. At the same time, a growing body of evidence has bolstered support for teaching social and emotional skills, showing that it can produce stronger academic achievement. The result has been endorsement by the federal government and funding from the likes of the Bill and Melinda Gates Foundation, the Robert Wood Johnson Foundation, and the Chan Zuckerberg Initiative.

Social-emotional learning can improve a range of children's skills, including their ability to recognize emotions, solve problems, make decisions, and demonstrate empathy, according to a review of more than 200 programs involving 270,000 children in kindergarten through high school. The few studies that measured impact on academic achievement found that social-emotional learning also made a difference in kids' ability to learn. Longterm, kids who got this kind of instruction were more likely to graduate from high school and college, less likely to get pregnant or contract a sexually transmitted infection, and less likely to be diagnosed with a clinical mental health disorder.

The CDC lists social-emotional learning in K–12 schools as one strategy for preventing sexual violence, and some programs have shown promise for directly addressing sexual harassment. Second Step, a social-emotional program for middle schoolers, contributed to a 56 percent decline in homophobic name-calling and a 39 percent decline in sexual violence in one of two states where it was tested.

Skeptics question whether schools should spend time on soft skills when kids—especially poor kids—need so much improvement in hard academics. "Emotional learning will be the downfall of society," reads the headline of a 2018 opinion piece in the right-leaning publication Townhall, written by Teresa Mull, a fellow at the conservative Heartland Institute. "SEL teaches kids to feel and not to think," Mull wrote. "Of course, feelings themselves are not bad or dangerous, but they can be when they aren't tempered with a sense of right and wrong. Traditional public schools, apparently determined not to teach kids history, how to read, spell, add, subtract, multiply, or anything useful, instead take on a role of psychotherapist (and not a good one)."

Social-emotional learning can certainly be done poorly, as can anything in schools. I know that from teaching middle school math early in my career and from covering education for most of my journalism career. But it can also be done powerfully, as at Maury, where fourth-graders are developing the vocabulary, experience, and confidence they need to navigate relationships and internal storms of emotion.

The boy with the chapped upper lip told me that in third grade, there was a lot of pushing and bullying. It was terrible, but no one ever told the teachers about it, and so it continued. Now, things were totally different. In fourth grade, his teachers' relentless focus on seven skills had helped kids be more kind to one another: courage, consistency, persistence, optimism, resilience, flexibility, and empathy.

I asked him which of the seven skills he'd been working on.

"Optimism. Also consistency. But I would say optimism is a little harder since my sister is annoying," he said, without cracking a smile. "It's hard to stay hopeful that she will stop."

He and his classmates—a diverse group both racially and socioeconomically—are not suffering academically. Their math and reading test scores are improving in the fourth grade, not declining.

I first met Duckett in 2014, when I was covering D.C. schools for the *Post*. A two-decade veteran of the classroom, she told me then that she had initially been skeptical of social-emotional learning. It seemed so fuzzy, so nebulous. But she was converted when her fourth-graders piloted Roots of Empathy, a Canadian program that brings babies into classrooms to teach kids how to recognize and deal with emotions in themselves and in their peers. Studies have found that Roots results in less aggression and bullying and more sharing and cooperation. Duckett found that the visits from the baby had helped her create an environment where kids were less likely to misbehave, more available for learning— and kinder to one another.

Since then, Duckett and her teaching partner Abby Sparrow, who together are responsible for about fifty kids, have doubled down on social-emotional learning. At first, they were just looking for a way to improve academic achievement and classroom harmony. Then they started to see their work as something much bigger. "This shapes who they will be in marriages and in the workplace," Duckett said. "I hope part of what we're raising them to believe is they should have deep, meaningful connections."

Besides hosting the baby in their classroom for Roots of Empathy, Duckett and Sparrow devote the first two weeks of school to helping their students understand the seven skills they want them to learn. And every Friday morning is dedicated to social-emotional learning, including the elementary school version of Second Step and a ceremony for recognizing students who demonstrate one of the seven skills. They are rewarded with a coveted foam crown—and a long, detailed, appreciative narrative from their teachers, delivered in front of all the other kids, about what they did to earn recognition.

Duckett and Sparrow are not working in a vacuum. Their whole school is attuned to the social and emotional needs of children, and in particular those who have been through the kind of trauma that can interfere with their ability to learn. Struggling children are paired with adults in the building who are not their teachers; they meet once a week, sometimes to talk about academic goals and sometimes just to play a board game and talk. The point is to open up avenues for children to build the kinds of trusting relationships that can buffer them from the effects of their adversity, including their propensity to act out violently.

Duckett and Sparrow also pick a few children each year—often kids who have more than their fair share of pain or difficulty at home—whom they ask to join a lunch club. Those children get to eat with their teachers once a week, and go on an outing—to a movie, or ice-skating, or a museum—once a month. It's another way to build the kind of relationships that can help inoculate a child against the toxic stress in his or her life.

In my visits, I saw that the power of these two teachers' approach lies less in any pre-cooked curriculum than in the fact that two tough, deeply adored teachers treat social and emotional skills as if they are just as critical as math, reading, and writing. They have created a common language to describe the aspirations they have for their students, and they constantly reinforce those aspirations.

"What matters the most to Ms. Sparrow and Ms. Duckett is kindness, caring, and not giving up," one of their students said in June, explaining to a group of third-graders what they could expect the following school year. He said when he moved up to fifth grade, his goal was to keep working on "feeling what other people are feeling."

Whenever a student throws a tantrum, or does or says something disrespectful, he has to reflect in writing on what he did, what he was feeling when he did it, how he's going to make amends, and what he's going to do differently next time.

"I used to get a lot of reflections because I didn't know what to do when I got angry," one boy told me. Now, he said, "I usually breathe. It really calms me down. Sometimes, I just walk away." It wasn't just anger he had learned to manage. On one of the days I visited, he knew he was feeling really sad, and he dealt with it by asking Sparrow for a hug—in front of the whole class. In the fourth grade at Maury, it was not embarrassing for boys or girls to have feelings, or to need comfort.

Figuring out how to negotiate life with classmates and friends is not actually all that different from figuring out how to negotiate a relationship with a lover, and class discussions organically go places that will prepare these kids for romantic encounters—without their talking about sex at all. On the wall hang artifacts from these discussions: A handwritten poster on what consent sounds like (Yes! Okay! Sounds great! Let's do it!), when it's necessary (giving hugs, borrowing things, touching another person, eating their stuff), what you do if you don't want to give consent (Nope. Stop. I'm good. Maybe later. I don't like that. No.). Another poster on handling uncomfortable situations—express how the other person made you feel, and make a request for how they should act next time.

On a visit close to the end of the year, one boy told me that he had learned in fourth grade to be more courageous about admitting when he messed up. "If you don't own up to your mistakes, you can lead the problem further," he told me. Another acknowledged that he needed to work on being less selfish. And yet another wrote, at the end of the year, that he had learned a lot about being open to taking help from other people. "I started this year not wanting help," he said. "Now I love getting help."

It's hard to see how teaching these skills—managing anger, holding oneself accountable, resisting the urge to be selfish, dealing with uncomfortable personal situations, asking for help when you need it—could lead to the "downfall of society." And easy to see how they could be helpful to boys—and girls—as they make their way through relationships, and through life.

Teaching Boys They Have a Gender, Too

In 1994, thousands of representatives from nearly 180 nations gathered in Cairo for a conference on how to deal with the global population explosion that was threatening the health and safety of the planet and its people. The International Conference on Population and Development marked a turning point in the global fight for gender equity. For the first time, the world recognized that the key to slowing population growth was empowering women in the realms of education, economic opportunity, and sexual and reproductive health. And women's empowerment couldn't be achieved without men, who had a responsibility to change their own beliefs and behavior with regard to everything from child care to violence against women.

Since then, scholars, funders, and international development agencies have increasingly turned their attention to reshaping gender norms, building evidence that helping men challenge rigid ideas about masculinity—helping them break down the walls of the Man Box—can increase support for gender equity and reduce violence against women. From South Africa to Canada, sexual-health and antiviolence interventions built on this foundation of questioning traditional gender norms have been shown to change boys' and mens' attitudes toward women and even reduce their perpetration of intimate-partner and dating violence. And there is some evidence that programs focused on challenging norms of masculinity also may improve men's health—by reducing, for example, their risk of contracting HIV.

These efforts to challenge gender inequality by helping boys broaden their ideas about what it means to be men are known, in the parlance of public health, as "gender-transformative." Even as gender-transformative programs have become a more common global strategy, they have gained little traction in this country, according to experts in the field. Now that's starting to change—a little bit. Organizations that specialize in working with boys in the United States have seen interest in their services skyrocket in the last couple of years, suggesting a pent-up desire for help navigating these fraught conversations.

"We can't keep up with the demand for our work now," said Matt Theodores, executive director of Maine Boys to Men, which sends employees into middle schools to work with boys, facilitating lessons on gender stereotypes, empathy, healthy relationships, and sexual consent. The organization believes it is critical to reach boys in early adolescence, when their ideas and attitudes are still fluid—not just to counter sexual violence, but to empower boys to stay connected to their own feelings and to other people.

Facilitator Ryan Tardiff, twenty-seven, told me that when he was thirteen—about the same age as the kids he works with now—child welfare officials briefly removed him from his abusive home. "I remember very distinctly measuring myself against other students a lot and really just giving up. I'm never going to be good at sports, so fuck sports, fuck kids who like sports—I'm going to do me, and I don't care. I'll do whatever I need to do to prove that you don't matter to me. That was kind of my attitude for the following four years," he said. "It's really important to catch kids before they get to that point. The more we can foster opportunities for students to be able to reflect and connect with each other, the better off they'll be. The less likely they'll be to close off and feel like nobody cares and feel they have to show that they don't care about other people. Most of the time they deeply do."

We still need more evidence about what works, as most evaluations of these kinds of efforts around the world haven't measured whether the changes last over the long term or affect boys' behavior in addition to their attitudes. But public health experts have come to see these kinds of efforts as a promising avenue. The U.S. government itself has promoted the notion that we must challenge norms of masculinity in order to improve men's health and reduce violence against women.

"In many societies, boys are raised to be men learning that violence is a way to demonstrate their masculinity and prove themselves to be 'real men,' often at great cost not only to the women and girls in their lives but also to themselves," reads a 2015 report by the U.S. Agency for International Development. "Offering men a positive vision of an alternative but culturally compelling male gender identity has proven effective in working with men to reject violence and adopt more gender equitable masculinities."

The language is academic and dry, but it is an unmistakable call to reexamine the lessons we teach boys about what it means to be a man.

* * *

The nonprofit Promundo, which has offices in Brazil, Portugal, the Democratic Republic of the Congo, and Washington, D.C., is a global leader in the field of promoting gender equity by engaging men and boys. The organization has adapted its work for boys and young men in the United States, but ran into obstacles as political winds shifted in the aftermath of President Trump's election in 2016.

Promundo introduced a program in Brazil nearly two decades ago that aimed to broaden boys' ideas about masculinity. The curriculum, called "Program H" (the H is for *homens* and *hombres*, the Portuguese and Spanish words for *men*), grew out of group interviews that Gary Barker, Promundo's founder and chief executive officer, had conducted with young men in Brazilian favelas.

Many of the men he spoke with were deeply and openly sexist, Barker told me. But then there were other guys who resisted that sexism—who spoke up and said it wasn't okay. These were the men Barker found most interesting. He believed they spoke for the majority of men, who were troubled by sexism but often too afraid to say so. What was it in these men's lives that had led them to question dominant ideas about gender? What was it that allowed them to challenge other young men who talked about women and girls—even very young girls—as sexual objects for their taking?

When he interviewed these men, he found they had some things in common. They had family members who themselves challenged gender norms. They had some kind of social group in their lives that allowed them space to consider and talk about alternatives to the gender status quo. And they were able to see the costs of traditional masculine norms because they had suffered at the hands of a man—often a father—who subscribed to them.

Program H attempts to create some of these conditions by giving boys a place to reflect on the unwritten rules that dictate how men and women are supposed to act—and how those rules can be harmful to both sexes. With attention to issues of race and class, it teaches boys to see imbalances in power. It emphasizes that every man and woman and boy and girl has bodily autonomy and a right to make their own decisions about sex and conception. And it appears to work.

Studies of the program's impact in eight countries, from Brazil to Mexico, India, and the Balkans, have shown change in participants' attitudes about gender equality and violence toward women. Boys report changes in their own behavior, such as a greater likelihood of using a condom (in India and the Balkans and Brazil), less violence against an intimate partner (Ethiopia, Chile, and Brazil), and fewer symptoms of sexually transmitted infections (Mexico). On the strength of results like these, Program H has spread to schools and communities in many countries with the support of key international development organizations—including the United Nations, the World Health Organization, and UNICEF—that have deemed it an effective way to get boys involved in undoing gender inequality.

In 2015, Promundo won a five-year, multimillion-dollar grant from the U.S. government to test whether the program could reduce teen pregnancies and sexual violence, particularly among young men of color. Called Manhood 2.0, its thirteen-hour curriculum has been tried on a small scale in a few cities, including Pittsburgh, New York, and Washington, D.C.

Adrian Ellerbe was in the eleventh grade at E. L. Haynes Public Charter School in Washington when he went through it. He said that the leaders of Manhood 2.0, two young men of color from the nonprofit Latin American Youth Center, managed to create something special: a space where he and his classmates could talk freely, without worrying that their secrets would be shared. "It was great being able to sit down with other guys and talk about things that men are expected to do versus what they really want to do," he said.

Adrian said he walked away from the group with a firm understanding of sexual consent—"I don't really do anything unless I'm told yes"—and a new understanding of LGBTQ people and homosexuality. Now a high school graduate planning to join the city police department's cadet training program, he said he had also come to see that men have emotions, and that showing them is not a bad thing. "It's okay to cry because crying makes you know that you have feelings, that you actually feel something," he said. "It's okay to say you're not okay."

*   *   *

Thanks to politics, it's hard to say whether Manhood 2.0 really works.

The grant Promundo was depending on to test its impact came from the Department of Health and Human Services' Teen Pregnancy Prevention Program, which the Obama administration established as a way to shift federal dollars from abstinence-only sex education to approaches backed by evidence of effectiveness. Public health experts saw that shift as a vote for science, but some conservative leaders argued it was a waste of taxpayer money resulting in programs that encouraged teens to have sex.

But in 2017, the Trump administration suddenly announced it would yank the pregnancy prevention funds from Promundo and eighty other organizations. Health and Human Services officials told CNN that they had reviewed results of an earlier round of funding and found "very weak evidence of positive impact of these programs."

The move, which came shortly after Trump appointed a leading advocate for abstinence-only sex education to a high-ranking post at HHS, caught the grantees by surprise. A class-action lawsuit filed on behalf of dozens of them argued that the decision to abruptly shut off the funding spigot was unlawful. A federal judge agreed in June 2018, concluding that the agency had violated its own regulations by withdrawing the money without giving a good reason.

Promundo filed its own separate suit in September 2018 and eventually recovered some of the lost funding. But the interruption and uncertainty meant that the organization had to downsize its D.C. program and give up on doing the expansive, rigorous study that it originally envisioned. A look just at the impact on boys in Pittsburgh, where the study continued with other funding, yielded mixed results. Sexual violence and relationship abuse declined among boys who took Manhood 2.0. But it also declined among boys in the control group, who had taken a job-skills training course that had nothing to do with gender. Both groups also saw slight improvements in their attitudes toward gender equity, while Manhood 2.0 participants made greater progress in recognizing abusive behavior.

Elizabeth Miller, a doctor who specializes in adolescent health at the Children's Hospital of Pittsburgh and who evaluated the city's Manhood 2.0 program, told me she isn't sure why there wasn't a bigger difference between the two groups. Maybe the job-skills course had an impact because of its discussions related to being careful online so as not to leave a digital footprint that would turn off a potential employer. (In fact, the boys who took the job-skills course were less likely to be sexually abusive online.) Or maybe the acceleration of the #MeToo movement meant that during the course of the study, all of the boys were exposed to more conversation and ideas related to sexual harassment and sexual violence. Whatever the explanation, she argues, the results show that boys' attitudes and behavior can change, and that makes her optimistic: "What we are seeing is some movement in this work."

Miller is one of the leading voices in public health arguing that the United States should follow the lead of countries around the world that have pioneered efforts to prevent sexual violence by helping boys see and transform the pressures they face to live up to rigid ideas of what it means to be a man. She knows that early-childhood experiences, particularly with abuse and family dysfunction, play a big role in whether a person develops a proclivity for violence. And she believes that public health experts have to continue looking for ways to address those problems. But interrupting deep-seated family cycles of violence is a difficult, long-term project, and if we don't also focus on shifting gender norms for boys, she said, we're missing an opportunity to make meaningful change now.

"I have been one of these researchers who digs her heels in to say, I'm unabashedly focused on challenging toxic masculinity," she said. "It's harmful for boys, it's harmful for girls, it's harmful for our society, and there's plenty of evidence to support that."

Teaching Boys to See Themselves as Change Agents

Chapter Seven described Mentors in Violence Prevention, an approach developed by activist Jackson Katz to teach people how to recognize sexual violence and intervene to stop it. MVP is gender-transformative in that it directly challenges gender norms and stereotypes. It is grounded in Katz's belief that we won't stop sexual violence until we rethink the ways we teach boys to be men, and we won't prevent sexual harassment and rape without also pushing back against misogynistic and homophobic language and jokes and other everyday sexism and hate.

Katz is not alone. Many other activists and scholars also believe that attacking the problem of sexual violence requires a social-justice approach that teaches people to recognize and challenge gender norms and homophobia. But there is another approach that skips all the gender stuff. It doesn't ask boys and men to deconstruct their masculinity, attack systemic misogyny, or stop laughing at sexist jokes. It just asks them—alongside girls and women—to recognize warning signs of an impending rape or sexual assault and then to do whatever it takes to stop it.

Green Dot is one of the most well-known programs that uses this approach. It was created by psychologist Dorothy Edwards, a self-described "radical feminist lesbian" who spent the first part of her career doing the sort of rape-prevention education that boiled down, she said, to instructing men not to rape and women not to get raped. Ten years in, she realized that nothing much was changing. Sexual violence on college campuses was still prevalent, and she could see that many men were not only disengaged from the movement to fight assault but alienated by it. They were tired of being treated as if they condoned rape or, worse, committed it.

Edwards came to see the way that she and other rape-prevention educators spoke to men as part of the problem; their defensiveness was justified, she thought. Seeking a different way to bring men in as allies, she came up with Green Dot—bystander intervention, but stripped of tripwire terms and concepts that repelled men.

You won't find any discussion of "gender-based violence" in a Green Dot training. Instead, it's "power-based personal violence." There is no mention of "consent." There's no instruction about gender stereotypes; no Man Box or Woman Box; no lectures about how our jokes, our music, and our media sustain "rape culture." It's too much, too fast, Edwards said, to ask boys and young men to unlearn what their culture has taught them about who they are and how to be—especially in the short time that most schools and colleges allot for violence prevention.

"Somebody is already defensive and doesn't quite care. You think in an hour they are super-receptive to deconstructing their fucking masculinity?" she told me in her office, tucked away among auto shops and construction-supply warehouses in northern Virginia, outside D.C.

Instead, Edwards thinks that rape prevention should start with what most everyone can agree on: rape is bad, and we should all try to stop it. "Programs like MVP and other programs that really get into masculinity . . . those are not bad things. Those are good things. The question is about readiness—it's about who's ready to hear that. If someone comes at you too hard, too quickly, and you're not receptive, you shut down. Not only do you shut down, but you dig your heels in."

Her own daughter was assaulted as a teenager in the presence of two bystanders, and if they had intervened to prevent that assault, she would have been grateful no matter what their beliefs about women or rape or about her own daughter's culpability. "I wouldn't care if they were blaming her. I wouldn't care if, after they got her to safety, they went home and played violent video games while telling each other sexist jokes and watching porn," Edwards said. If she could get more men to prevent violence by suppressing her urge to lecture them about their masculinity, then so be it. "Do you want to be right?" she says. "Or do you want to be effective?"

Green Dot teaches young people to be on the lookout for signs of sexual assault and dating violence, and then to figure out a way to stop the assault from happening. If it's too awkward or dangerous to directly confront a potential assaulter, then Green Dot teaches it's perfectly okay to delegate responsibility—ask someone else to help—or create a distraction that interrupts the situation.

One student at the University of Kentucky, where Edwards was working when she developed Green Dot, told her that when he saw his fraternity brother taking a drunk girl upstairs during a party, he lied and told the guy his car was being towed. The frat brother went off to check on his car, and the girl's friends had time and space to usher her out of the house. The bystander didn't smash the patriarchy, obviously. But maybe he stopped a rape from happening. And for Edwards, that's enough.

She also believes that for many men, this is the first step toward broader progress. Once a guy feels invested enough to step in and prevent an assault, he'll be more likely to think of himself as an ally to women, more likely to challenge casual misogyny. He may never stop laughing at sexist jokes, may never stop watching porn—but that doesn't mean he can't be a force for good.

"Look, I spent my whole life immersed in this issue, caring about this issue, and I will still laugh at the sexist joke. . . . I will *tell* a sexist joke if it's super-funny," she said. It seemed both hypocritical and unrealistic, she said, for her to then stand up in front of a group of boys and tell them not to do the same.

To Jackson Katz and other sexual violence prevention advocates, Green Dot and programs like it are maddening. They see it as trying to fight violence by skirting the truth about social norms that encourage and sustain violence in the first place. When the Obama administration unveiled It's On Us, an initiative to fight campus sexual violence that echoed Green Dot's gender-neutral approach, some survivors and activists rolled their eyes.

"The campaign's tips—like guiding your friends away from perpetrators at parties—might help an individual woman avoid a rapist in an individual instance, but it won't stop that rapist from turning to the next girl down the bar," wrote Dana Bolger, cofounder of the national student organization Know Your IX, on the blog *Feministing*, in 2014. She continued:

> It makes the problem seem discrete and manageable, with a quick fix that fits comfortably within an existing structure of how our world works, who has power, and who doesn't. It enlists men, for instance, to protect their female friends at a bar but not to recognize their own power and privilege, the subtle ways in which they enact violence all the time. It's On Us is so appealing precisely because it doesn't require us to disrupt the status quo.

Without singling out any one program, Katz offers withering criticism of the gender-neutral approach. "I think talking about the cultural ideology of manhood and womanhood is the heart of the matter. This is not just some add-on," he told me. "The presumption of people who don't want to talk about gender is that men can't handle the truth. . . . It's a factually incorrect statement that men can't handle the discussion. Men can handle the truth. And let's face it, the culture has deep misogyny, deep sexism. Boys and men absorb that in the air that they breathe. At what point do they become conscious of this and try to figure out how to work against it and work toward the fairness and justice they say they believe in?"

But Green Dot has something rare in the world of sexual violence: a wealth of data from years of rigorous evaluation that suggest the program actually reduces sexual violence.

With the help of millions of dollars in funding from the CDC, researchers gathered data from twenty-six Kentucky high schools over the course of five years. Half went through Green Dot, and half didn't. Real culture change takes time, and in the first two years, sexual violence rates remained about the same at both groups of schools. But in the third and fourth years, they diverged. Kids in the schools with Green Dot reported significantly less sexual violence—including coerced sex, physically forced sex, alcohol- and drug-facilitated sex, sexual harassment, and dating violence. Perpetration rates were 17 percent lower in year three, and 21 percent lower in year four, which translates into hundreds of sexually violent events that didn't happen in schools with Green Dot.

But there is, it seems, a cost to leaving out discussion of gender norms and homophobia. The same research team found that Green Dot was more effective for straight than for sexual-minority boys and girls, and suggested that the program should expand to instruction that would reduce homophobia and homophobic teasing.

Edwards said that she is now collaborating with a diverse team of people to redesign the program—initially created by a group of middle-class white women—to be more relevant to and effective for nonwhite students and LGBTQ teens. Whether that can be done without acknowledging gender and masculinity remains to be seen.

Boys Leading Boys

I vividly remember a conversation at the end of my senior year in high school with a classmate who confessed he was mortified by the prospect of going off to college as a virgin. His admission astonished me.

It was beyond my comprehension. Why would anyone in college even know whether he'd had sex? And why would they care?

More than two decades later, I am more empathetic. With great patience, boys have explained to me what it is like to live in a world where every other guy knows whether you have had sex, and how much and what kind, and that these experiences are a big part of what determines your place in the pecking order of teenage life.

"If two people are having an argument, one easy demeaning roast is 'Oh, you're still a virgin.' That's such a big thing to say," one California high school senior told me. I asked for clarification, not understanding how a guy would know whether another guy had ever put his penis into another person. "It's always there," another boy said. "You're always aware, who's doing what." Virgins are the lowest of the low, and guys who hook up with a lot of girls float above everyone else. I asked these boys where guys with steady girlfriends fit in, and they looked at me blankly. There aren't many of those guys, apparently.

In Maine, a group of young people lamented how high school boys are always talking about their "body count," the number of girls they've had sex with. Who knows if they're telling the truth. It doesn't matter. The talk makes every boy feel as if he's supposed to be sexually active and he's supposed to want a lot of partners. Of course, not every boy does.

One of the Mainers said that there was no "body count" talk in his high school, but that he was worried about confronting it in college. He was worried what that pressure would do to him. "I'm scared as a young male to think that I might be going to a college where that's prevalent, and all of a sudden that becomes a part of who I am," he said. "I mean, I'm going to be a college freshman. Am I going to be comfortable enough to say I'm not going to be involved in this? That's kind of scary to me."

Jacob Greene, a high school senior from Washington, D.C., told me that starting in his sophomore year, he had felt pressure to have sex. But he also felt he wasn't ready. "I felt like, Oh, look, I have to be sexually active to fit in. Even though I kind of didn't want to do that, and it wasn't good for my mental health," he said.

Until now, boys have been living in a world where there aren't many places for them to talk about the pressures and stereotypes they face. Without room for those conversations, it's easy for boys to believe that while they don't buy into those pressures and stereotypes, the people around them definitely do. It's easy for them to believe that most boys are seeking and having a lot of sex. Then their behavior shifts as they try to live up to what they perceive to be the group norm.

If boys came to understand how many of them actually aren't having sex, how many of them aren't even sure they're ready for sex, they might feel more empowered to make their own choices rather than being swept along by peer pressure. Same with every other idea about how boys are, or think they're supposed to be. If boys saw how those ideas are caricatures that everyone recognizes but few actually believe in, perhaps the caricatures wouldn't be so powerful.

That's the basic theory of what's known as the social norms approach, articulated in the 1980s by psychologist Alan Berkowitz. There's a gap between what we think is normal in our social group and what is actually normal, and if we can shine a light on that gap, we can help people make healthier decisions for themselves. For example, multiple studies have shown that college students think their fellow students party harder and drink more than they do, and that misperception prods them to drink more than they otherwise would. Men tend to believe that other men aren't as bothered as they are by misogynistic comments; if they are shown that other men are just as troubled by such comments as they are, there is some evidence that they are more likely to intervene.

If we can give boys space for conversations about masculinity, sex, consent, and porn—if we give them a chance to see the gap between what they *think* other boys believe and what other boys *actually* believe—then maybe they'd feel less tension between what they feel in their guts and the messages they think they're getting from the world about how to be.

This is the theory that a lot of violence-prevention programs for boys are based on. But it is one thing for adults—men or women—to stand up in front of a group of boys and tell them it's time to shake off stereotypes and embrace a new masculinity. It's entirely another when boys broach those topics together, among themselves. They can create conversations that they say feel less accusatory than searching, and are more likely to trigger reflection than defensiveness. It is particularly powerful when the guys who are leading those conversations have a lot of social capital.

Alex Thompson is one of those guys: a handsome, popular soccer and lacrosse player who, as a senior at Georgetown Day School, cofounded a group for male students to talk about their role in fighting sexual harassment and assault.

Another student, Jacob Greene, said when he first showed up, he was happily surprised to see who was there. He thought that it was going to be a small group preaching to themselves, the converted. But it was a large group of a few dozen, including most of the soccer team and lacrosse team. "I was like, Whoa, these guys never are in any of these conversations. Why are they here now?"

They were there because—at a time when plenty of young men were pushing back against the #MeToo movement, fearing they were endangered by it—Alex and his cofounder, a fellow athlete, had made it cool, or at least acceptable, to be there. The two of them were moved to lead the group after a summit on sexual consent at Georgetown Day drew hundreds of students and faculty from other high schools—almost all of them female. "There were two-hundred-plus people and only ten of us guys, on an issue that is ninety-plus percent initiated by and the problem of men," Alex told me. "It doesn't make sense for less than five percent of the people at these kinds of educational workshops to be guys."

Called Boys Leading Boys, the group meets a couple of times a month, opening up a place where guys can talk about "a lot of nitty-gritty stuff," as Alex, who is now in college, put it. Not just what it means to intervene, as a bystander, but what your options are if it's too awkward or intimidating to step in directly. Not just the rules of consent, but how they actually work in real life. How do you know if a girl really wants to grind with you at the school dance? Is it cool to hook up with a girl who's two years younger than you, or is the power dynamic too weird?

They talk about what it means to be a stereotypical "good man," and what it means to be a "real man," and how those ideals can be contradictory and confusing for a boy trying to figure things out. They talk about how the media romanticizes sexual coercion, and they talk about porn—about how it's not real, about how it leaves out consent and foreplay, about how it affects what you think girls like and how you think men are supposed to look and behave.

Boys Leading Boys is not universally beloved by Georgetown Day students; the school's feminist group has criticized the boys for thinking they can make real progress without including and listening to women. "It feels congratulatory, like if you're in here, you're a good man and you have no more work to do," one member of the feminist group told me.

The boys are protective of their all-male space, which they say is necessary in order for guys to feel comfortable asking questions or saying things they're not sure are okay to say. "These conversations are hard. But because it's a male space, it's okay to make mistakes or get vulnerable and say, 'Oh, I did this wrong,' and feel not everyone's judging them or people are gonna be like, 'Oh, look, you're a terrible person,'" Jacob said. "I'm not saying that that actually happens. But there's a fear of that."

Since its founding, Boys Leading Boys has spread to other private schools in D.C. Meanwhile, Alex Thompson is trying to bring what he has learned about talking to boys about masculinity, sex, and sexual violence to his fraternity at the University of North Carolina–Chapel Hill. He runs the peer-education program on sexual violence for new pledges, and he's working with a small group of other like-minded guys to bring that education to leaders of Greek organizations across campus—young men who hold powerful positions now and are on a path toward influence after college, too.

He has spent a lot of energy figuring out what it takes to get through to everyone—not just guys who already agree with him, but other guys who roll their eyes at talk of sexual assault.

"I definitely heard in high school some stuff about, like, I'm not going to rape anyone, why do I have to talk about this. I'm sick of being over-scrutinized. But I hear a lot more of that at Chapel Hill," he said. Real buy-in from young men doesn't come from the online training modules that incoming freshmen are required to click through, Alex said. It comes from conversations among students who feel comfortable enough with one another to speak honestly.

Alex said that, within his fraternity, he has tried to depoliticize the conversation, so that both liberal and conservative students feel as if they are part of it. And he has tried to steer clear of saying that guys should care about sexual violence because they care about their sisters and their mothers and wouldn't want them to be victims. That trope is worn-out and misguided, he said.

He thinks about it differently. Boys and young men should care about this, and should intervene to stop other people from being hurt, because it's the right and honorable thing to do. Most consider themselves to be moral people. They consider themselves to be good. And given tools, given support, they can *do* good, too.

Epilogue

My son wakes up most days around 5:30 a.m. I can hear his first snuffles and shrieks of delight and despair, and then finally his calls for mama, mama. My cue, dragging me out of sleep. I creep into the room he shares with his big sister, pick him up along with whatever stuffed-animal menagerie he is clutching, and carry him back to the warm dark cocoon of my bed until a more decent hour.

One recent morning he was holding a fox and an elephant. Instead of returning to bed, where his dad was sleeping fitfully, we went downstairs to the living room. We climbed onto the small orange couch, pulled a fleece blanket over us, and watched the tiny white Christmas lights on our porch, blinking against a dark sky that turned blue and bruised-looking and finally dawned gray.

He turned his face toward mine, and I said: *I love you, Gus!*

He took my face in his two small hands, squinched his eyes at me, and smiled.

At two and almost a half years old, he is still too young to have learned to be anyone but himself. He is unselfconscious and piercingly honest about what he wants and what he thinks.

But he is also on the cusp of understanding more about how the world works, including that he is a boy, and that being a boy comes with certain rules he's supposed to follow, certain assumptions about what's important to him, how he should act and who he should be.

In the quiet morning moments that he and I share, I think about what that new understanding will mean for him, how it will shape the man he will become.

I am afraid, more than anything, that he'll learn to be someone who is not him. I have the same fear for his sister, but the contours are different. I worry the world will teach her that she must be likable and sweet, that she's only as valuable as her beauty. I worry that Gus will learn that he must be tough and lustful, that he will have to be hard in every way and all the time. I worry that to navigate the world he will stitch himself an armor that shields him from feeling all the things a human can feel, all the huge joy and fierce pain of connecting sincerely with people—with girls, with other boys, with himself. I worry that because of his gender, sometimes people will assume the worst about him. I worry that he will be lonely.

But over the last year, in the days and weeks I spent away from him and his sister, working on this book, these fears of mine have been joined by a whole lot of hope. I feel lucky to be raising a boy now, in this moment.

Boys today are on their way to learning a lesson that my generation was never really taught: that every person gets to decide whether they want to be touched or not. A whole army of children across the country are now growing up hearing parents and teachers tell them, over and over, that their bodies are their own. Yes, that means society will hold my son accountable for his sexual behavior in a way that earlier generations never had to deal with. But I don't see that as a loss.

I hope that the growing concern about sexual violence will be accompanied by real change: recognition that our sons need better sex education, earlier, as well as frank conversations about porn, consent, and handling rejection. And I hope now that more people are questioning their assumptions about boys and pushing back against old-fashioned ideas about how we teach them to be men, our sons will have more latitude to explore who they want to be and what life they want to create.

While girls have long been allowed and even encouraged to be boy-ish, we are finally starting to rethink the penalty we've made boys pay for being girlish. More parents and teachers and coaches are starting to realize that we owe our sons the same message we are trying to give our daughters: *you can become whoever you want and pursue whatever you dream.* You are allowed to love basketballs and city buses and tow trucks, just as you are allowed to delight in wearing your sister's pink hand-me-downs and dressing up as Wonder Woman. You can be girly, because when we say girly we really mean fully human, capable of both strength and vulnerability, anger and empathy, laughter and tears, a ca-reer and a family.

Halfway through my work on this book, I met an old friend for coffee. I told him what I have already told you: that when my daughter was born, I knew exactly how I wanted to raise her so that she would see that she is not bound by old-fashioned stereotypes about what it means to be a woman. That I didn't have any of the same instinct about raising my son. That I had taught my girl to proclaim that she was strong and fearless, and that I had no idea what to teach my boy.

My friend is a writer who fixes up old houses, a father of two girls who runs ultramarathons in wild places, a husband who has moved across the country multiple times with his wife. The two of them have left jobs and lives to support each other's dreams and aspirations. He is handsome and self-assured and reflective and sometimes uncertain. He is in many ways the kind of person I hope my son will be. He told me that when he was growing up, his mother always told him that he was strong and gentle. That was her mantra for him, and he said it stuck. It is how he thinks of himself now. It is also who he is.

And so I am stealing this from my friend, or from his mother. It is what I am telling my son now, *you are strong and gentle,* and it is what I am urg-ing him to proclaim about himself. If strong is something boys are told they should be, and gentle is something supposedly for girls, then I hope that he will grow up seeing that he can be both, and that the lines between what we think of as "masculine" or "feminine" are lines we have drawn ourselves and can erase.

I hope my daughter will see the same thing, that she doesn't have to reject the qualities traditionally associated with women in order to succeed. I've stopped urging her to be strong and fearless. Everyone is afraid sometimes, and she has no more duty to pretend at fearlessness than my son. I want them both to be strong and gentle. Ambitious and kind. Confident and caring. Courageous and reflective.

I am hardly the first to think this way. Four decades ago, the pioneering and controversial feminist psychologist Sandra Bem articulated a new theory of gender, arguing that it was not a simple continuum, with masculine qualities at one pole and feminine qualities at the other. Instead, masculinity and femininity exist independent of each other, on separate dimensions, she said—so a person can be super-masculine and not very feminine, like a stereotypical football player. Or the opposite, super-feminine and not very masculine. But it is not a zero-sum game; a person can have a lot of "masculine" and "feminine" traits at the same time. Bem termed these people "androgynous."

An androgynous person might be an ambitious leader who likes taking risks while simultaneously being compassionate and emotionally expressive. People like this simply have more tools with which to respond to whatever they encounter in the world, and social scientists have found that it gives them an advantage on many fronts, from self-esteem to marital satisfaction. They tend to be more flexible, more adaptable, and more creative.

Psychologist Mihaly Csikszentmihalyi—who coined the term "flow" to describe intense, productive mental focus—wrote a 1996 book based on interviews with ninety-one exceptionally creative people who made major contributions in the arts, sciences, business, or government. They included Denise Levertov, the poet; astronomer Vera Rubin; the musician Ravi Shankar; and Jonas Salk, the scientist who developed the vaccine for polio. They tended to exhibit strong qualities that crossed stereotypical gender lines, Csikszentmihalyi wrote: "When tests of masculinity/femininity are given to young people, over and over one finds that creative and talented girls are more dominant and tough than other girls, and creative boys are more sensitive and less aggressive than their male peers."

The notion of androgyny eventually lost its luster among feminist scholars, who argued that while Bem may have been interested in blurring the lines between men and women, her ideas actually reinforced the idea that behavior can be defined as essentially "masculine" or "feminine" instead of simply "human." Bem came to agree.

But I still find the concept useful. We still tell stories about how boys are supposed to be and about how girls are supposed to be, stories we all begin to learn by heart from before we can talk. Sandra Bem worked to rewrite those stories in her own life and for her two children. In her memoir, *An Unconventional Family*, she recounted her efforts to "inoculate" her son and daughter against gender and sex stereotypes. She and her husband rotated being the parent "on duty" who played the traditionally female role of being in charge of all decisions about and for the kids. They made sure both their children played with trucks and dolls and both wore pink and blue. To counteract the messages delivered by books in which boys are always heading out for adventures while girls stay home, Bem transformed characters from one sex to the other with Wite-Out and markers. As her children grew, she spoke to them more directly about the ways in which gender stereotypes showed in and shaped the world around them.

For her memoir, she interviewed her son Jeremy. He had grown up to be a gifted mathematician who also loved literature and languages, and he had an affinity for what he described as "emotionally intense discussion of the inner details of life." His mother asked him how she should have raised him differently.

"If you were doing it all over again, I would advise you to make it clearer to me that it's okay to have conventional desires as well as unconventional ones," he said. He said it was sometimes hard for him to pursue women, because he was so aware of the history of men pressuring women for sex, and he didn't want to be that way. But he said overall, he was grateful for his mother's approach.

"I get to be a complete person," he told her. "That's what it comes down to."

Acknowledgments

As a reporter, I depend on the time and incredible generosity of strangers who are willing to share their experiences and their expertise. This book would not exist without the help of hundreds of people—parents and their sons, teachers, principals, coaches, young men, and scholars—who answered my phone calls and let me into their classrooms and their homes. Some are named in these pages, but many who helped shape my questions and my thinking are not. I am grateful to each of them.

I am also grateful to the many people in my life who helped me find my way to writing and reporting, especially my family. My father, Mike Brown, worked as a journalist for the *Louisville Courier-Journal*, first in Kentucky and later as the Capitol Hill correspondent in Washington. My mother, Margaret Brown, worked as a librarian and encouraged me to keep a journal. Ours was a house of books and words, and my parents were always my first readers and most benevolent critics.

In my late twenties, I made a career shift from teaching middle school math to reporting the news. It was a harebrained scheme that never would have worked out if not for my writing group in Juneau, Alaska, especially Rebecca Braun and Ali McKenna, who gave me confidence to pursue what seemed like a ridiculous path. I also owe my life as a working writer and reporter to the Graduate School of Journalism at the University of California-Berkeley—and more specifically, to the mentorship and friendship of Lydia Chavez, a gifted reporter and exacting professor. Lydia assigned me to do things that scared me, and in doing so she forced me—because I wanted to impress her—to push past my own boundaries. I am deeply grateful to her and to so many others who gave me opportunities to learn: Carolyn Ross, who taught my first college writing class; Jodi Peterson, who gave me my first journalism internship at *High Country News*; and John Daniel and Frank and Bradley Boyden, who gave me the gift of a wilderness writing residency along Oregon's Rogue River, two hours' drive from anywhere.

I landed at the *Washington Post* as an intern in 2009. The *Post* is my hometown newspaper, and I am so lucky to work there. Over the past decade, my bosses have mostly been men. All of them are deeply involved parents who showed me how to balance a demanding job with caring for family. Adam Bernstein, Craig Timberg, Nick Anderson, Josh White, Mike Semel, and Eric Rich: they have cheered me on, challenged me, and given me opportunities to grow.

Top editors at the *Post* gave me a year's leave to write this book, time that I have appreciated deeply.

The *Post* has also given me colleagues who have become friends who buoy me in small and big ways.

Joe Heim, who is calm and funny and always willing to go for a walk around the block. Jonathan O'Connell, who brought me ice cream during one particularly hard stretch. Julie Tate, who not only fact-checked this manuscript but also listens well and makes me laugh.

Beth Reinhard is a stalwart friend who refused to allow me to lose confidence. Valerie Strauss basically became one of my limbs, I relied on her so much. She encouraged me constantly, read every word of this book before it was published, and gave me the gift of her astute editing.

This book would not exist without two people who believed in it from the beginning: Bridget Wagner Matzie, my literary agent, and Julia Cheiffetz of One Signal Publishers.

It also would never have come to be without June and Gus, the incredible little human beings who turned me into a mom, and the rest of my family—including my parents, the most generous human beings I know,

ACKNOWLEDGMENTS

who lifted me up constantly and helped care for June and Gus while I was traveling and writing; my mother-in-law, Suzanne Carreiro, who played an indispensable role in caring for our children; my three brothers, who first taught me how complicated, wonderful, and loving boys are; and my sister, who always knows just what I need to hear. Finally, my husband, journalist Jacob Fenston, who has always been an equal partner in caring for our family, became the primary parent and housekeeper during the many months that I worked on this project. I could not have written this book, or any book, without a partner who gave his time and energy as selflessly as Jacob did.

Endnotes

PROLOGUE

1 *first stories about Harvey Weinstein's alleged predation:* Weinstein has denied all allegations of nonconsensual sex. Jodi Kantor and Megan Twohey, "Harvey Weinstein Paid Off Sexual Harassment Accusers for Decades," *New York Times*, October 5, 2017, https://www.nytimes.com/2017/10/05/us/harvey-weinstein-harassment-allegations.html; Ronan Farrow, "From Aggressive Overtures to Sexual Assault: Harvey Weinstein's Accusers Tell Their Stories," *New Yorker*, October 10, 2017, https://www.newyorker.com/news/news-desk/from-aggressive-overtures-to-sexual-assault-harvey-weinsteins-accusers-tell-their-stories.

2 *the journalist "who had gained my trust":* "Kavanaugh Hearing: Transcript," courtesy of Bloomberg Government, *Washington Post*, September 27, 2018, https://www.washingtonpost.com/news/national/wp/2018/09/27/kavanaugh-hearing-transcript/.

2 *the boys had laughed "maniacally":* Emma Brown, "California Professor, Writer of Confidential Brett Kavanaugh Letter, Speaks Out About Her Allegation of Sexual Assault," *Washington Post*, September 16, 2018, https://www.washingtonpost.com/investigations/california-professor-writer-of-confidential-brett-kavanaugh-letter-speaks-out-about-her-allegation-of-sexual-assault/2018/09/16/46982194-b846-11e8-94eb-3bd52dfe917b_story.html.

2 *the* Post *published her allegations:* Ibid.

3 *"Privilege comes with responsibility. . .":* Liam Chalk, Jonah Chang, and Simon Palmore, "Stand Up St. Albans," *Saint Albans News*, September 2018.

7 *less likely to have had sexual intercourse than teen girls:* Gladys M. Martinez and Joyce C. Abma, "Sexual Activity and Contraceptive Use Among Teenagers Aged 15–19 in the United States, 2015–2017," National Center for Health Statistics (Hyattsville, MD), 2020, https://www.cdc.gov/nchs/products/databriefs/db366.htm. Data from the National Survey of Family Growth show that between 2015 and 2017, 42 percent of teen girls aged fifteen to nineteen had had sexual intercourse, compared to 38 percent of teen boys—a decline, for boys, of 17 percent since 2002.

7 *sexually assaulting or harassing more than a dozen women:* Danielle Kurtzleben, "Here's the List of Women Who Accused Donald Trump of Sexual Misconduct,"

NPR, October 20, 2016, https://www.npr.org/2016/10/13/497799354/a-list-of
-donald-trumps-accusers-of-inappropriate-sexual-conduct.

7 *grabbing women by the "pussy"*: David A. Fahrenthold, "Trump Recorded Having
Extremely Lewd Conversation About Women in 2005," *Washington Post*, October 8, 2016, https://www.washingtonpost.com/politics/trump-recorded-having
-extremely-lewd-conversation-about-women-in-2005/2016/10/07/3b9ce776-8cb
4-11e6-bf8a-3d26847eeed4_story.html.

7 *insulted television anchor Megyn Kelly*: Philip Rucker, "Trump Says Fox's Megyn
Kelly Had 'Blood Coming Out of Her Wherever,'" *Washington Post*, August 8, 2015,
https://www.washingtonpost.com/news/post-politics/wp/2015/08/07/trump
-says-foxs-megyn-kelly-had-blood-coming-out-of-her-wherever/.

8 *Girls weren't even welcome at public high schools until the 1820s*: Kirstin Olsen,
Chronology of Women's History (Westport, CT: Greenwood Press, 1994), 113.

8 *more likely than men to enroll in and graduate from college*: Joel McFarland et al.,
"The Condition of Education 2019. NCES 2019-144," National Center for Education Statistics, 2019, https://nces.ed.gov/pubs2019/2019144.pdf, xxxv, 147.

8 *more than half of the nation's master's and doctoral degrees*: William J. Hus-
sar and Tabitha M. Bailey, "Projections of Education Statistics to 2027. NCES
2019-001," National Center for Education Statistics, 2019, https://nces.ed.gov
/pubs2019/2019001.pdf.

8 *closer than we used to be*: According to U.S. Census data published by the National
Committee on Pay Equity, https://www.pay-equity.org/info-time.html.

8 *Chance the Rapper postponed his 2019 tour*: Samantha Schmidt, "Chance the
Rapper Postpones Tour for Paternity Leave after Birth of Second Daughter,"
The Washington Post, September 10, 2019, https://www.washingtonpost.com
/lifestyle/2019/09/10/chance-rapper-postpones-tour-paternity-leave-after-birth
-second-daughter/.

8 *Alexis Ohanian—took sixteen weeks' paid paternity leave*: Alexis Ohanian, "Alexis
Ohanian: Paternity Leave Was Crucial after the Birth of My Child, and Every
Father Deserves It," *The New York Times*, April 15, 2020, https://www.nytimes
.com/2020/04/15/parenting/alexis-ohanian-paternity-leave.html.

8 *"That's why I took the leave"*: Recode Decode, hosted by Kara Swisher, podcast
audio. Ohanian: all parents, including dads, should have six months of paid family leave. https://www.vox.com/recode-podcasts.

8 *proportion of dads who stay at home full-time*: Gretchen Livingston, "Stay-at-Home
Moms and Dads Account for About One-in-Five U.S. Parents," Pew Research
Center, September 24, 2018, https://www.pewresearch.org/fact-tank/2018/09/24
/stay-at-home-moms-and-dads-account-for-about-one-in-five-u-s-parents/.

8 *three times as many hours on childcare*: Gretchen Livingston and Kim Parker, "8
Facts About American Dads," Pew Research Center, June 12, 2019, https://www
.pewresearch.org/fact-tank/2019/06/12/fathers-day-facts/.

8 *proportion of male registered nurses*: Men accounted for 2.7 percent of registered
nurses in 1970, according to the U.S. Census Bureau. By 2011, that figure had risen
to 9.6 percent. Liana Christin Landivar, "Men in Nursing Occupations: American
Community Survey Highlight Report," U.S. Census Bureau, 2013, https://www
.census.gov/content/dam/Census/library/working-papers/2013/acs/2013_Landi
var_02.pdf. In 2018, men accounted for 11.4 percent of registered nurses, according to the Bureau of Labor Statistics, "Labor Force Statistics from the Current
Population Survey," https://www.bls.gov/cps/cpsaat11.htm.

9 *7 percent of fathers*: Livingston, "Stay-at-Home Moms and Dads Account for
About One-in-Five U.S. Parents."

9 *far less time than moms on childcare and housework:* Ibid. Mothers spent about 75 percent more time on childcare and housework than fathers did.

9 *11 percent of the field:* Bureau of Labor Statistics, "Labor Force Statistics from the Current Population Survey."

9 *4 percent of dental assistants, 6 percent of childcare workers:* Data on dental assistants and childcare workers are from the Bureau of Labor Statistics. Data on elementary school teachers are from the National Center for Education Statistics, which issues an annual compendium, "The Condition of Education." Data on sex of teachers over time are from a subsection of that report, "Characteristics of Public School Teachers," 2020, https://nces.ed.gov/programs/coe/indicator_clr.asp.

9 *"acting like a girl":* This figure comes from a rare survey of adolescents aged ten to nineteen carried out by the public opinion research firm PerryUndem for the nonprofit Plan International USA in 2018, "The State of Gender Equality for U.S. Adolescents," 2018, https://www.planusa.org/docs/state-of-gender-equality-2018.pdf.

9 *more than one-third of boys believe:* Ibid.

10 *often even more than they want sex:* "I want to have that experience [sex], but I want it to mean something," one fifteen-year-old told a team of researchers led by David L. Bell, a professor at Columbia University's school of public health and a physician who runs the Young Men's Clinic at New York Presbyterian Hospital. "I want it to be something we both want to do, not because we just want the experience of doing it. I want to look back on that and see like, I really care for her and not look back on her like, oh, I had sex with her." David L. Bell, Joshua G. Rosenberger, and Mary A. Ott, "Masculinity in Adolescent Males' Early Romantic and Sexual Heterosexual Relationships," *American Journal of Men's Health* 9, no. 3 (2015): 201–8, https://doi.org/10.1177/1557988314535623, retrieved from https://pdfs.semanticscholar.org/2771/384507b3666a29947b9736d5ee6bfe50a200.pdf.

10 *has tracked groups of teen boys:* The description of Way's research comes from my interview with her and from her book: Niobe Way, *Deep Secrets: Boys' Friendships and the Crisis of Connection* (Cambridge, MA: Harvard University Press, 2013).

11 *remarkable similarities across the globe:* Venkatraman Chandra-Mouli et al., "Implications of the Global Early Adolescent Study's Formative Research Findings for Action and for Research," *Journal of Adolescent Health* 61, no. 4 (2017): S5–9, https://www.jahonline.org/article/S1054-139X(17)30358-0/fulltext.

11 *tough and strong and sexually dominant:* Sara De Meyer et al., " 'Boys Should Have the Courage to Ask a Girl Out': Gender Norms in Early Adolescent Romantic Relationships," *Journal of Adolescent Health* 61, no. 4 (2017): S42–47, https://doi.org/10.1016/j.jadohealth.2017.03.007.

11 *for girls who play soccer:* Chunyan Yu et al., "Marching to a Different Drummer: A Cross-Cultural Comparison of Young Adolescents Who Challenge Gender Norms," *Journal of Adolescent Health* 61, no. 4 (2017): S48–54, https://www.sciencedirect.com/science/article/pii/S1054139X17303312.

11 *higher levels of physical violence, neglect, and sexual abuse:* Robert W. Blum, Mengmeng Li, and Gia Naranjo-Rivera, "Measuring Adverse Child Experiences Among Young Adolescents Globally: Relationships with Depressive Symptoms and Violence Perpetration," *Journal of Adolescent Health* 65, no. 1 (January 2019): 86–93, https://www.sciencedirect.com/science/article/pii/S1054139X1930062X.

ENDNOTES

12 *United States is lagging other countries:* See Chapter Eight.

12 *India and South Africa:* Ibid.

14 *no one cause of sexual violence:* Andra Teten Tharp et al., "A Systematic Qualitative Review of Risk and Protective Factors for Sexual Violence Perpetration," *Trauma, Violence, & Abuse* 14, no. 2 (December 2012): 133–67, https://doi.org/10.1177/1524838012470031.

CHAPTER ONE: WHAT WE DON'T SEE

17 *Five boys, football players at a high school:* Dan Morse and Donna St. George, "Five Teens Charged with Rape Counts Amid Damascus Football Hazing Investigation," *The Washington Post*, November 2, 2018, https://www.washingtonpost.com /local/public-safety/three-male-teens-charged-with-rape-amid-damascus-foot ball-hazing-investigation/2018/11/02/1dae6656-dec2-11e8-85df-7a6b4d25cfbb _story.html.

17 *It had happened on the last day of October:* The account of the attack at Damascus High is based on arrest warrants filed in Montgomery County District Court that I obtained, and on prosecutors' descriptions of the incident as reported in the *Washington Post*. Dan Morse and Donna St. George, "'Astonishingly Cruel': Prosecutor Describes Locker Room Sex Assault Case at Damascus High School," *Washington Post*, November 26, 2018, https://www.washingtonpost.com/local /public-safety/extraordinarily-violent-and-cruel-prosecutor-describes-sex -assault-case-at-damascus-high-school/2018/11/26/a48dde98-f19d-11e8-aeea -b85fd44449f5_story.html.

17 *"It's time":* This is according to a prosecutor's statement in court, as reported by the *Washington Post*: Morse and St. George, "'Astonishingly Cruel.'"

18 *watching the horror unspool:* Dan Morse and Donna St. George, "A Football Locker Room, a Broomstick and a Sex Assault Case Roil a School," *Washington Post*, March 29, 2019, https://www.washingtonpost.com/local/crime/a-football-locker -room-a-broomstick-and-a-sex-assault-case-roil-a-school/2019/03/29/01500f30 -2fc8-11e9-8ad3-9a5b113ecd3c_story.html.

18 *Gatlinburg, Tennessee, 2015:* According to lawsuit filed by the victim in *John Doe v. Hamilton County Board of Education et al.*, in federal district court in Tennessee. This case also was covered in great detail by local media, especially the *Chattanooga Times Free Press*.

18 *La Vernia, Texas, 2017:* According to complaints filed in federal court by parents of two alleged victims in *John Doe et al v. La Vernia Independent School District* in the U.S. District Court of the Western District of Texas. The case has also been extensively covered in the local media, as in Lauren Caruba and Caleb Downs, "Mugshots: La Vernia Athletics Scandal Arrests Climb to 13," *San Antonio Express-News*, April 12, 2017, https://www.mysanantonio.com /news/local/crime/article/3-more-students-arrested-La-Vernia-hazing-scan dal-11068363.php.

18 *Bixby, Oklahoma, 2018:* Samantha Vicent, "Former Bixby Players Accused of Raping Teammate Ordered to Pay $300 in Restitution on Amended Assault Charge, Court Records Show," *Tulsa World*, February 20, 2019, https://www.tulsaworld .com/news/local/crime-and-courts/former-bixby-players-accused-of-raping -teammate-ordered-to-pay/article_7ea7c7f2-5518-5cc4-a218-d6a32881c832 .html.

18 *In one study of thirteen thousand children:* Ateret Gewirtz-Meydan and David Finkelhor, "Sexual Abuse and Assault in a Large National Sample of Children

ENDNOTES

and Adolescents," *Child Maltreatment* 25, no. 2 (May 2020): 203–14, https://doi .org/10.1177/1077559519873975. Among girls who experience assault or abuse, 88 percent of offenders are boys. For boys, 46 percent of offenders are other boys, and 54 percent are girls. Of the 13,000 or more study subjects, surveys for those nine years and under were filled out by the subjects' parents. This meant—because it's common for children not to tell anyone that they've been abused—that some incidents were not counted. Children aged ten to seventeen filled out the survey themselves, and their responses show that two-thirds of sexual assault and abuse incidents had never been reported to a parent or another adult.

18 *as many as one in six boys:* The figure comes from a landmark study of adverse childhood experiences conducted by the CDC and Kaiser Permanente in the 1990s, "The CDC-Kaiser Permanente Adverse Childhood Experiences (ACE) Study," which relied upon surveys of more than seventeen thousand Californians, most of whom were white and had more than a high school education. Centers for Disease Control and Prevention, "About the CDC-Kaiser Ace Study," accessed September 27, 2019, https://www.cdc.gov/violenceprevention/childabuseandne glect/acestudy/about.html.

Some other attempts to measure the prevalence of child sexual abuse among boys have yielded lower estimates. In 2013, for example, a team led by David Finkelhor of the University of New Hampshire's Crimes Against Children Research Center found that one in twenty boys experience sexual abuse before age eighteen. Finkelhor told me via email that researchers haven't "pursued more precision on the issue" because there is a general consensus that 1) a substantial number of males are victims, and 2) though it is not as frequent a problem for boys as it is for girls, it is common enough that boys should be considered and included in any prevention/education efforts. David Finkelhor, Anne Shattuck, Heather A. Turner, and Sherry L. Hamby, "The Lifetime Prevalence of Child Sexual Abuse and Sexual Assault Assessed in Late Adolescence," *Journal of Adolescent Health* 55, no. 3 (2014): 329–33, https://doi.org/10.1016/j.jadohealth.2013.12.026.

18 *About one in four men:* Sharon G. Smith et al., "National Intimate Partner and Sexual Violence Survey: 2015 Data Brief—Updated Release," National Center for Injury Prevention and Control, Centers for Disease Control and Prevention, 2018, https://www.cdc.gov/violenceprevention/pdf/2015data-brief508.pdf, 2-3. Forty-four percent of women say they have been sexually victimized during their lifetimes, compared to 25 percent of men, according to the Centers for Disease Control and Prevention.

18 *more than 40 percent of gay men:* These figures refer to non-rape sexual violence. The survey was not able to estimate comparable rates of rape victimization among gay and bisexual men. Mikel L. Walters, Jieru Chen, and Matthew J. Breiding, "National Intimate Partner and Sexual Violence Survey: 2010 Findings on Victimization by Sexual Orientation," National Center for Injury Prevention and Control and Centers for Disease Control and Prevention, 2013, https://www.cdc .gov/violenceprevention/pdf/nisvs_sofindings.pdf, 1.

19 *4 million men (and 5.6 million women):* Smith et al., "National Intimate Partner and Sexual Violence Survey: 2015 Data Brief."

19 *majority of male rape victims:* According to the CDC's National Intimate Partner and Sexual Violence survey, 87 percent of male rape victims report male perpetrators. But 79 percent of males who were made to penetrate reported female perpetrators, as did 82 percent of men subjected to sexual coercion and 53 percent of men subjected to unwanted sexual contact. Sharon G. Smith, et al.,

ENDNOTES

"National Intimate Partner and Sexual Violence Survey: 2010–2012 State Report," National Center for Injury Prevention and Control, Centers for Disease Control and Prevention, 2017, https://www.cdc.gov/violencepre vention/pdf/NISVS StateReportBook.pdf, 31–32.

20 *his victims spoke through tears*: The description of the victims' testimony and direct courtroom quotes are from audio files of a February 26, 2019, hearing in Utah's Sixth District juvenile court, obtained via public records request.

20 *"The worst of it all was when he squoze"*: Ibid.

21 *"I was going to tell her"*: From Martin's deposition, filed in connection with his lawsuit, *John Doe vs. Hamilton County Board of Education*, U.S. District Court for the Eastern District of Tennessee, Doc 139-15, 52.

21 *JJ's Hideaway*: Details come from documents filed in court in connection with Martin's lawsuit against Hamilton County schools, including sworn depositions and judge's orders. August 6, 2018, order by Judge Sandy Mattice, https://cdn .atixa.org/website-media/atixa.org/wp-content/uploads/2018/08/12192020/248 -Ct-Order-on-Motions-for-Summary-Judgment2-1.pdf.

22 *"Don't be a pussy!"*: Ibid.

22 *"belittle me"*: Martin's deposition, 61.

22 *the argument that scholars make in academic circles*: Susan Stuart, "Warriors, Machismo, and Jockstraps: Sexually Exploitative Athletic Hazing and Title IX in the Public School Locker Room," *Western New England Law Review* 35, no. 2 (2013): 377–423, https://digitalcommons.law.wne.edu/cgi/viewcontent.cgi?article=1710 &context=lawreview.

23 *emasculate their teammates*: "What better way to diminish the autonomy and the worth of someone than to call them a girl, a woman, a bitch, or a pussy, or to sexually abuse them through penetration?" said Jennifer Waldron, a professor of kinesiology and graduate dean at the University of Northern Iowa, in an interview with me. Waldron has researched and written about boys' ritualized sexual violence.

23 *nine months recovering*: Judge Mattice's August 6, 2018, order.

23 *One of the attackers was convicted*: Kendi A. Rainwater, "All Three Defendants in Ooltewah Rape Case Found Guilty, Two Receive Reduced Charges," *Chattanooga Times Free Press*, August 30, 2016, https://www.timesfreepress.com/news/local /story/2016/aug/30/all-three-defendants-ooltewah-rape-case-found-guilty-two -reduced-charges/384141/#document_1661.

23 *filed charges of aggravated rape*: Travis Dorman, "Judge Tosses Perjury Charges Against Gatlinburg Detective in Ooltewah Rape Case," *Knoxville News Sentinel*, November 28, 2017, https://www.knoxnews.com/story/news/crime/2017/11/28 /judge-tosses-perjury-charges-against-gatlinburg-detective-ooltewah-rape -case/903329001/.

23 *"something stupid that kids do"*: Video of this portion of Burns's testimony is available online: "Ooltewah Assault Hearing Part 3," Law & Crime Network, February 15, 2016, https://www.youtube.com/watch?v=8G-epfmV_xA. See comments beginning at 20:30.

23 *"To me it was an assault"*: Ibid.

23 *"no rape or torture, no screams of anguish"*: See the video of Burns's testimony online at "Full Preliminary Hearing: Ooltewah Assault," WRCB Chattanooga, 2016, https://www.youtube.com/watch?v=eE5b0fJq8HE. "There was no rape or torture": 2:13:55. "What this case actually is": 2:14:42. Burns's claim that there were "no screams of anguish" seemed to conflict with his own police report, in which he wrote that a victim "screamed in pain." A grand jury indicted Burns

on two counts of aggravated perjury after Chattanooga prosecutor Neil Pinkston asked for an investigation of his statement. The charges were ultimately dropped, and now Burns has sued Pinkston for allegedly defaming him by accusing him of lying. Dorman, "Judge Tosses Perjury Charges."

23 *"smaller than what it's been blown up to be"*: I called Burns to ask him to explain what he meant when he said this. He said that he was unable to comment due to a pending civil lawsuit related to the incident, and referred me to his lawyer. His lawyer did not respond.

23 *lawyers representing the school board asked the judge:* A spokesman for the school board said that neither the board nor its lawyers had any involvement in this particular motion or in any of the legal proceedings, as the court case was taken over by the school district's liability insurance carrier.

23 *settled with Martin for $750,000:* The insurance carrier also settled for an undisclosed amount with another student who was victimized during the same basketball tournament.

24 *Kids who play organized sports do better in school:* Kelsey Logan and Steven Cuff, "Organized Sports for Children, Preadolescents, and Adolescents," *Pediatrics* 143, no. 6 (2019): e20190997, https://doi.org/10.1542/peds.2019-0997.

24 *according to social scientists:* According to interviews with, for example, psychologist and hazing expert Susan Lipkins and B. Elliot Hopkins, director of sports, sanctioning, and student services for the National Federation of State High School Associations.

25 *Sexualized hazing:* See Stuart, "Warriors, Machismo, and Jockstraps."

25 *the first and so far only national survey of high school hazing:* Nadine C. Hoover and Norman J. Pollard, "Initiation Rites in American High Schools: A National Survey," Alfred University, 2000, https://www.alfred.edu/about/news/studies/high-school-hazing/index.cfm.

25 *they were stymied:* According to an interview with Norman Pollard of Alfred University, who coled the study.

25 *The players had been sodomized:* Susan Lipkins, *Preventing Hazing* (San Francisco: Jossey-Bass, 2006), 11.

27 *Lipkins recalled a football player:* Lipkins described this story to me in an interview, and she also reported it in *Preventing Hazing,* 41–43.

27 *"I had enough of this birthday thing":* Ibid., 42.

28 *David Smith:* This is a pseudonym.

28 *suspended for five days:* According to documents filed in the case *Child Doe v. Washington Public Schools et al.*

29 *"Fuck you, I am going to kill you":* A copy of the text message was filed in court attached to Document 103, the defendant's motion for partial summary judgment, as Exhibit 20.

29 *"What do you want me to do, hold his hand?":* McPherson admitted during a sworn deposition that he did make this statement to David Smith. He said he meant that he couldn't walk with the child through the hallways or sit in class with him. He also admitted that he didn't know that the school district had a policy requiring school officials to make accommodations to protect bullying victims from retaliation. The deposition is Exhibit 21 attached to the Smiths' motion for partial summary judgment, Document 103. The relevant pages are 32 and 81.

29 *"I did not think it was sexual":* Ibid., 36.

29 *the defendants argued that they had taken the incidents seriously:* Defendants' motion for summary judgment, Document 102.

29 *they said they didn't have enough information:* Defendants' answer to amended

complaint, Document 21, page 4. "Defendants are without knowledge or information sufficient to admit or deny the allegations."

29 *"I don't remember saying that":* Document 103, Exhibit 21, page 41.

30 *the agent, Josh Dean, said:* The deposition was taken in Oklahoma City on July 8, 2019, and was filed as Exhibit 16 attached to the Smiths' motion for partial summary judgment in *Child Doe v. Washington Public Schools et al.* The Oklahoma State Bureau of Investigation's findings were not previously made public, as OSBI investigations are confidential under state law. The agency denied my request for a copy of its final report on Washington Middle School, and did not respond to questions about Dean's deposition. Ultimately, two students were criminally charged with rape by instrumentation, according to Dean. The district attorney's office wouldn't confirm whether that was true, citing state law requiring confidentiality of juvenile cases.

30 *two students were criminally charged:* Smiths' motion for partial summary judgment, Doc. 103, page 15.

31 *the myths we continue to believe about male victims:* This review describes male rape myths and compares the degree to which men and women endorsed them in 1992 versus 2008. Rates of endorsement were strikingly similar. Jessica A. Turchik and Katie M. Edwards, "Myths About Male Rape: A Literature Review," *Psychology of Men & Masculinities* 13, no. 2 (2012): 211.

32 *One student at the Massachusetts Institute of Technology told me:* A few years ago, for a *Washington Post* project on campus sexual assault, several of my colleagues and I interviewed dozens of survivors of college sexual assault, including many men. Some interviews in this section come from that project. Nick Anderson, Emma Brown, Steve Hendrix, and Sudan Svrluga, "Sexual Assault Survivors Tell Their Stories," *Washington Post*, June 5, 2015, http://www.washingtonpost.com /graphics/local/sexual-assault/?j=story-5.

32 *fraternity brothers are at greater risk:* Rita C. Seabrook, L. Monique Ward, and Soraya Giaccardi, "Why Is Fraternity Membership Associated with Sexual Assault? Exploring the Roles of Conformity to Masculine Norms, Pressure to Uphold Masculinity, and Objectification of Women," *Psychology of Men & Masculinities* 19, no. 1 (2018): 3–13, https://doi.org/10.1037/men0000076.

32 *fraternity members are at greater risk than other students:* Claude A. Mellins, et al., "Sexual Assault Incidents Among College Undergraduates: Prevalence and Factors Associated with Risk," PLOS ONE 12, no. 11 (2017): e0186471, https://journals .plos.org/plosone/article?id=10.1371/journal.pone.0186471#pone.0186471.ref064.

32 *In a study of fraternity men at one midwestern college:* Maya Luetke, Stacey Giroux, Debby Herbenick, Christina Ludema, and Molly Rosenberg, "High Prevalence of Sexual Assault Victimization Experiences among University Fraternity Men," *Journal of Interpersonal Violence* (January 2020), https://doi .org/10.1177/0886260519900282.

32 *A 2018 survey of twelve hundred adults:* Scott M. Walfield, " 'Men Cannot Be Raped': Correlates of Male Rape Myth Acceptance," *Journal of Interpersonal Violence*, December 2018, https://doi.org/10.1177/0886260518817777.

33 *from media to medicine and law and scholarship:* Turchik and Edwards, "Myths About Male Rape."

33 *recognized that men could be raped:* FBI, "Attorney General Eric Holder Announces Revisions to the Uniform Crime Report's Definition of Rape," news release, January 6, 2012, https://archives.fbi.gov/archives/news/pressrel/press-re leases/attorney-general-eric-holder-announces-revisions-to-the-uniform-crime -reports-definition-of-rape.

ENDNOTES

33 *Scholars studying sexual violence:* The first national survey of sexual violence on college campuses found shocking levels of rape and sexual assault. It introduced the notion of date rape to the national lexicon, thereby changing the conversation about campus rape. But it only asked women about victimization by men, and only asked men about perpetration of women. So same-sex sexual violence, as well as perpetration by women and victimization of men, went undetected. Mary P. Koss, Christine A. Gidycz, and N. M. Wisniewski, "The Scope of Rape: Incidence and Prevalence of Sexual Aggression and Victimization in a National Sample of Higher Education Students," *Journal of Consulting and Clinical Psychology* 55, no. 2 (1987): 162–70, doi:10.1037/0022-006x.55.2.162/. Full text available at https://pdfs.semanticscholar.org/45ff/86fabeffa72408deb2 ba6fc298e6c332adf2.pdf?_ga=2.35477409.1254083838.1590431837-386207941 .1590431837.

33 *one survey of three hundred college men:* Jessica A. Turchik, "Sexual Victimization Among Male College Students: Assault Severity, Sexual Functioning, and Health Risk Behaviors," *Psychology of Men & Masculinities* 13, no. 3 (2012): 243–55, https://doi.org/10.1037/a0024605.

33 *attacked five men in a suburb:* John Porretto, "Rapist Preys on Men in Suburban Houston," Associated Press, December 27, 2006, https://www.foxnews.com /printer_friendly_wires/2006Dec27/0,4675,MaleRapes,00.html.

I learned of this AP article from a reference to a version of it in Lara Stemple and Ilan H. Meyer, "The Sexual Victimization of Men in America: New Data Challenge Old Assumptions," *American Journal of Public Health* 104, no. 6 (2014): E19–26.

33 *Bill Maher noted:* Bill Maher (@billmaher), "Michael Cohen famously said 'I'd take a bullet for Donald Trump.' Well, now that he's looking at prison time, we'll see if he's willing to take a dick," Twitter, April 21, 2018.

34 *men's rights activists argue:* Lisa Gotell and Emily Dutton, "Sexual Violence in the 'Manosphere': Antifeminist Men's Rights Discourses on Rape," *International Journal for Crime, Justice and Social Democracy* 5, no. 2 (2016): 65–80, https://doi .org/10.5204/ijcjsd.v5i2.310.

34 *as Stemple argues:* Stemple and Meyer, "The Sexual Victimization of Men in America" New Data Challenge Old Assumptions," *American Journal of Public Health* 104, no. 6 (2014): E19–26.

34 *"a loathsome, vile piece of human garbage":* This post has been deleted from the website but is still available via the Internet Archive's Wayback Machine: Paul Elam, "The Fembots Are Already Bent out of Shape," *A Voice for Men*, June 28, 2011, https://web.archive.org/web/20170207052110/https://www.avoiceformen .com/mens-rights/activism/the-fembots-are-already-bent-out-of-shape/.

34 *refuse to recognize male victimhood:* Hannah Wallen, "Feminists Define Rape to Exclude Male Victims," *A Voice for Men*, July 18, 2013, https://www.avoiceformen .com/feminism/feminist-lies-feminism/double-standard-rapeib/.

36 *The principal pleaded guilty:* "Judge Sentences Ex-Tampa Day School Principal to 10 Years for Sex Assault," *Tampa Bay Times*, April 30, 2015, https://www.tam pabay.com/news/courts/criminal/judge-sentences-ex-principal-to-10-years-for -sex-assault/2227724/?outputType=amp%3FoutputType%3Damp%3Foutput Type%3Damp%3FoutputType%3Damp%3FoutputType%3Damp%3FoutputTyp e%3Damp?outputType=amp.

37 *actor Kevin Spacey:* Chris Francescani, "The Rise and Fall of Kevin Spacey: A Timeline of Sexual Assault Allegations," ABC News, June 3, 2019, https://abc news.go.com/US/rise-fall-kevin-spacey-timeline-sexual-assault-allegations /story?id=63420983.

ENDNOTES

37 *film director Bryan Singer:* Alex French and Maximillian Potter, "'Nobody Is Going to Believe You,'" *The Atlantic*, March 2019, https://www.theatlantic.com/magazine/archive/2019/03/bryan-singers-accusers-speak-out/580462/.

37 *more than three hundred Ohio State University students:* Associated Press, "Lawyer in Ohio State Abuse Scandal Says Number of Accusers Has Surpassed 300," *New York Times*, August 23, 2019, https://www.nytimes.com/2019/08/23/sports/ohio-state-richard-strauss-sex-abuse.html.

38 *In 2019 an independent investigation:* "Report of the Independent Investigation: Sexual Abuse Committed by Dr. Richard Strauss at the Ohio State University," submitted by Caryn Trombino and Markus Funk of Perkins Coie LLP, May 15, 2019, https://presspage-production-content.s3.amazonaws.com/uploads/2170/reportoftheindependentinvestigationaccessible-376071.pdf?10000.

38 *committed nearly fifteen hundred acts of sexual abuse:* Jennifer Smola, "Number of Sex Crimes at Ohio State, Michigan State 'Unprecedented' Due to Richard Strauss, Larry Nassar Cases," *Columbus Dispatch*, October 6, 2019, https://www.dispatch.com/news/20191006/number-of-sex-crimes-at-ohio-state-michigan-state-unprecedented-due-to-richard-strauss-larry-nassar-cases.

38 *including forty-seven acts of rape:* Rick Maese, "With Ohio State Facing Latest Sex Abuse Suit, Attorney Says May Report 'Barely Scratches the Surface,'" *Washington Post*, November 7, 2019, https://www.washingtonpost.com/sports/2019/11/07/with-ohio-state-facing-latest-sex-abuse-suit-attorney-says-may-report-barely-scratches-surface/.

39 *most do not go on to lives of violence:* Cathy Spatz Widom, "The Cycle of Violence," *Science* 244, no. 4901 (1989): 160–66, https://www.jstor.org/stable/1702789?seq=1.

39 *victimized children are at greater risk of doing harm:* Natalie Wilkins et al., "Connecting the Dots: An Overview of the Links Among Multiple Forms of Violence," Centers for Disease Control and Prevention and Prevention Institute, July 2014, https://www.cdc.gov/violenceprevention/pdf/connecting_the_dots-a.pdf, 9.

39 *an older girl molested him:* R. Kelly, *Soulacoaster: The Diary of Me* (New York: SmileyBooks, 2012), 32–33.

39 *In 2016, he told GQ:* Chris Heath, "The Confessions of R. Kelly," *GQ*, January 2016, https://www.gq.com/story/r-kelly-confessions.

40 *their teammate Brad:* Brad is a pseudonym.

41 *the twenty-three-page report he eventually compiled:* The report mostly details interviews with male victims but also includes information from several girls who said that Brad had harassed them, threatening to kill himself if they didn't send him nude photographs of themselves.

41 *one count each of forcible sexual abuse:* Nate Carlisle, "Three Teens Accused of Sexually Abusing Other Gunnison Valley High School Students Convicted," *Salt Lake Tribune*, Jan. 17, 2019, https://www.sltrib.com/news/education/2019/01/17/teens-accused-sexually/.

42 *I'll call him Robert:* Robert is a pseudonym I am using to protect the identity of his son.

43 *a Utah law that allows some public access:* According to the general provisions of the Juvenile Court Act, Utah Code Title 78a, Chapter 6, Part 1, https://le.utah.gov/xcode/Title78A/Chapter6/78A-6-S114.html?v=C78A-6-S114_2020051220200701.

44 *Cox had spoken to a Salt Lake City television news reporter:* Michael Locklear, "Mom Details Son's Sexual Abuse at Gunnison Football Practice; 8 More Victims Report Abuse," KUTV, October 1, 2018, https://kutv.com/news/local/mom-says-her-freshman-sons-report-sparked-gunnison-valley-hs-sex-assault-investigation.

ENDNOTES

44 *The district agreed to settle:* According to documents filed in U.S. District Court for the District of Utah in *Misty Cox v. South Sanpete School District et al.* Case No. 4:18-cv-00070-DN-PK, Document 64.

CHAPTER TWO: BOYS WILL BE MEN

47 *We pay more attention to boy's anger and less to their fear:* Tara M. Chaplin, Pamela M. Cole, and Carolyn Zahn-Waxler, "Parental Socialization of Emotion Expression: Gender Differences and Relations to Child Adjustment," *Emotion* 5, no. 1 (2005): 80–88, https://doi.org/10.1037/1528-3542.5.1.80.

47 *less likely to talk with them about how they feel:* Ana Aznar and Harriet R. Tenenbaum, "Gender and Age Differences in Parent–Child Emotion Talk," *British Journal of Developmental Psychology* 33, no. 1 (2015): 148–55, https://doi.org/10.1111/bjdp.12069.

47 *stronger and more physically capable than they really are:* Emily R. Mondschein, Karen E. Adolph, and Catherine S. Tamis-LeMonda, "Gender Bias in Mothers' Expectations About Infant Crawling," *Journal of Experimental Child Psychology* 77, no. 4 (December 2000): 304–16, http://www.sciencedirect.com/science/article/pii/S0022096500925979.

47 *The more television a four-year-old watches:* May Long Halim, Diane N. Ruble, and Catherine S. Tamis-LeMonda, "Four-Year-Olds' Beliefs About How Others Regard Males and Females," *British Journal of Developmental Psychology* 31, no. 1 (March 2013): 128–35, https://doi.org/10.1111/j.2044-835X.2012.02084.x.

47 *nudges teen boys to tolerate sexual harassment:* L. Monique Ward and Jennifer Stevens Aubrey, "Watching Gender: How Stereotypes in Movies and on TV Impact Kids' Development," Common Sense, 2017, https://www.commonsensemedia.org/sites/default/files/uploads/pdfs/2017_commonsense_watchinggender_full report_0620.pdf.

48 *a famous experiment that psychologist Edward Tronick conducted:* Brigid Schulte, "Effects of Child Abuse Can Last a Lifetime: Watch the 'Still Face' Experiment to See Why," *Washington Post*, September 16, 2013, https://www.washingtonpost.com/blogs/she-the-people/wp/2013/09/16/affects-of-child-abuse-can-last-a-lifetime-watch-the-still-face-experiment-to-see-why/.

48 *"It might be nice to be a girl":* Niobe Way et al., "'It Might Be Nice to Be a Girl . . . Then You Wouldn't Have to Be Emotionless': Boys' Resistance to Norms of Masculinity During Adolescence," *Psychology of Men & Masculinities* 15, no. 3 (2014): 241–52, https://doi.org/10.1037/a0037262.

49 *needed more help to calm down:* M. Katherine Weinberg, Edward Z. Tronick, Jeffrey F. Cohn, and Karen L. Olson, "Gender Differences in Emotional Expressivity and Self-Regulation During Early Infancy," *Developmental Psychology* 35, no. 1 (1999): 175–88, https://doi.org/10.1037/0012-1649.35.1.175.

50 *one of the clearest ways in which boys and girls differ:* Judith E. Owen Blakemore, Sheri A. Berenbaum, and Lynn S. Liben, *Gender Development* (New York: Taylor & Francis Group, 2009), 125.

50 *as young as nine months:* Brenda K. Todd, John A. Barry, and Sara A. O. Thommessen, "Preferences for 'Gender-Typed' Toys in Boys and Girls Aged 9 to 32 Months," *Infant and Child Development* 26, no. 3 (2017): e1986, https://doi.org/10.1002/icd.1986.

51 *more likely to choose "masculine" options:* Sheri A. Berenbaum and Melissa Hines, "Early Androgens Are Related to Childhood Sex-Typed Toy Prefer-

ENDNOTES

ences," *Psychological Science* 3, no. 3 (May 1992): 203–6, https://doi.org/10.1111/j.1467-9280.1992.tb00028.x.

51 *modestly more aggressive:* Blakemore, Berenbaum, and Liben, *Gender Development,* 158.

51 *higher activity levels:* Vickie Pasterski et al., "Increased Aggression and Activity Level in 3- to 11-Year-Old Girls with Congenital Adrenal Hyperplasia (CAH)," *Hormones and Behavior* 52, no. 3 (2007): 368–74, https://doi.org/10.1016/j.yhbeh.2007.05.015.

51 *tracked about one hundred:* Carolyn T. Halpern et al., "Testosterone and Pubertal Development as Predictors of Sexual Activity: A Panel Analysis of Adolescent Males," *Psychosomatic Medicine* 55, no. 5 (1993): 436–47, https://journals.lww.com/psychosomaticmedicine/Fulltext/1993/09000/Testosterone_and_pubertal_development_as.7.aspx.

52 *the power of social expectations:* Carolyn Tucker Halpern et al., "Testosterone and Religiosity as Predictors of Sexual Attitudes and Activity Among Adolescent Males: A Biosocial Model," *Journal of Biosocial Science* 26, no. 2 (1994): 217–34, https://doi.org/10.1017/S0021932000021258.

52 *determining "boyishness":* Lise Eliot, *Pink Brain, Blue Brain: How Small Differences Grow into Troublesome Gaps—and What We Can Do About It* (New York: Houghton Mifflin Harcourt, 2009), 35–37, Kindle Edition. Studies on CAH girls are also described in Blakemore, Berenbaum, and Liben, *Gender Development,* 152–53.

53 *the notion that men are wired in fundamentally different ways:* See, for example, the 2003 book *The Essential Difference: The Truth About the Male and Female Brain* (New York: Basic Books, 2003), by Simon Baron-Cohen, a renowned professor of psychopathology at the University of Cambridge.

53 *millions of images of brains:* Lise Eliot, "Sex/Gender Differences in the Brain and Their Relationship to Behavior," in *Cambridge International Handbook on Psychology of Women,* ed. Fanny M. Cheung and Diane F. Halpern (Cambridge: Cambridge University Press, 2020), 63–80.

54 *"hot sun of our highly gendered society":* Eliot, *Pink Brain, Blue Brain,* 252.

54 *more likely to rate newborn baby boys:* Jeffrey Z. Rubin, Frank J. Provenzano, and Zella Luria, "The Eye of the Beholder: Parents' Views on Sex of Newborns," *American Journal of Orthopsychiatry* 44, no. 4 (1974): 512–19, http://dx.doi.org/10.1111/j.1939-0025.1974.tb00905.x.

54 *but they rebuff boys:* Beverly I. Fagot, "The Influence of Sex of Child on Parental Reactions to Toddler Children," *Child Development* 49, no. 2 (1978): 459–65, https://doi.org/10.2307/1128711. http://www.jstor.org/stable/1128711.

55 *predict how steep a ramp:* This study was highlighted by Eliot, *Pink Brain, Blue Brain,* and by Blakemore, Berenbaum, and Liben, *Gender Development.* See also Mondschein, Adolph, and Tamis-LeMonda, "Gender Bias in Mothers' Expectations About Infant Crawling."

55 *Fathers of young children:* Tara M. Chaplin, Pamela M. Cole, and Carolyn Zahn-Waxler, "Parental Socialization of Emotion Expression: Gender Differences and Relations to Child Adjustment," *Emotion* 5, no. 1 (2005): 80–88, https://doi.org/10.1037/1528-3542.5.1.80.

55 *In one study of toddlers playing in a group:* Hildy Ross, Caroline Tesla, Brenda Kenyon, and Susan Lollis, "Maternal Intervention in Toddler Peer Conflict : The Socialization of Principles of Justice," *Developmental Psychology* 26, no. 6 (1990): 994–1003.

ENDNOTES

58 *California activist Paul Kivel:* Michael A. Messner, Max A. Greenberg, and Tal Peretz, *Some Men: Feminist Allies and the Movement to End Violence Against Women* (New York: Oxford University Press, 2015), 71.

59 *publicly promoted new guidelines:* American Psychological Association, "APA Guidelines for Psychological Practice with Boys and Men," Boys and Men Guidelines Group, August 2018, http://www.apa.org/about/policy/psychological-practice-boys-men-guidelines.pdf.

59 *"Are you a filthy juden":* Levant sent me a copy of this email after we spoke by phone. He later published the email in a book. Ronald F. Levant and Shana Pryor, *The Tough Standard: The Hard Truths About Masculinity and Violence* (New York: Oxford University Press, 2020).

59 *an ad asking men to call out sexual harassment:* Gillette, "We Believe: The Best Men Can Be," 2019, https://www.youtube.com/watch?v=koPmuEyP3a0.

59 *"Let boys be damn boys":* Piers Morgan (@piersmorgan), "I've used @Gillette razors my entire adult life but this absurd virtue-signalling PC guff may drive me away to a company less eager to fuel the current pathetic global assault on masculinity. Let boys be damn boys. Let men be damn men," Twitter, January 14, 2019, https://twitter.com/piersmorgan/status/1084891133757587456?lang=en.

59 *in 2015, when Target announced:* "What's in Store: Moving Away from Gender-Based Signs," news release, 2015, https://corporate.target.com/article/2015/08/gender-based-signs-corporate.

60 *wrote on Target's Facebook page:* Target, "Sonos makes a picnic pop. Turn it up and even the bugs will be boppin," Facebook, August 8, 2016, https://www.facebook.com/target/photos/a.127542808119/10153593329408120.

60 *deep convictions in some quarters:* Kimberly Parker, Juliana Menasce Horowitz, and Renee Stepler, "On Gender Differences, No Consensus on Nature vs. Nurture," Pew Research Center, December 5, 2017, https://www.pewsocialtrends.org/2017/12/05/on-gender-differences-no-consensus-on-nature-vs-nurture/. Beliefs about American boyhood often cleave along partisan lines, with Republicans more likely to argue that biology is the cause of differences between boys and girls, and Democrats more likely to point to socialization.

60 *lags behind the average girl in reading:* According to the National Assessment of Educational Progress, administered every other year to fourth graders and eighth-graders across the country. David Reilly, David L. Neumann, and Glenda Andrews, "Gender Differences in Reading and Writing Achievement: Evidence from the National Assessment of Educational Progress (NAEP)," *American Psychologist* 74, no. 4 (2019): 445–58, https://doi.org/10.1037/amp0000356.

60 *Boys are more likely to drop out of high school:* Joel McFarland et al., "The Condition of Education 2019. NCES 2019-144," National Center for Education Statistics, 2019, https://nces.ed.gov/pubs2019/2019144.pdf, xxxv, 147.

60 *this "boy crisis" in education:* See, for example, Peg Tyre, *The Trouble with Boys: A Surprising Report Card on Our Sons, Their Problems at School, and What Parents and Educators Must Do* (New York: Crown, 2008).

60 *boys have less confidence in their own reading skills:* Francesca Muntoni, Jenny Wagner, and Jan Retelsdorf, "Beware of Stereotypes: Are Classmates' Stereotypes Associated with Students' Reading Outcomes?," *Child Development*, February 2020, https://srcd.onlinelibrary.wiley.com/doi/full/10.1111/cdev.13359.

62 *One-quarter believe that "men should use violence":* The survey was conducted by the U.S. arm of Promundo, a nonprofit organization that has been a global

leader in advocating for engaging men and boys in pushing for gender equity and violence prevention, in partnership with Unilever, maker of the men's deodorant Axe. Brian Heilman, Gary Barker, and Alexander Harrison, "The Man Box: A Study on Being a Young Man in the US, UK, and Mexico," 2017, rev. December 15, 2018, Promundo-US and Unilever, https://promundoglobal.org/resources /man-box-study-young-man-us-uk-mexico/.

62 *the guys who live inside the Man Box:* Heilman, Barker, and Harrison, "The Man Box."

62 *more likely to physically or sexually abuse their dating partners:* See, for example, "Sexual Violence: Risk and Protective Factors," Centers for Disease Control and Prevention, accessed September 27, 2019, http://www.cdc.gov/ViolencePreven tion/sexualviolence/riskprotectivefactors.html, and Rachel M. Smith, Dominic J. Parrott, Kevin M. Swartout, and Andra Teten Tharp, "Deconstructing Hegemonic Masculinity: The Roles of Antifemininity, Subordination to Women, and Sexual Dominance in Men's Perpetration of Sexual Aggression," *Psychology of Men & Masculinities* 16, no. 2 (2015): 160–69, https://doi.org/10.1037/a0035956. https:// www.ncbi.nlm.nih.gov/pubmed/29950930.

62 *208 men in their twenties and thirties:* Smith, Parrott, Swartout, and Tharp, "De-constructing Hegemonic Masculinity."

62 *developed and refined over many years by Ronald Levant:* Ronald Levant, Linda Hirsch, Elizabeth Celentano, and Tracy Cozza, "The Male Role: An Investigation of Contemporary Norms," *Journal of Mental Health Counseling* 14 (1992): 325–37; Ronald F. Levant et al., "Evaluation of the Factor Structure and Construct Validity of Scores on the Male Role Norms Inventory—Revised (MRNI-R)," *Psychology of Men & Masculinities* 11, no. 1 (2010): 32, table 1.

63 *eight basic gender stereotypes:* Dominic J. Parrott, professor and director of the Center for Research on Interpersonal Violence at Georgia State University, in an email to the author, August 1, 2020.

64 *symptoms of depression:* Heilman, Barker, and Harrison, "The Man Box."

64 *One large-scale study found that people wedded to sexist beliefs:* Tyler Reny, "Mas-culine Norms and Infectious Disease: The Case of COVID-19," *Politics & Gender,* 2020, 1–23, doi:10.1017/S1743923X20000380.

65 *victims of violent crime:* Rachel E. Morgan and Barbara A. Oudekerk, "Crimi-nal Victimization, 2018," Bureau of Justice Statistics, U.S. Department of Justice, 2019, https://www.bjs.gov/content/pub/pdf/cv18.pdf.

65 *more likely to die from heart disease:* Women are more likely to die of Alzheimer's disease, and the sexes are equally susceptible to dying from stroke or hyperten-sion. Will H. Courtenay, *Dying to Be Men: Psychosocial, Environmental and Biobe-havioral Directions in Promoting the Health of Men and Boys,* Routledge Series on Counseling and Psychotherapy with Boys and Men, vol. 10 (New York: Routledge, 2011), 4.

65 *four times more likely than women to kill themselves or be killed by someone else:* Ibid.

65 *Men die earlier than women across the globe:* Global Health Observatory data repository: life expectancy and healthy life expectancy, data by coun-try, World Health Organization, http://apps.who.int/gho/data/view.main.SDG 2016LEXREGv?lang=en.

65 *five years shorter:* Elizabeth Arias and Jiaquan Xu, "National Vital Statistics Re-ports: United States Life Tables," 2017, National Center for Health Statistics, 2019, https://www.cdc.gov/nchs/data/nvsr/nvsr68/nvsr68_07-508.pdf.

ENDNOTES

65 *more stereotypically "masculine" ways:* Holly B. Shakya et al., "Adolescent Gender Norms and Adult Health Outcomes in the USA: A Prospective Cohort Study," *The Lancet Child & Adolescent Health* 3, no. 8 (2019): 529–38, https://doi.org/10.1016/S2352-4642(19)30160-9.

65 *less likely to seek psychological help:* Joel Y. Wong et al., "Meta-Analyses of the Relationship between Conformity to Masculine Norms and Mental Health-Related Outcomes," *Journal of Counseling Psychology* 64, no. 1 (2017): 80–93, http://dx.doi.org/10.1037/cou0000176.

66 *how to examine their testicles:* Courtenay, *Dying to Be Men,* 36–37.

66 *"fired" from the team:* Judy Y. Chu, *When Boys Become Boys: Development, Relationships and Masculinity* (New York: New York University Press, 2014), 131.

66 *"There's no way to get off the Mean Team":* Ibid., 133.

66 *surveys of thousands of adolescents:* Michael D. Resnick et al., "Protecting Adolescents from Harm: Findings from the National Longitudinal Study on Adolescent Health," *JAMA* 278, no. 10 (1997): 823–32, https://doi.org/10.1001/jama.1997.03550100049038.

67 *William:* William is a pseudonym.

69 *"There's no person in the whole world like you":* This is how Fred Rogers described closing his program in 1963, when he testified in support of National Public Television before a U.S. Senate subcommittee. PBS published the clip on November 22, 2019, as part of an episode of the program MetroFocus, https://www.pbs.org/video/mister-rogers-goes-washington-ycjrnx/.

69 *"We'll see how long that lasts":* Sarah L. Kaufman, "Lara Spencer Apologizes for Ridiculing Prince George and Ballet, but the Damage Has Been Done," *Washington Post,* August 26, 2019, https://www.washingtonpost.com/entertainment/tv/lara-spencer-apologizes-for-ridiculing-prince-george-and-ballet-but-the-damage-has-been-done/2019/08/26/989ed7d2-c798-11e9-8067-196d9f17af68_story.html.

71 *parents of preschoolers:* Emily W. Kane, "'No Way My Boys Are Going to Be Like That!': Parents' Responses to Children's Gender Nonconformity," *Gender and Society* 20, no. 2 (2006): 149–76, http://www.jstor.org/stable/27640879. See also Emily W. Kane, *The Gender Trap: Parents and the Pitfalls of Raising Boys and Girls* (New York: New York University Press, 2012).

71 *"a little 'quiffy' thing":* Kane, "'No Way,'" 166.

71 *"I would probably see that as a failure as a dad":* Ibid., 163.

71 *"I wanted to prepare him":* Michael Schulman, "EJ Johnson Is 'Not Just Some Other Rich Girl,'" *New York Times,* September 2, 2017, https://www.nytimes.com/2017/09/02/style/ej-johnson-rich-kids-of-beverly-hills.html.

72 *"This is child abuse":* "Boy Wonder," https://boy-wonder.com.

72 *the "pussification of men":* These comments were made in response to a post about Boy Wonder by the market research company Dose. Facebook, April 19, 2019, https://www.facebook.com/Dose/posts/2292046570889868?comment_tracking=%7B%22tn%22%3A%22O%22%7D.

73 *boys who witness violence in their home:* There is a large body of research that finds links between experiencing and witnessing violence and dysfunction at home in childhood and later perpetration of various kinds of violence. Every additional adverse childhood experience adds to the risk of adolescent interpersonal violence and self-harm by 35 to 144 percent: Naomi N. Duke, Sandra L. Pettingell, Barbara J. McMorris, and Iris W. Borowsky, "Adolescent Violence Perpetration: Associations with Multiple Types of Adverse Childhood Experi-

ences," *Pediatrics* 125, no. 4 (2010): e778–86, https://doi.org/10.1542/peds.2009 -0597, https://pediatrics.aappublications.org/content/pediatrics/125/4/e778.full .pdf. Children who are neglected or physically or sexually abused are more likely to perpetrate youth violence and intimate partner violence: Xiangming Fang and Phaedra S. Corso, "Child Maltreatment, Youth Violence, and Intimate Partner Violence: Developmental Relationships," *American Journal of Preventive Medicine* 33, no. 4 (2007): 281–90, https://doi.org/10.1016/j.amepre.2007.06.003. Experiencing violence in childhood or adolescence puts individuals at greater risk of perpetrating intimate partner violence (and being a victim of it): Anu Manchikanti Gómez, "Testing the Cycle of Violence Hypothesis: Child Abuse and Adolescent Dating Violence as Predictors of Intimate Partner Violence in Young Adulthood," *Youth & Society* 43, no. 1 (2011/03/01 2010): 171–92, https://doi .org/10.1177/0044118X09358313.

74 *More likely to abuse their dating partners:* Elizabeth A. Mumford, Weiwei Liu, and Bruce G. Taylor, "Parenting Profiles and Adolescent Dating Relationship Abuse: Attitudes and Experiences," *Journal of Youth and Adolescence* 45, no. 5 (February 2016): 959–72, https://doi.org/10.1007/s10964-016-0448-8.

74 *Dads who challenge:* Megan Fulcher, Lisa M. Dinella, and Erica S. Weisgram, "Constructing a Feminist Reorganization of the Heterosexual Breadwinner/ Caregiver Family Model: College Students' Plans for Their Own Future Families," *Sex Roles* 73, no. 3 (August 2015): 174–86, https://doi.org/10.1007/s11199 -015-0487-8.

74 *College men who can recall:* Ibid.

75 *No matter the sexual orientation of parents:* Megan Fulcher, Erin L. Sutfin, and Charlotte J. Patterson, "Individual Differences in Gender Development: Associations with Parental Sexual Orientation, Attitudes, and Division of Labor," *Sex Roles* 58, no. 5 (March 2008): 330–41, https://doi.org/10.1007/s11199-007-9348-4.

75 *As Fulcher and her colleagues write:* Fulcher, Dinella, and Weisgram. "Constructing a Feminist Reorganization," p. 184.

75 *a 2016 poll:* Curtis M. Wong, "50 Percent of Millennials Believe Gender Is a Spectrum, Fusion's Massive Millennial Poll Finds," *HuffPost*, February 5, 2015, https:// www.huffpost.com/entry/fusion-millennial-poll-gender_n_6624200.

75 *more than a quarter of California teens were gender-nonconforming:* Bianca D. M. Wilson et al., "Characteristics and Mental Health of Gender Nonconforming Adolescents in California," Williams Institute at UCLA School of Law and UCLA Center for Health Policy Research, December 2017, https://williamsinstitute.law .ucla.edu/publications/gnc-youth-ca/.

75 *A survey of high school seniors:* Joanna Pepin and David Cotter, "Trending Toward Traditionalism? Changes in Youths' Gender Ideology," Council on Contemporary Families, March 30, 2017, https://contemporaryfamilies.org/2-pepin-cotter-tra ditionalism/.

76 *2 percent of toys in the Sears catalog:* Elizabeth Sweet, "Toys Are More Divided by Gender Now Than They Were 50 Years Ago," *The Atlantic*, December 9, 2014, https://www.theatlantic.com/business/archive/2014/12/toys-are-more-divided -by-gender-now-than-they-were-50-years-ago/383556/.

76 *The industry stopped giving out separate awards:* Elissa Strauss, "Why Girls Can Be Boyish but Boys Can't Be Girlish," CNN, April 12, 2018, https://www.cnn .com/2018/04/12/health/boys-girls-gender-norms-parenting-strauss/index .html.

76 *Disney used to separate the toys for sale:* As of 2012, Disney's website categorized toys by gender; those that appeared only in the boys' category were more

ENDNOTES

likely to be bold-colored action toys and weapons, whereas those only in the girls' category were more likely to be pastel-colored and more likely to be dolls or related to beauty and cosmetics. When I checked the Disney website in June 2019, shoppers got the exact same list of toys whether they clicked on "for boys" or "for girls." Carol J. Auster and Claire S. Mansbach, "The Gender Marketing of Toys: An Analysis of Color and Type of Toy on the Disney Store Website," *Sex Roles* 67 (June 2012): 375–88, https://doi.org/10.1007/s11199 -012-0177-8.

76 *a popular doll that eats:* Baby Alive, https://babyalive.hasbro.com/en-us.

76 *A Hasbro video advertisement from Brazil shows boys:* Alexandra Jardine, "Hasbro's 'Baby Alive' Ad Encourages Boys to Play with Dolls Too," *AdAge*, April 24, 2019, https://adage.com/creativity/work/hasbro-we-can-all-take-care/2166141.

77 *"Creatable World" dolls:* Eliana Dockterman, "'A Doll for Everyone': Meet Mattel's Gender-Neutral Doll," *Time*, September 25, 2019, https://time.com/5684822 /mattel-gender-neutral-doll/.

77 *"I think if we could have a hand in creating the idea":* Ibid.

78 *Wade started using the pronoun "she":* Minyvonne Burke, "Dwyane Wade Says Trans Daughter Zaya Knew Gender Identity Since She Was 3 Years Old," NBC News, February 19, 2020, https://www.nbcnews.com/feature/nbc-out/dwyane -wade-says-trans-daughter-zaya-knew-gender-identity-she-n1138196.

78 *Wade said on a sports podcast: All the Smoke,* Podcast audio, "D-Wade! Dwyane Wade Talks Big Three, Retirement and Family!" December 19, 2019.

78 *"My job as a father is to facilitate their lives":* Ramin Setoodeh, "NBA Star Dwyane Wade on Supporting His Son's Attendance at Miami Pride," *Variety*, June 18, 2019, https://variety.com/2019/biz/news/dwyane-wade-miami -pride-1203246328/.

78 *the boys' group that Phyllis Fagell runs:* I visited the group and several of Fagell's classes. Andrew Reiner first reported on the boys' group for the *New York Times*: Andrew Reiner, "Boy Talk: Breaking Masculine Stereotypes," *New York Times*, October 24, 2018, https://www.nytimes.com/2018/10/24/well/family/boy-talk-break ing-masculine-stereotypes.html.

79 *Men of Strength clubs:* The "dominant story of masculinity" quote comes from a brochure published on the Men Can Stop Rape website, https://mcsr.org/men-of -strength-most-club.

79 *a summer camp for boys:* C. Brian Smith, "A Masculinity Camp for Boys That Starts at 8," *MEL Magazine*, 2017, https://melmagazine.com/en-us/story/a-ma sculinity-camp-for-boys-that-starts-at-age-8.

CHAPTER THREE: THE SEX ED CRISIS

82 *Harvard University's Making Caring Common project:* Richard Weissbourd, Trisha Ross Anderson, Alison Cashin, and Joe McIntyre, "The Talk: How Adults Can Promote Young People's Healthy Relationships and Prevent Misogyny and Sexual Harassment," Making Caring Common Project, Harvard Graduate School of Education, https://static1.squarespace.com/static/5b7c56e255b02c683659fe43/t /5bd51a0324a69425bd079b59/1540692500558/mcc_the_talk_final.pdf.

83 *another national survey on sex ed:* Laura Duberstein Lindberg, Isaac Maddow-Zimet, and Heather Boonstra, "Changes in Adolescents' Receipt of Sex Education, 2006–2013," *Journal of Adolescent Health: Official Publication of the Society for Adolescent Medicine* 58, no. 6 (2016): 621–27, https://doi.org/10.1016/j.jado health.2016.02.004.

83 *only 28 percent of boys:* "The State of Gender Equality for U.S. Adolescents," Plan International USA, 2018, https://www.planusa.org/docs/state-of-gender-equality -2018.pdf.

83 *boys start watching porn at age thirteen:* Debby Herbenick et al., "Diverse Sexual Behaviors and Pornography Use: Findings from a Nationally Representative Probability Survey of Americans Aged 18 to 60 Years," *Journal of Sexual Medicine* 17, no. 4 (April 2020), https://doi.org/https://doi.org/10.1016/j .jsxm.2020.01.013.

84 *a remarkable evaporation of sex education:* This interview with Guttmacher Institute expert Laura Lindberg prompted me to look more closely at the CDC data: Rafael Heller, "Trends in Adolescent Sexual Behavior, Health, and Education: A Conversation with Laura Lindberg," *Phi Delta Kappan* 100, no. 2 (2018): 35–39, https://www.kappanonline.org/heller-laura-lindberg-trends-adolescent-sexual -behavior-health-education-interview/. Full data sets for the CDC's School Health Policies and Practices for 2000 are at Laura Kann, Nancy D. Brener, and Diane D. Allensworth, "Health Education: Results from the School Health Policies and Programs Study 2000," *Journal of School Health* 71, no. 7 (October 2009): 266–78, https://doi.org/10.1111/j.1746-1561.2001.tb03504.x; for 2014, see "Results from the School Health Policies and Practices Study 2014," Centers for Disease Control and Prevention, 2015, https://www.cdc.gov/healthyyouth/data/shpps/pdf /SHPPS-508-final_101315.pdf, 21.

84 *Instruction has dwindled :* A CDC spokeswoman provided the data in this paragraph to me in response to my request. The CDC had previously published data from its 2000 and 2014 School Health Policies and Practices Study in a way that made it impossible to compare findings across years.

84 *singularly ineffective at changing much of anything:* Sarah DeGue et al., "A Systematic Review of Primary Prevention Strategies for Sexual Violence Perpetration," *Aggression and Violent Behavior* 19, no. 4 (July–August 2014): 346–62, https://doi .org/https://doi.org/10.1016/j.avb.2014.05.004.

84 *a nosedive since 2000:* According to a CDC spokeswoman, the number of schools teaching abstinence declined 20 percent between 2000 and 2014.

85 *committed some act of sexual violence:* Laura F. Salazar et al., "Precollege Sexual Violence Perpetration and Associated Risk and Protective Factors among Male College Freshmen in Georgia," *Journal of Adolescent Health: Official Publication of the Society for Adolescent Medicine* 62, no. 3 (2018): S51–57, https://doi .org/10.1016/j.jadohealth.2017.09.028.

86 *Of eight hundred incoming male freshmen:* Jacquelyn W. White and Paige Hall Smith, "Sexual Assault Perpetration and Reperpetration: From Adolescence to Young Adulthood," *Criminal Justice and Behavior* 31, no. 2 (2004): 182–202.

86 *At a different college, it was 14 percent:* Heidi M. Zinzow and Martie Thompson, "A Longitudinal Study of Risk Factors for Repeated Sexual Coercion and Assault in US College Men," *Archives of Sexual Behavior* 44, no. 1 (2015): 213–22.

86 *Just 41 percent of young women:* The figures on how much teen sex is "wanted" comes from CDC data published here: Gladys Martinez, Casey E. Copen, and Joyce C. Abma, "Teenagers in the United States: Sexual Activity, Contraceptive Use, and Childbearing, 2006–2010 National Survey of Family Growth," National Center for Health Statistics, 2011, 31, https://www.cdc.gov/nchs/data/series /sr_23/sr23_031.pdf.

86 *In a national sample of a thousand adolescents:* Michele L. Ybarra and Kimberly J. Mitchell, "Prevalence Rates of Male and Female Sexual Violence Perpetrators in

ENDNOTES

a National Sample of Adolescents," *JAMA Pediatrics* 167, no. 12 (2013): 1125–34, https://doi.org/10.1001/jamapediatrics.2013.2629.

86 *only twenty-nine states in the nation:* This figure (as well as the thirteen states that require medically accurate sex ed and stats on states that require instruction on sexual orientation) comes from data on state laws and policies compiled by the Guttmacher Institute, which does research on and advocates for sexual and reproductive health rights. "State Laws and Policies: Sex and HIV Education," Guttmacher Institute, updated September 1, 2019, https://www.guttmacher.org/state-policy/explore/sex-and-hiv-education.

86 *only eleven (plus D.C.):* Sarah Shapiro and Catherine Brown, "Sex Education Standards Across the States," Center for American Progress, updated May 10, 2019, accessed September 27, 2019.

87 *together enroll nearly 10 million children:* "Laws That Prohibit the 'Promotion of Homosexuality': Impacts and Implications (Research Brief)," GLSEN, 2018, https://www.glsen.org/sites/default/files/2019-10/GLSEN-Research-Laws-that-Prohibit-Promotion-of-Homosexuality-Implications.pdf.

87 *requires teachers to emphasize that homosexuality:* Jonece Starr Dunigan, "How Alabama's Current Sex Ed Law Harms LGBTQ Youth," Al.com, May 15, 2019, https://www.al.com/news/2019/05/how-alabamas-current-sex-ed-law-harms-lgbtq-youth.html.

87 *Democrats are generally more supportive:* Leslie Kantor and Nicole Levitz, "Parents' Views on Sex Education in Schools: How Much Do Democrats and Republicans Agree?," *PLOS ONE* 12, no. 7 (2017): e0180250, https://doi.org/10.1371/journal.pone.0180250.

87 *Most parents, regardless of their party affiliation:* Ibid.

88 *the National Longitudinal Study of Adolescent to Adult Health:* A systematized review of ninety-three studies using Add Health data found that the strength of parent-teen relationships predicts a range of health outcomes. Teens who have warm, close relationships with their parents are less likely to be depressed or contemplate suicide or have substance abuse problems, and more likely to have high self-esteem and make healthy choices about sex later on.

Andrew C. Pool and Carol A. Ford, "Longitudinal Associations Between Parent-Teen Relationship Quality and Adult Health Outcomes: A Review of Add Health Data," paper presented at the Psychological Well-Being: International Transcultural Perspectives, Washington, D.C., 2019, https://www.jahonline.org/article/S1054-139X(18)30693-1/fulltext.

Examples of individual research projects that have used Add Health data:

Teens who have stronger relationships with their parents are more likely to have greater self-esteem and stronger intimate relationships of their own. Matthew D. Johnson and Nancy L. Galambos, "Paths to Intimate Relationship Quality from Parent-Adolescent Relations and Mental Health," *Journal of Marriage and Family* 76, no. 1 (January 2014): 145–60, https://doi.org/10.1111/jomf.12074.

Young people who are less connected to their parents are more likely to have unmet mental health needs. Kelly A. Williams and Mimi V. Chapman, "Unmet Health and Mental Health Need Among Adolescents: The Roles of Sexual Minority Status and Child-Parent Connectedness," *American Journal of Orthopsychiatry* 82, no. 4 (2012): 473, doi:10.1111/j.1939-0025.2012.01182.x.

Teens have fewer sexual partners over the long term when they have strong connections with their parents, and/or when their parents are religious or disapprove of teen sex. Emily Cheshire, Christine E. Kaestle, and Yasuo Miyazaki, "The

Influence of Parent and Parent-Adolescent Relationship Characteristics on Sexual Trajectories into Adulthood," *Archives of Sexual Behavior* 48 (2019): 893–910, https://doi.org/10.1007/s10508-018-1380-7.
See also https://www.cpc.unc.edu/projects/addhealth/publications.

88 *Feeling close to parents and connected to school helps protect teen boys:* Michael D. Resnick et al., "Protecting Adolescents from Harm: Findings from the National Longitudinal Study on Adolescent Health," *JAMA* 278, no. 10 (1997): 823–32, https://doi.org/10.1001/jama.1997.03550100049038. Michael D. Resnick, Marjorie Ireland, and Iris Borowsky, "Youth Violence Perpetration: What Protects? What Predicts? Findings from the National Longitudinal Study of Adolescent Health," *Journal of Health Economics* 35 (2004): 424–33, https://doi.org/10.1016/j.jadohealth.2004.01.011.

88 *teens who watch a lot of porn:* Paul J. Wright, Debby Herbenick, and Bryant Paul, "Adolescent Condom Use, Parent-Adolescent Sexual Health Communication, and Pornography: Findings from a U.S. Probability Sample," *Health Communication* (August 2019): 1–7, https://doi.org/10.1080/10410236.2019.1652392.

89 *88 percent of scenes from popular porn movies:* Ana J. Bridges, Robert Wosnitzer, Erica Scharrer, Chyng Sun, and Rachael Liberman, "Aggression and Sexual Behavior in Best-Selling Pornography Videos: A Content Analysis Update," *Violence Against Women* 16, no. 10 (2010): 1065–85. https://doi.org/10.1177/1077801210382866. Full text at https://pdfs.semanticscholar.org/db43/7a7a4a975603690bd5921286c7831b487d10.pdf.

89 *One seventeen-year-old boy told researchers:* Emily F. Rothman, Courtney Kaczmarsky, Nina Burke, Emily Jansen, and Allyson Baughman, "'Without Porn . . . I Wouldn't Know Half the Things I Know Now': A Qualitative Study of Pornography Use among a Sample of Urban, Low-Income, Black and Hispanic Youth," *Journal of Sex Research* 52, no. 7 (2015): 736–46, https://doi.org/10.1080/00224499.2014.960908.

90 *a massive study of campus sexual violence:* Jennifer S. Hirsch and Claude A. Mellins, "Sexual Health Initiative to Foster Transformation (SHIFT): Final Report," 2019, https://sexualrespect.columbia.edu/files/sri/content/shift_final_report_4-11-19_1.pdf.

90 *20 percent of Columbia students:* Precollege victimization rates are also described in Hirsch and Mellins, "Sexual Health Initiative to Foster Transformation (SHIFT): Final Report." They are drawn from John S. Santelli et al., "Does Sex Education Before College Protect Students from Sexual Assault in College?," *PLOS ONE* 13, no. 11 (2018): e0205951, https://doi.org/10.1371/journal.pone.0205951.

90 *One woman told the SHIFT team:* Jennifer S. Hirsch and Shamus Khan, *Sexual Citizens: A Landmark Study of Sex, Power, and Assault on Campus* (New York: W. W. Norton & Company, 2020), 46–52.

90 *pushed right past her objections:* Ibid., 6–7.

90 *having sex with a blackout-drunk woman:* Ibid., 152–57.

90 *"sexual assault is a predictable consequence":* Ibid., xiii.

93 *"emerging and potentially normal" part of teens' sexual development:* Eli Rosenberg, "One in Four Teens Are Sexting, a New Study Shows. Relax, Researchers Say, It's Mostly Normal," *Washington Post*, February 27, 2018, https://www.washingtonpost.com/news/the-switch/wp/2018/02/27/a-new-study-shows-one-in-four-teens-are-sexting-relax-experts-say-its-mostly-normal/.

94 *one in eight has forwarded a sext:* Sheri Madigan et al., "Prevalence of Multiple Forms of Sexting Behavior among Youth: A Systematic Review and Meta-Analysis," *JAMA Pediatrics* 172, no. 4 (2018): 327–35, https://doi.org/10.1001/jamapediat rics.2017.5314. https://www.ncbi.nlm.nih.gov/pmc/articles/PMC5875316/.

94 *higher than average risk of being sexually assaulted:* Megan K. Maas, Bethany C. Bray, and Jennie G. Noll, "Online Sexual Experiences Predict Subsequent Sexual Health and Victimization Outcomes among Female Adolescents: A Latent Class Analysis," *Journal of Youth and Adolescence* 48, no. 5 (May 01 2019): 837–49, https://doi.org/10.1007/s10964-019-00995-3.

95 *concern about a "sex recession":* Kate Julian, "Why Are Young People Having So Little Sex?," *The Atlantic,* December 2018, https://www.theatlantic.com/magazine /archive/2018/12/the-sex-recession/573949/.

95 *nearly tripled, to 28 percent:* Christopher Ingraham, "The Share of Americans Not Having Sex Has Reached a Record High," *Washington Post,* March 29, 2019, https://www.washingtonpost.com/business/2019/03/29/share-americans-not -having-sex-has-reached-record-high/.

95 *a survey of nearly 500 college men:* Chyng Sun, Ana Bridges, Jennifer A. John-son, and Matthew B. Ezzell, "Pornography and the Male Sexual Script: An Analy-sis of Consumption and Sexual Relations," *Archives of Sexual Behavior* 45, no. 4 (2016/05/01 2016): 983–94, https://doi.org/10.1007/s10508-014-0391-2.

96 *Ideally . . . boys would get this advice before they get to college:* Maas has written on her blog about how to talk to kids about pornography. She has also written a downloadable e-book: Megan Maas, "Preparing for the Porn Talk: 1 of 3," *Dr. Megan Maas,* 2014, http://www.meganmaas.com/blog/preparing-for-the-porn-talk -part-1-of-3.

97 *teenagers who learned how to say no:* Santelli et al., "Does Sex Education Before College Protect Students from Sexual Assault in College?," e0205951.

97 *The SHIFT team argues that it can:* Madeline Schneider and Jennifer S. Hirsch, "Comprehensive Sexuality Education as a Primary Prevention Strategy for Sexual Violence Perpetration," *Trauma, Violence, & Abuse* 21, no. 3 (EPub May 2, 2020): 439–55, doi:10.1177/1524838018772855.

98 *set aside any doubts:* "National Sexuality Education Standards: Core Content and Skills, K–12," a special publication of the *Journal of School Health,* Future of Sex Education Initiative, 2012, http://www.futureofsexeducation.org/documents /josh-fose-standards-web.pdf.

100 *having sex for the first time when they are very young:* Laura D. Lindberg, Isaac Maddow-Zimet, and Arik V. Marcell, "Prevalence of Sexual Initiation before Age 13 Years Among Male Adolescents and Young Adults in the United States," *JAMA Pediatrics* 173, no. 6 (2019): 553–60, https://doi.org/10.1001/jamapedia trics.2019.0458.

100 *"sexual abuse of Black boys receives little or no attention":* bell hooks, *We Real Cool: Black Men and Masculinity* (New York: Routledge, 2004), 76.

101 *nearly one in ten boys:* Ibid.

101 *According to the most recent national data available:* The National Survey of Fam-ily Growth—S Listing, National Center for Health Statistics, https://www.cdc .gov/nchs/nsfg/key_statistics/s.htm#sexeducation.

101 *six states across the political spectrum:* Catherine Brown and Abby Quirk, "Momentum Is Building to Modernize Sex Education," Center for American Progress, 2019, https://www.americanprogress.org/issues/education-k-12/reports /2019/05/29/469886/momentum-building-modernize-sex-education/.

ENDNOTES

102 *laws in twenty-eight states:* "State Laws and Policies: Sex and HIV Education," Guttmacher Institute, updated September 1, 2019, https://www.guttmacher.org /state-policy/explore/sex-and-hiv-education.

102 *in 1995, 81 percent of teen boys:* Lindberg, Maddow-Zimet, and Boonstra, "Changes in Adolescents' Receipt of Sex Education, 2006–2013"; John S. Santelli et al., "Abstinence-Only-Until-Marriage: An Updated Review of U.S. Policies and Programs and Their Impact," *Journal of Adolescent Health* 61, no. 3 (2017): 273–80, https://doi.org/10.1016/j.jadohealth.2017.05.031. Results from the school health policies and practices Study 2014, Centers for Disease Control and Prevention, 2015, https://www.cdc.gov/healthyyouth/data/shpps/pdf /shpps-508-final_101315.pdf.

102 *no strong evidence that . . . keeps young people safe:* Santelli et al., "Abstinence-Only-Until-Marriage: An Updated Review of U.S. Policies and Programs and Their Impact"; John Santelli et al., "Abstinence and Abstinence-Only Education: A Review of U.S. Policies and Programs," *Journal of Adolescent Health* 38, no. 1 (January 2006): 72–81, https://doi.org/https://doi.org/10.1016/j.jado health.2005.10.006.

102 *including at the CDC:* Helen B. Chin et al, "The Effectiveness of Group-Based Comprehensive Risk-Reduction and Abstinence Education Interventions to Prevent or Reduce the Risk of Adolescent Pregnancy, Human Immunodeficiency Virus, and Sexually Transmitted Infections: Two Systematic Reviews for the Guide to Community Preventive Services," *American Journal of Preventive Medicine* 42, no. 3 (March 2012): 272–94, https://doi.org/10.1016/j .amepre.2011.11.006.

102 *"programs promoting abstinence-only until heterosexual marriage occurs are ineffective":* Cora C. Breuner and Gerri Mattson, "Sexuality Education for Children and Adolescents," *Pediatrics* 138, no. 2 (2016): e20161348, https://doi.org/10.1542 /peds.2016-1348.

102 *Teens who get comprehensive sex ed:* Chin et al., "The Effectiveness of Group-Based Comprehensive Risk-Reduction and Abstinence Education Interventions."

104 *talking about pornography didn't persuade them to start watching it:* Findings in this paragraph are from Emily F. Rothman et al., "A Pornography Literacy Class for Youth: Results of a Feasibility and Efficacy Pilot Study," *American Journal of Sexuality Education* 13, no. 1 (February 2018): 1–17, https://doi.org/10.1080/155 46128.2018.1437100.

105 *this new approach and its promising results:* Maggie Jones, "What Teenagers Are Learning from Online Porn," *New York Times Magazine,* February 7, 2018, https:// www.nytimes.com/2018/02/07/magazine/teenagers-learning-online-porn-liter acy-sex-education.html.

105 *the porn effects disappeared:* Laura Vandenbosch and Johanna M. F. van Oosten, "The Relationship Between Online Pornography and the Sexual Objectification of Women: The Attenuating Role of Porn Literacy Education," *Journal of Communication* 67, no. 6 (December 2017): 1015–36, https://doi.org/10.1111 /jcom.12341.

105 *DARE, the ineffective antidrug program:* Christopher Ingraham, "A Brief History of Dare, the Anti-Drug Program Jeff Sessions Wants to Revive," *Washington Post,* July 12, 2017, https://www.washingtonpost.com/news/wonk/wp/2017/07/12/a -brief-history-of-d-a-r-e-the-anti-drug-program-jeff-sessions-wants-to-revive/.

106 *Watching porn underage is associated with:* Starting sex at a younger age: see Laura Vandenbosch and Steven Eggermont, "Sexually Explicit Websites and

ENDNOTES

Sexual Initiation: Reciprocal Relationships and the Moderating Role of Pubertal Status," *Journal of Research on Adolescence* 23, no. 4 (2013): 621–34, https://doi .org/10.1111/jora.12008.

Not using condoms (boys who watched more porn were less likely to use condoms): Marie-Thérèse Luder et al., "Associations Between Online Pornography and Sexual Behavior Among Adolescents: Myth or Reality?," *Archives of Sexual Behavior* 40, no. 5 (October 2011): 1027–35, https://doi.org/10.1007/s10508-010 -9714-0.

Viewing women as sex objects, believing in gender stereotypes: Jochen Peter and Patti M. Valkenburg, "Adolescents' Exposure to a Sexualized Media Environment and Their Notions of Women as Sex Objects," *Sex Roles* 56, no. 5 (March 2007): 381–95, https://doi.org/10.1007/s11199-006-9176-y.

Having more sex partners: Kyler R. Rasmussen and Alex Bierman, "Risk or Release?: Porn Use Trajectories and the Accumulation of Sexual Partners," *Social Currents* 5, no. 6 (2018): 566–82, https://doi.org/10.1177/2329496518780929.

Believing in rape myths: John D. Foubert, Matthew W. Brosi, and R. Sean Bannon, "Pornography Viewing Among Fraternity Men: Effects on Bystander Intervention, Rape Myth Acceptance and Behavioral Intent to Commit Sexual Assault," *Sexual Addiction & Compulsivity* 18, no. 4 (2011/10/01 2011): 212–31, https://doi.org/10.1080/10720162.2011.625552.

See also Rita C. Seabrook, L. Monique Ward, and Soraya Giaccardi, "Less Than Human? Media Use, Objectification of Women, and Men's Acceptance of Sexual Aggression," *Psychology of Violence* 9, no. 5 (2019): 536–45.

106 *interest in casual sex and having more sex partners:* Peter and Valkenburg, "Adolescents' Exposure to a Sexualized Media Environment and Their Notions of Women as Sex Objects"; Rasmussen and Bierman, "Risk or Release?"

106 *the more pornography a boy used, the worse his grades:* Ine Beyens, Laura Vandenbosch, and Steven Eggermont, "Early Adolescent Boys' Exposure to Internet Pornography: Relationships to Pubertal Timing, Sensation Seeking, and Academic Performance," *Journal of Early Adolescence* 35, no. 8 (2015): 1045–68, https://doi .org/10.1177/0272431614548069.

But the research on this question is equivocal. More recently, a study of Croatian teens found no such association between porn use and academic performance, though it did find that grades suffered when boys spent a lot of time on social media sites: Sandra Šević, Jasmina Mehulić, and Aleksandar Štulhofer, "Is Pornography a Risk for Adolescent Academic Achievement? Findings from Two Longitudinal Studies of Male Adolescents," *European Journal of Developmental Psychology* 17, no. 2 (2020): 275–292, https://doi.org/10.1080/17405629.2019.15 88104.

106 *almost six times more likely to be sexually aggressive:* Michele L. Ybarra et al., "X-Rated Material and Perpetration of Sexually Aggressive Behavior among Children and Adolescents: Is There a Link?," *Aggressive Behavior* 37, no. 1 (2011): 1–18, https://doi.org/10.1002/ab.20367.

106 *tenth-grade boys who watched violent porn were three times more likely to sexually abuse a dating partner:* These boys were also twice as likely to themselves be the victims of sexual and physical dating violence. The findings do not show that porn *caused* the abuse, but the strong connection held true even when the researchers controlled for other relevant factors, like boys' attitudes about masculinity, their belief in rape myths, and their history of substance use and suspension and expulsion from school. The effects of violent porn were much more pronounced for boys than girls. Whitney L. Rostad et al., "The Association Between Exposure

to Violent Pornography and Teen Dating Violence in Grade 10 High School Students," *Archives of Sexual Behavior* 48, no. 7 (October 2019): 2137–47, https://doi.org/10.1007/s10508-019-1435-4.

106 *no connection between watching porn and risky sexual behavior:* Goran Milas, Paul Wright, and Aleksandar Štulhofer, "Longitudinal Assessment of the Association Between Pornography Use and Sexual Satisfaction in Adolescence," *Journal of Sex Research* 57, no. 1 (2020): 16–28, https://doi.org/10.1080/0022 4499.2019.1607817. Goran Koletić, Taylor Kohut, and Aleksandar Štulhofer, "Associations Between Adolescents' Use of Sexually Explicit Material and Risky Sexual Behavior: A Longitudinal Assessment," *PLOS ONE* 14, no. 6 (2019): e0218962. https://doi.org/10.1371/journal.pone.0218962.

The study on Dutch teens that found a relationship between watching porn and reduced sexual satisfaction: Jochen Peter and Patti M. Valkenburg, "Adolescents' Exposure to Sexually Explicit Internet Material and Sexual Satisfaction: A Longitudinal Study," *Human Communication Research* 35, no. 2 (April 2009): 171–94, https://doi.org/10.1111/j.1468-2958.2009.01343.x.

The study on Canadian teens, which found a connection between watching pornography and having multiple partners, is cited above: Rasmussen and Bierman, "Risk or Release?"

107 *that was not the case in another 2019 study:* Ivan Landripet, Vesna Buško, and Aleksandar Štulhofer, "Testing the Content Progression Thesis: A Longitudinal Assessment of Pornography Use and Preference for Coercive and Violent Content among Male Adolescents," *Social Science Research* 81 (July 2019): 32–41, https://doi.org/10.1016/j.ssresearch.2019.03.003.

107 *understand and explore their sexuality:* Porn "helped me feel less confused about myself," one college student told researchers in this study: Mark McCormack and Liam Wignall, "Enjoyment, Exploration and Education: Understanding the Consumption of Pornography Among Young Men with Non-Exclusive Sexual Orientations," *Sociology* 51, no. 5 (2017): 975–91, https://doi.org/10.1177/0038038516629909.

107 *a growing number of states (and the national Republican Party):* Lindsay Whitehurst and Jonathan J. Cooper, "A Growing Number of States Call Porn a Public Health Crisis," Associated Press, May 9, 2019, https://www.apnews.com/9c91cfd2 8a7b461b87948f36117a432e.

CHAPTER FOUR: SHAPING YOUNG MINDS

111 *bruised, disheveled and . . . covered in semen:* This letter was one of many OCR documents first made public in April 2019 by Tyler Kingkade, a reporter who has covered sexual violence among K–12 and college students for many years. Kingkade obtained dozens of OCR letters of finding and resolution through Freedom of Information Act requests, and then he not only wrote about his findings for the online education site The 74 Million but also posted the underlying documents for all to read—a real public service. https://docs.google.com/spreadsheets/d/1qB5ORjooRtn-wMGPOz0TWJIqj-M7Bu13ZSziEzmTpkI/edit#gid=0.

The account is from Letter to Kristen M. Howard of Detroit Public Schools, U.S. Education Department Office for Civil Rights, 2018, https://www2.ed.gov/about/offices/list/ocr/docs/investigations/more/15161041-a.pdf. Kingkade also described the Detroit case in his story summarizing what he learned from the documents he obtained via FOIA: Tyler Kingkade, "Exclusive: New Documents

Show the Trump Administration Has Confronted Dozens of School Districts Across the Country for Mishandling Sexual Assault Cases," The 74 Million, April 24, 2019, https://www.the74million.org/article/exclusive-new-documents-show -the-trump-administration-has-confronted-dozens-of-school-districts-across -the-country-for-mishandling-sexual-assault-cases/.

111 *the school district did not even have a policy for handling such complaints:* In an email, a spokeswoman for the school system told me that these "unfortunate incidents" happened when Detroit Public Schools was run by a state emergency manager who was primarily concerned with financial oversight, and who often left students' needs unmet. Now, there is a locally elected school board that has adopted policies for handling sexual misconduct and staffed a new office to respond to complaints.

112 *Hammond, Indiana:* Letter to Dr. Walter Watkins, Superintendent of Schools in Hammond, Indiana, U.S. Department of Education Office for Civil Rights, 2017, https://www2.ed.gov/about/offices/list/ocr/docs/investigations/more/05155001 -a.pdf. This letter was one of the OCR documents made public by Tyler Kingkade.

112 *A boy choked a girl:* The incidents in this paragraph were described in a letter of findings after the U.S. Education Department investigated sexual violence in Chicago Public Schools. Letter to Dr. Janice K. Jackson, Chief Executive Officer of Chicago Public Schools: U.S. Department of Education Office for Civil Rights, 2019, https://www2.ed.gov/about/offices/list/ocr/docs/investigations /more/05151178-a.pdf.

112 *a scathing investigative series published by the* Chicago Tribune: David Jackson, Jennifer Smith Richards, Gary Marx, and Juan Perez Jr., "Special Report: Chicago Public Schools Fails to Protect Students from Rape and Sexual Abuse," *Chicago Tribune*, June 1, 2018, https://www.chicagotribune.com/investigations/ct-chicago -public-schools-sexual-abuse-story.html. The full series is available online at http://graphics.chicagotribune.com/chicago-public-schools-sexual-abuse/gaddy.

112 *an investigation by the U.S. Education Department:* See letter of findings in note above.

113 *Kenneth Marcus, an assistant secretary of education for civil rights:* Erica L. Green, "Chicago Public Schools Ordered to Toughen Sexual Misconduct Policies," *New York Times*, September 12, 2019 2019, https://www.nytimes.com/2019/09/12/us /politics/chicago-schools-sexual-misconduct.html.

113 *nearly one in ten boys between the ages of ten and eighteen:* Elizabeth A. Mumford, Nnenna Okeke, and Emily Rothman, "Young Men's Attitudes and Neighborhood Risk Factors for Sexual Harassment Perpetration in the United States," *Journal of Community Health* 45 (2020): 245–51, https://doi.org/10.1007/s10900-019-00 738-2.

114 *Nearly half of middle school and high school students:* "Crossing the Line: Sexual Harassment at School," American Association of University Women, 2011, https://www.aauw.org/files/2013/02/Crossing-the-Line-Sexual-Harassment-at -School.pdf.

115 *a 2017 national survey of high school students:* Laura Kann, Tim McManus, and William A. Harris, "Youth Risk Behavior Surveillance—United States, 2017," Centers for Disease Control and Prevention, 2018, https://www.cdc.gov/healthyy outh/data/yrbs/pdf/2017/ss6708.pdf.

115 *they are at even higher risk:* Meredith Dank, Pamela Lachman, Janine M Zweig, and Jennifer Yahner, "Dating Violence Experiences of Lesbian, Gay, Bisexual, and Transgender Youth," *Journal of Youth and Adolescence* 43, no. 5 (2014): 846–57, https://doi.org/10.1007/s10964-013-9975-8.

115 *far-reaching effects on teens' mental and physical health:* Deinera Exner-Cortens, John Eckenrode, and Emily Rothman, "Longitudinal Associations Between Teen Dating Violence Victimization and Adverse Health Outcomes," *Pediatrics* 131, no. 1 (2013): 71–78, https://doi.org/10.1542/peds.2012-1029.

115 *academic struggles and poor educational outcomes:* Victoria L. Banyard and Charlotte Cross, "Consequences of Teen Dating Violence: Understanding Intervening Variables in Ecological Context," *Violence Against Women* 14, no. 9 (September 2008): 998–1013, https://doi.org/10.1177/1077801208322058.

116 *A study of 150 teenagers who were killed:* Avanti Adhia et al., "Intimate Partner Homicide of Adolescents," *JAMA Pediatrics* 173, no. 6 (2019): 571–77, https://doi.org/10.1001/jamapediatrics.2019.0621.

116 *High school principals across the country are unprepared:* Jagdish Khubchandani et al., "Preventing and Responding to Teen Dating Violence: A National Study of School Principals' Perspectives and Practices," *Violence and Gender* 4, no. 4 (December 2017): 144–51, https://doi.org/10.1089/vio.2017.0043.

116 *"harassment often happens while many people watch":* Nan Stein, "Sexual Harassment in School: The Public Performance of Gendered Violence," *Harvard Educational Review* 65, no. 2 (1995): 145–63.

118 *Davis was LaShonda Davis:* The description of LaShonda's allegations and of her case are drawn from Supreme Court records in *Davis v. Monroe County Board of Education,* 526 U.S. 629 (1999).

119 *"They make you send your kids to school":* David Firestone, "When a Tormented Child Cried Stop," *New York Times,* May 25, 1999, https://archive.nytimes.com/www.nytimes.com/library/politics/scotus/articles/052599harass-mom.html.

119 *"routine problems of adolescence" . . . "A teacher's sexual overtures":* These quotes are from Kennedy's dissent.

119 *a slightly wordier way of saying:* Boys will be boys: Through the Supreme Court's public information office, I asked Justice Kennedy if he would be willing to talk with me about this dissent and how he sees it now. He declined.

120 *"I'm sure that school children nationwide tease each other":* Audio of the oral argument is available at "Davis v. Monroe County Board of Education," https://www.oyez.org/cases/1998/97-843.

120 *the Trump administration announced new rules:* Erica L. Green, "Devos's Rules Bolster Rights of Students Accused of Sexual Misconduct," *New York Times,* May 6, 2020, https://www.nytimes.com/2020/05/06/us/politics/campus-sexual-misconduct-betsy-devos.html.

121 *A ninth-grader who is suspended just one time:* Robert Balfanz, Vaughan Byrnes, and Joanna Hornig Fox, "Sent Home and Put Off Track: The Antecedents, Disproportionalities, and Consequences of Being Suspended in the Ninth Grade," *Journal of Applied Research on Children: Informing Policy for Children at Risk* 5, no. 2 (2014): 17–30, https://digitalcommons.library.tmc.edu/childrenatrisk/vol5/iss2/13.

121 *researchers have made a strong case:* Russell J. Skiba, Mariella I. Arredondo, and Natasha T. Williams, "More Than a Metaphor: The Contribution of Exclusionary Discipline to a School-to-Prison Pipeline," *Equity & Excellence in Education* 47, no. 4 (2014): 546–64, https://doi.org/10.1080/10665684.2014.958965.

122 *borne the brunt of the crackdown in schools:* Information in this paragraph comes from an analysis of federal civil rights data. "K–12 Education: Discipline Disparities for Black Students, Boys, and Students with Disabilities," U.S. Government Accountability Office, 2018, https://www.gao.gov/assets/700/690828.pdf.

ENDNOTES

122 *Black boys are suspended at more than* three times *the rate of white boys:* Eighteen percent of Black boys were suspended during the 2013–2014 school year, according to federal civil rights data, compared to 5.2 percent of white boys: ibid.

123 *his classmates both teased him—they thought he seemed gay—and leaned on him for help:* Deposition of Student B in *John Doe 2 v. Fairfax County School Board,* filed in U.S. District Court for the Eastern District of Virginia. The deposition was filed April 19, 2019, as Exhibit 10 to John Doe's 2 opposition to the school board's motion for summary judgment. Pages 23–24, 37.

124 *The previous principal:* Peggy Fox, "Feds Investigating Virginia School after Sex Harassment Complaints against Coach," WUSA9, January 4, 2018, https://www.wusa9.com/article/news/local/virginia/feds-investigating-virginia-school-after-sex-harassment-complaints-against-coach/504918719. "Lake Braddock Principal Retiring Following Federal Investigation into Sex Harassment by Coach," WUSA9, February 2, 2018, https://www.wusa9.com/article/news/local/virginia/lake-braddock-principal-retiring-following-federal-investigation-into-sex-harassment-by-coach/65-513958354.

124 *News stories had claimed:* Jacob Bogage, "At Lake Braddock, Sexual Harassment Accusations, Personnel Changes and Lingering Resentment," *The Washington Post,* June 29, 2017, https://www.washingtonpost.com/sports/highschools/at-lake-braddock-sexual-harassment-accusations-personnel-changes-and-lingering-resentment/2017/06/29/59a3d00e-5536-11e7-a204-ad706461fa4f_story.html.

124 *John admitted making these crude statements:* John Doe 2's complaint in *John Doe 2 v. Fairfax County School Board,* filed in U.S. District Court for the Eastern District of Virginia.

124 *"I guess everybody does it:"* Transcript of John Doe 2's hearing before a school district hearing officer. Appended as an exhibit to Fairfax County School Board's motion for summary judgment, page 121.

124 *"committed serious repeated offenses":* Letter from hearing officers to John Doe 2's parents, March 23, 2018. Appended to Fairfax County School Board's motion for summary judgment, page 180.

125 *which he described as "traumatic" and "horrible":* John Doe 2 deposition, part of the Defendant's Motion for Summary Judgment, p. 1243.

125 *"I regularly consider harming myself":* Declaration of John Doe 2, p. 3.

126 *she called the case "sad" and "troubling":* Transcript of motion hearing, September 7, 2018, Document 22, p. 3.

126 *The district's investigation was flawed:* May 29, 2019. Memorandum Opinion by Judge Leonie Brinkema, granting defendant's motion for summary judgment. Document 145.

127 *fair and impartial investigations:* The full statement from Fairfax County Public Schools:

> Regardless of gender, FCPS conducts fair and impartial investigations that protect the rights of the victims and the accused. Consequences are also assigned in a fair and impartial manner. The severity of consequences is not based on gender.
>
> FCPS has established a Title IX coordinator and enhanced Title IX training for all of our employees. We are finishing a complete overhaul of our Title IX policies and regulations.
>
> The School Board approved a revised [Student Rights and Responsibilities] to include mandatory reporting language and a modified health cur-

riculum in high school to include bystander awareness and intervention training.

Two of the Title IX cases we have recently defended involved male students who were appropriately suspended and reassigned to different high schools for sexually harassing female classmates.

FCPS won summary judgment in both cases. Those cases show that we defend and protect victims of harassment, and we will continue to do so.

We regularly train our teachers and administrators on the prevention of bullying and sexual harassment.

The superintendent has also sent a clear message to our organization that bullying and sexual harassment will not be tolerated in our schools or our school system.

127 *just one of those teams billed $176,000*: Notice of attorney's charging lien, document 69.

128 *"No one ever sat John down"*: Lawyer Amanda DeFede's letter to the Fairfax County School Board, March 29, 2018, filed as an exhibit with the school system's motion for summary judgment, p. 835.

128 *"destroy the rest of my life"*: Declaration of John Doe 2, p. 3.

128 *"accepted into a good college"*: John Doe 2 deposition, p. 1244.

128 *boys who might otherwise be recruited as allies*: For one teenage boy, being wrongly accused and punished for sexual harassment at school began a series of events that led to his falling briefly within the ideological grasp of online extremists on 4chan and Reddit. Anonymous, "What Happened after My 13-Year-Old Son Joined the Alt-Right," *Washingtonian*, May 5, 2019, https://www.washingto nian.com/2019/05/05/what-happened-after-my-13-year-old-son-joined-the-alt -right/.

129 *we could do better by victims and offenders alike*: Kathleen Daly, "Restorative Justice and Sexual Assault: An Archival Study of Court and Conference Cases," *British Journal of Criminology* 46, no. 2 (2005): 334–56, https://doi.org/10.1093/bjc /azi071.

Kathleen Daly, "A Tale of Two Studies: Restorative Justice from a Victim's Perspective," in *New Directions in Restorative Justice: Issues, Practice, Evaluation*, ed. Elizabeth Elliott and Robert M. Gordon (Cullompton, UK: Willan, 2005), 11, https://research-repository.griffith.edu.au/bitstream/handle/10072/165/kdaly _part2_paper7.pdf?sequence=2.

Daly, a professor at Griffith University in Brisbane, Australia, studied the outcomes of four hundred juvenile sexual violence cases in South Australia, where restorative conferences are an option. Cases sent to court took twice as long to resolve as those sent to conference—and even then, only 51 percent of court cases resulted in a conviction for a sexual offense. So half of the offenders whose cases ended up in court walked away without any punishment at all, and half the victims walked away without any acknowledgment of what they had endured. The most serious crime, rape, was the one least likely to result in a conviction.

In contrast, every conference began with the offender's admission of guilt. And every conference included an agreement, created with input from the victim, to repair the harm done in some way. Conferences were more likely than court to result in an apology to the victim and a stay-away order for the offender. And importantly, conferences also were more likely to require counseling for the offender.

We think of courts as having the power to punish severely for severe crimes. In the 116 cases Daly studied that resulted in convictions in court, however, only 20 percent resulted in a sentence of detention—and in all but three of those cases, the detention was suspended. For victims, the justice system wasn't bringing much in the way of justice at all.

131 *the smaller boy, Darren:* Darren and Malik are pseudonyms.

CHAPTER FIVE: THE PROBLEM WITH "CONSENT"

136 *his criminal defense lawyer: The Daily,* podcast audio, "The Woman Defending Harvey Weinstein," February 7, 2020, https://www.nytimes.com/2020/02/07/pod casts/the-daily/weinstein-trial.html.

137 *LegalFling and Consent Amour:* Edward C. Baig, "Does 'Yes' Mean 'Yes?' Can You Give Consent to Have Sex to an App?," *USA Today,* September 26, 2018, https://www.usatoday.com/story/tech/columnist/baig/2018/09/26/proof-yes-means -yes-sexual-consent-apps-let-users-agree-have-sex/1420208002/.

138 *consent is a low bar:* Sex educator Shafia Zaloom emphasized this when I interviewed her for this book: When it comes to what we hope for young people navigating their sexual lives, mere consent should be considered the floor, not the ceiling. Zaloom has written a book for parents seeking guidance on talking about sex with their kids. Shafia Zaloom, *Sex, Teens and Everything in Between: The New and Necessary Conversations Today's Teenagers Need to Have About Consent, Sexual Harassment, Healthy Relationships, Love and More* (Naperville, Illinois: Sourcebooks, 2019).

139 *his comeback:* Ansari's public remarks come from *Aziz Ansari Right Now,* a Netflix recording of his 2019 comedy tours.

140 *An abridged version of her story:* The summary of the story and quotes come from Katie Way, "I Went on a Date with Aziz Ansari. It Turned into the Worst Night of My Life," Babe.net, January 13, 2018, https://babe.net/2018/01/13 /aziz-ansari-28355.

141 *"misread things in the moment:"* Ibid.

141 *"What you have done is appalling":* Banfield read her letter on the January 16, 2018, episode of *Crime & Justice,* her show on HLN, a cable news channel owned by CNN, https://www.cnn.com/videos/us/2018/01/16/open-letter-to-aziz-ansari -sexual-assault-accuser-banfield.hln.

142 *"That's on you":* Bari Weiss, "Aziz Ansari Is Guilty. Of Not Being a Mind Reader," *New York Times,* January 15, 2018, https://www.nytimes.com/2018/01/15/opin ion/aziz-ansari-babe-sexual-harassment.html.

142 *professional assassination by an anonymous woman:* Caitlin Flanagan, "The Humiliation of Aziz Ansari," *The Atlantic,* January 14, 2018.

144 *"that's when rape comes up":* Mary Kirtley Righi, Katherine W. Bogen, Caroline Kuo, and Lindsay M. Orchowski, "A Qualitative Analysis of Beliefs About Sexual Consent among High School Students," *Journal of Interpersonal Violence* (EPub April 2019): 0886260519842855, https://doi .org/10.1177/0886260519842855.

145 *"It would have been rude":* This study was part of Columbia's SHIFT study on sexual violence, described further in Chapter Four. Jennifer S. Hirsch, Shamus R. Khan, Alexander Wamboldt, and Claude A. Mellins," Social Dimensions of Sexual Consent Among Cisgender Heterosexual College Students: Insights from Ethnographic Research," *Journal of Adolescent Health* 64, no. 1 (2019): 26–35, https://doi.org/10.1016/j.jadohealth.2018.06.011.

146 *By analyzing conversational patterns:* Celia Kitzinger and Hannah Frith, "Just Say No? The Use of Conversation Analysis in Developing a Feminist Perspective on Sexual Refusal," *Discourse & Society* 10, no. 3 (July 1999): 293–316, https://doi.org /10.1177/0957926599010003002.

147 *"The behavior of a Harvey Weinstein is simple to condemn":* James Hamblin, "This Is Not a Sex Panic," *The Atlantic,* January 17, 2018, https://www.theatlantic.com /entertainment/archive/2018/01/this-is-not-a-sex-panic/550547/.

148 *A review of dozens of surveys of more than 25,000 college men:* RaeAnn E. Anderson et al., "The Frequency of Sexual Perpetration in College Men: A Systematic Review of Reported Prevalence Rates from 2000 to 2017," *Trauma, Violence, & Abuse* (EPub July 2019): 1524838019860619, https://doi .org/10.1177/1524838019860619. Studies of young men who are not enrolled in college have found similarly high rates of sexual aggression and similarly low rates of men who believe they have committed rape. Antonia Abbey and Pam McAuslan, "A Longitudinal Examination of Male College Students' Perpetration of Sexual Assault," *Journal of Consulting and Clinical Psychology* 72, no. 5 (2004): 747.

148 *an average of about one-third:* Ibid.

150 *half of all sexual assaults on college campuses involve alcohol:* Antonia Abbey, "Alcohol-Related Sexual Assault on College Campuses: A Continuing Problem," in *Addressing Violence Against Women on College Campuses,* ed. Catherine Kaukinen, Michelle Hughes Miller, and Ráchael A. Powers (Philadelphia: Temple University Press, 2017), 78–94.

150 *Drunk people also suffer from what researchers call "alcohol myopia":* According to an interview with Antonia Abbey. And see Abbey, "Alcohol-Related Sexual Assault on College Campuses: A Continuing Problem."

151 *more likely to see women who have been drinking as sexually available:* Abbey, "Alcohol-Related Sexual Assault on College Campuses: A Continuing Problem."

151 *"The perfect beer for removing 'no' from your vocabulary":* Ibid.

151 *relationship between the density of liquor stores and the prevalence domestic violence:* Lynne Peeples, "Liquor Store Density Linked to Domestic Violence," Reuters, December 17, 2010, https://www.reuters.com/article/us-liquor-violence /liquor-store-density-linked-to-domestic-violence-idUSTRE6BG5E520101217.

152 *college men listened to a 6.5-minute audiotape:* Jeffrey A. Bernat, Karen S. Calhoun, and Stephanie Stolp, "Sexually Aggressive Men's Responses to a Date Rape Analogue: Alcohol as a Disinhibiting Cue," *Journal of Sex Research* 35, no. 4 (1998/11/01 1998): 341–48, https://doi.org/10.1080/00224499809551952.

154 *some young men and professors have raised concerns:* Emily Yoffe, "The Question of Race in Campus Sexual-Assault Cases," *The Atlantic,* September 11, 2017, www.theatlantic.com/education/archive/2017/09/the-question-of-race-in-cam pus-sexual-assault-cases/539361/.

154 *two Black football players at Sacred Heart University:* Daniel Tepfer, "Suits Claim Shu Violated Contract in False Rape Case," *Connecticut Post,* October 30, 2018, https://www.ctpost.com/local/article/Suits-claim-SHU-violated-contract-in -false-rape-13349201.php.

154 *She later admitted to lying:* Daniel Tepfer, "Yovino Sentenced to 1 Year in False Rape Case," *Connecticut Post,* August 24, 2018, https://www.ctpost.com/news/ar ticle/Yovino-sentenced-to-1-year-in-false-rape-case-13177363.php.

155 *young American men are having less sex:* Ingraham, "The Share of Americans Not Having Sex Has Reached a Record High."

CHAPTER SIX: RACISM, VIOLENCE, TRAUMA

158 *BAM boosts boys' high school graduation rate by 19 percent:* Sara B. Heller et al., "Thinking, Fast and Slow? Some Field Experiments to Reduce Crime and Dropout in Chicago," NBER Working Paper 21178, National Bureau of Economic Research, Cambridge, MA, 2015, https://doi.org/10.3386/w21178. http://www.nber.org/papers/w21178.

160 *a growing body of research on implicit bias:* Cheryl Staats, "State of the Science: Implicit Bias Review 2013," Kirwan Institute for the Study of Race and Ethnicity, Ohio State University, 2013, http://www.kirwaninstitute.osu.edu/reports/2013/03_2013_SOTS-Implicit_Bias.pdf.

160 *assumptions that people like me often don't realize we are making:* Ibid.

160 *news reporting that echoes stereotypes of Black men as threatening:* Michael Oshiro and Pamela Valera, "Framing Physicality and Public Safety: A Study of Michael Brown and Darren Wilson," in *Inequality, Crime, and Health Among African American Males*, Research in Race and Ethnic Relations, Vol. 20, ed. Marino A. Bruce and Darnell F. Hawkins (Bingley, UK: Emerald Publishing Limited, 2018), 207–28.

160 *Black children are 3.6 times more likely to be suspended:* "2013–2014 Civil Rights Data Collection: A First Look," U.S. Department of Education Office for Civil Rights, 2016, https://www2.ed.gov/about/offices/list/ocr/docs/2013-14-first-look.pdf.

160 *Researchers at Yale University tried to answer that question:* Emma Brown, "Yale Study Suggests Racial Bias among Preschool Teachers," *Washington Post*, September 27, 2016, https://www.washingtonpost.com/news/education/wp/2016/09/27/yale-study-suggests-racial-bias-among-preschool-teachers/.

160 *Gilliam told me:* Ibid.

161 *Black boys are more likely to see Black men celebrated:* "Social Science Literature Review: Media Representations and Impact on the Lives of Black Men and Boys," The Opportunity Agenda, 2011, https://www.racialequitytools.org/resourcefiles/Media-Impact-onLives-of-Black-Men-and-Boys-OppAgenda.pdf.

162 *no similarly strong narrative about Black men as victims:* Alexander Weiss and Steven M. Chermak, "The News Value of African-American Victims: An Examination of the Media's Presentation of Homicide," *Journal of Crime and Justice* 21, no. 2 (1998): 71–88, https://doi.org/10.1080/0735648X.1998.9721601.

162 *More Black boys and men . . . die of homicide than any other cause:* "Leading Causes of Death by Age Group, Black Males, United States, 2015," Centers for Disease Control and Prevention, 2015, https://www.cdc.gov/healthequity/lcod/men/2015/black/index.htm.

162 *murdered at nearly fifteen times the rate of white boys and men:* "National Violent Death Reporting System," Centers for Disease Control and Prevention, https://wisqars.cdc.gov:8443/nvdrs/nvdrsDisplay.jsp.

163 *landmark study by the CDC and Kaiser Permanente:* Vincent J. Felitti et al., "Relationship of Childhood Abuse and Household Dysfunction to Many of the Leading Causes of Death in Adults: The Adverse Childhood Experiences (ACE) Study," *American Journal of Preventive Medicine* 14, no. 4 (1998): 245–58, https://doi.org/10.1016/S0749-3797(98)00017-8.

163 *the more likely he is to struggle with poor health:* Ibid.

163 *outside-the-home adversities that were just as toxic:* "A Guide to Toxic Stress," Center for the Developing Child, Harvard University, https://developingchild.harvard.edu/resources/aces-and-toxic-stress-frequently-asked-questions/.

ENDNOTES

163 *the push to address childhood trauma as a serious health risk:* Nadine Burke Harris, "Adverse Childhood Experiences: The Role of Philanthropy: 2014 Grantmakers in Health Annual Meeting on Health Philanthropy Plenary Address," Grantmakers in Health, 2014, https://www.gih.org/files/FileDownloads/2014_Annual_Meeting_Plenary_BurkeHarris.pdf.

163 *chronic state of overdrive takes a toll:* "Excessive Stress Disrupts the Architecture of the Developing Brain: Working Paper 3, Updated Edition, National Scientific Council on the Developing Child, 2005/2014, https://developingchild.harvard.edu/wp-content/uploads/2005/05/Stress_Disrupts_Architecture_Developing_Brain-1.pdf.

163 *hormones and wiring inside children's brains:* Jack P. Shonkoff et al., "The Lifelong Effects of Early Childhood Adversity and Toxic Stress," *Pediatrics* 129, no. 1 (2012): e232, https://doi.org/10.1542/peds.2011-2663.

164 *violent to others as he grows up:* Charles L. Whitfield, Robert F. Anda, Shanta R. Dube, and Vincent J. Felitti, "Violent Childhood Experiences and the Risk of Intimate Partner Violence in Adults: Assessment in a Large Health Maintenance Organization," *Journal of Interpersonal Violence* 18, no. 2 (February 2003): 166–85, https://doi.org/10.1177/0886260502238733. See also Natalie Wilkins et al., "Connecting the Dots: An Overview of the Links among Multiple Forms of Violence," Centers for Disease Control and Prevention, Prevention Institute, 2014, 8–9, https://www.cdc.gov/violenceprevention/pdf/connecting_the_dots-a.pdf.

164 *according to an analysis of shootings since 1966:* Jillian Peterson and James Densley, "We Have Studied Every Mass Shooting Since 1966. Here's What We've Learned About the Shooters," *Los Angeles Times*, August 4, 2019, https://www.latimes.com/opinion/story/2019-08-04/el-paso-dayton-gilroy-mass-shooters-data.

164 *prevent some violence in the world—including sexual violence:* "Gang violence is connected to bullying is connected to school violence is connected to intimate partner violence is connected to child abuse is connected to elder abuse. It's all connected," Deborah Prothrow-Stith, a doctor who has led efforts to treat youth violence as a public health issue, wrote in 2011. Deborah Prothrow-Stith, "Preventing Violence in the Next Decade: Five Lessons for the Movement," Remarks from the CDC's Striving to Reduce Youth Violence Everywhere (STRYVE), 2011, https://www.preventioninstitute.org/sites/default/files/publications/Preventing%20Violence%20in%20the%20Next%20Decade%20Five%20Lessons.pdf.

164 *feeling connected to a caring adult:* Joy D. Osofsky, "The Impact of Violence on Children," *Future of Children* 9, no. 3 (1999): 33–49, https://doi.org/10.2307/1602780.

164 *Research suggests:* Christina Bethell et al., "Positive Childhood Experiences and Adult Mental and Relational Health in a Statewide Sample: Associations Across Adverse Childhood Experiences Levels," *JAMA Pediatrics* 173, no. 11 (2019): e193007, https://doi.org/10.1001/jamapediatrics.2019.3007.

165 *Three-quarters of U.S. public schools:* Rachel Hansen and Melissa Diliberti, "Explore Data on Mental Health Services in K–12 Public Schools for Mental Health Awareness Month," *NCES Blog*, National Center for Education Statistics, May 30, 2018, https://nces.ed.gov/blogs/nces/post/explore-data-on-mental-health-services-in-k-12-public-schools-for-mental-health-awareness-month.

165 *two-thirds of subjects reported having at least one:* Felitti et al., "Relationship of Childhood Abuse and Household Dysfunction to Many of the Leading Causes of Death in Adults."

ENDNOTES

165 *Black children accumulate significantly more adverse experiences than white children:* Kameron J. Sheats et al., "Violence-Related Disparities Experienced by Black Youth and Young Adults: Opportunities for Prevention," *American Journal of Preventive Medicine* 55, no. 4 (August 2018): 462–69, https://doi.org/10.1016/j.amepre.2018.05.017.

165 *"Violence worked in his world":* John Rich, *Wrong Place, Wrong Time: Trauma and Violence in the Lives of Young Black Men* (Baltimore: Johns Hopkins University Press, 2011), 57.

166 Ultimately, I believe that if we want to make ourselves safe: Ibid. p. 201.

166 *When Arne Duncan left his job as President Obama's education secretary:* Emma Brown, "Arne Duncan Calls for Addressing Gun Violence in Final Speech as Education Secretary," *Washington Post*, December 30, 2015, https://www.washingtonpost.com/local/education/arne-duncan-calls-for-addressing-gun-violence-in-final-speech-as-education-secretary/2015/12/30/de05521c-ada5-11e5-b711-1998289ffcea_story.html.

167 *"If we were to fix every police department today in need of help":* Juan Perez Jr., "Arne Duncan Calls for Changes to Police Training," *Chicago Tribune*, December 30, 2015, https://www.chicagotribune.com/news/ct-arne-duncan-chicago-violence-speech-met-20151231-story.html.

167 *a spike in murders that left 769 people dead:* "Chicago Police Department Annual Report 2017," Chicago Police Department, 2017, 13, https://home.chicagopolice.org/wp-content/uploads/2019/03/Chicago-Police-Department-Annual-Report-2017.pdf.

167 *working for the after-school tutoring program his mother ran:* KK Ottesen, "Arne Duncan on Effecting Change for Kids and Gun Violence: 'We Lack the Courage,' " *Washington Post*, December 11, 2018, https://www.washingtonpost.com/lifestyle/magazine/arne-duncan-on-effecting-change-for-kids-and-gun-violence-we-lack-the-courage/2018/12/07/70fc9606-e6b6-11e8-b8dc-66cca409c180_story.html.

167 *Activists working in the streets:* Fran Spielman, "Lightfoot Names Two More $165k-a-Year Deputy Mayors for Public Safety, Infrastructure," *Chicago Sun-Times*, June 25, 2019, https://chicago.suntimes.com/city-hall/2019/6/25/18758640/lightfoot-deputy-mayors-public-safety-infrastructure-susan-lee-anne-sheahan.

168 *Duncan told me in 2016:* Emma Brown, "Arne Duncan Will Focus on Improving Opportunities for Chicago Youth," *Washington Post*, March 17, 2016, https://www.washingtonpost.com/news/education/wp/2016/03/17/arne-duncan-says-he-will-focus-on-improving-opportunities-for-chicago-youth/.

169 *The organization has reached nearly 350 young men:* Data in this paragraph is from an internal CRED document, "Reducing Gun Violence in Chicago: Update on the Citywide Response by Private Funders," July 2019.

169 *Homicides in Chicago fell 15 percent between 2016 and 2017:* Annual Report 2017, Chicago Police Department, https://home.chicagopolice.org/wp-content/uploads/2019/03/Chicago-Police-Department-Annual-Report-2017.pdf; *CPD End-of-Year Crime Statistics: 2018,* Chicago Police Department, December 31, 2018, https://home.chicagopolice.org/cpd-end-of-year-crime-statistics-2018/; Eric Levenson and Jason Hanna, "Chicago's Homicide Rate Decreases for the Third Straight Year," CNN, December 31, 2019, https://www.cnn.com/2019/12/31/us/chicago-murders-drop-2019/index.html.

170 *The Boston Consulting Group estimated:* CRED, "Reducing Gun Violence in Chicago."

171 *someone also let twenty-seven of the thirty horses out of their stables:* Rosemary R. Sobol, "Two Chicago Police Horses Injured During Break-in at Stable," *Chicago Tribune,* September 17, 2012, https://www.chicagotribune.com/news/ct-xpm -2012-09-17-chi-2-chicago-police-horses-injured-during-break-in-at-stables -20120917-story.html.

171 *cruelty to a police animal:* According to Cook County Criminal Court records.

174 *stabbed to death by his girlfriend:* David Struett, "Man Stabbed to Death in Rose-land Fight," *Chicago Sun-Times,* October 21, 2018, https://chicago.suntimes.com /news/fatal-roseland-stabbing/.

174 *apparently killed his girlfriend and then killed himself:* According to Merrillville Police Department police report obtained via public records request.

175 *rooted in intimate relationships:* "Why Relationships Matter for In-Risk Men: Identifying and Responding to Intersections between Intimate Partner Conflict and Community Violence," Alliance of Local Service Organizations, 2014, http:// also-chicago.org/also_site/wp-content/uploads/2015/08/Why-Relationships -Matter-for-In-Risk-Men_042014.pdf.

176 *a felony charge for illegal firearm possession:* According to Cook County Criminal Court records.

177 *the history that author Ta-Nehisi Coates laid out:* Ta-Nehisi Coates, "The Case for Reparations," *The Atlantic,* June 2014, https://www.theatlantic.com/magazine /archive/2014/06/the-case-for-reparations/361631/.

179 *Bill Gates:* In 2019, Gates wrote on Instagram of the time he spent with BAM students: "Although some of the guys talked about typical teenage frustrations—a teacher was treating them unfairly, or they kept dying in a video game—others had tragic stories. One had just watched a family member go to jail. Another spoke about a friend who had been shot. It was inspiring to see these young men working on dealing with their anger much earlier than I did. I was touched by the respect they had for each other and the intimacy they allowed them-selves. I left thinking: This is how every classroom in the world should feel." https://www.instagram.com/p/BuO0dBXgf7j/?utm_source=ig_share_sheet &igshid=1liwwary0imol.

181 *what the Nobel Prize–winning psychologist Daniel Kahneman called "slow think-ing":* Daniel Kahneman, *Thinking, Fast and Slow* (New York: Farrar, Straus and Giroux, 2011).

181 *"This exercise, like many in the program":* Heller et al., "Thinking, Fast and Slow?"

184 *one of sixty-four people shot that weekend, one of eleven killed:* Craig Wall and Diane Pathieu, "Chicago Shootings: 64 Shot, 11 Fatally in Weekend Violence," ABC 7 Chicago, July 13, 2020, https://abc7chicago.com/chicago-shooting-shoot ings-this-weekend-violence-how-many-shot-in/6314582/.

CHAPTER SEVEN: WHY HARRY NEEDS SALLY

186 *four of those men are graduates of all-male high schools:* Corey Mitchell, "The Supreme Court Justices Are All Ivy Law Grads, but What About High School?," *Education Week,* July 12, 2018, https://www.edweek.org/ew/articles/2018/07/12 /the-supreme-court-justices-are-all-ivy.html.

186 *a confidential survey of administrators at more than 330 schools:* 2019 IBSC Mem-ber Survey, MMG Education, 2019, p. 95.

187 *the St. Albans yearbook had also featured sexist slurs:* Nick Anderson, "Sex-ist Slurs and Coded Insults: St. Albans School 2015 Yearbook Stirred Outrage,"

Washington Post, October 3, 2018, https://www.washingtonpost.com/local/edu cation/sexist-slurs-and-coded-insults-st-albans-school-2015-yearbook-stirred -outrage/2018/10/03/39c788d0-c4ab-11e8-b1ed-1d2d65b86d0c_story.html# comments-wrapper.

187 *circulated a Google document describing sexual misconduct:* Nick Anderson, "Accounts of 'Unwanted Sexual Advances' and Other Incidents Roil Two Private Schools," *Washington Post*, December 22, 2014, https://www.washingtonpost.com /local/education/accounts-of-unwanted-sexual-advances-and-other-incident s-roil-two-private-schools/2014/12/22/9f7e786e-89f9-11e4-a085-34e9b9f09a58 _story.html?itid=lk_inline_manual_28.

187 *"Truly reprehensible":* Ibid.

187 *in a speech to parents:* Jason Robinson, "Boys' Schools: Beginning a New Conversation. Remarks from the St. Albans Annual Parent Dinner," International Boys School Coalition, January 23, 2019, https://www.theibsc.org/news/ideas/new -conversation.

190 *the number of single-sex public schools and classrooms grew:* Motoko Rich, "Old Tactic Gets New Use: Public Schools Separate Girls and Boys," *New York Times*, November 13, 2014, https://www.nytimes.com/2014/12/01/education/single-sex -education-public-schools-separate-boys-and-girls.html?module=inline.

191 *met with fierce criticism:* "Education Equality," Feminist Majority Foundation, http://www.feminist.org/education/SexSegregation.asp.

191 *a group of feminist scholars, mostly in psychology:* Diane F. Halpern et al., "The Pseudoscience of Single-Sex Schooling," *Science* 333, no. 6050 (2011): 1706, https://doi.org/10.1126/science.1205031.

191 *The ACLU pointed to writings:* "Sex-Segregated Schools: Separate and Unequal," American Civil Liberties Union, https://www.aclu.org/sex-segregated-schools -separate-and-unequal.

191 *boys' spatial skills are boosted by multiple testosterone surges a day:* Michael Gurian and Arlette C. Ballew. *The Boys and Girls Learn Differently Action Guide for Teachers* (San Francisco: Jossey-Bass, 2003) p. 100.

191 *He also wrote that girls "often cannot master physics or calculus in high school":* Ibid, p. 100.

191 *it turns out there isn't much difference at all:* Erin Pahlke, Janet Shibley Hyde, and Carlie M. Allison, "The Effects of Single-Sex Compared with Coeducational Schooling on Students' Performance and Attitudes: A Meta-Analysis," *Psychological Bulletin* 140, no. 4 (2014): 1042–72, https://doi.org/http://dx.doi.org/10.1037 /a0035740.

191 *"strong opinions thrive in the absence of much evidence":* Alice Sullivan, Heather Joshi, and Diana Leonard, "Single-Sex and Co-Educational Secondary Schooling: What Are the Social and Family Outcomes, in the Short and Longer Term?," *Longitudinal and Life Course Studies* 3, no. 1 (2011): 21, https://doi.org/10.14301/llcs .v3i1.148.

192 *fewer mixed-gender friendships and more anxiety in mixed-gender groups:* Wang Ivy Wong, Sylvia Yun Shi, and Zhansheng Chen, "Students from Single-Sex Schools Are More Gender-Salient and More Anxious in Mixed-Gender Situations: Results from High School and College Samples," *PLOS ONE* 13, no. 12 (2018), https://doi.org/https://doi.org/10.1371/journal.pone.0208707.

192 *graduates of all-boys schools were more likely to have been divorced:* Sullivan et al., "Single-Sex and Co-Educational Secondary Schooling."

193 *a sickening video was posted to social media:* "St Michaels: Alleged Gang Sex As-

sault Shocks Canada," BBC News, November 19, 2018, https://www.bbc.com/news/world-us-canada-46268978.

193 *he told Canadian media:* Rachael D'Amore, "Former St. Michael's Student Says He Endured 'Sexualized Initiation' in the 1980s," CTV News Toronto, November 16, 2018, https://toronto.ctvnews.ca/former-st-michael-s-student-says-he-endured-sexualized-initiation-in-the-1980s-1.4180752.

193 *On Facebook, he urged his fellow alumni:* Liam Mather, Facebook, November 21, 2018, https://www.facebook.com/liam.mather/posts/10160860014090411.

194 *questioned whether anyone in charge really wanted cultural change:* St. Michael's officials did not respond to my request for an interview.

194 *the school chose a man with a long career in Catholic education:* "St. Michael's College School Appoints New Principal," news release, 2019, https://www.stmichaelscollegeschool.com/stories/~board/stories/post/st-michaels-college-school-appoints-new-principal.

194 *established an independent committee to examine its culture:* St. Michael's College School Independent Respect and Culture Review Committee, August 2019, https://smcsrespectandculture.com/wp-content/uploads/2019/08/Final-Report-of-the-Independent-Respect-and-Culture-Review-Committee.pdf.

196 *sex offender who was convicted of molesting a child under the age of fourteen:* Matthias Gafni, "De La Salle Sex Assault Case: Suspect's Father, a Registered Sex Offender, Defends Son," *East Bay Times,* December 1, 2016, https://www.eastbaytimes.com/2016/12/01/victim-of-alleged-de-la-salle-sex-assault-speaks-out/.

196 *he told the* East Bay Times: Ibid.

196 *she managed to record her refusal in a ten-second Snapchat file:* Matthias Gafni, "Former De La Salle Football Player Guilty of Raping Carondolet Student; Victim Recorded Assault," *The Mercury News,* September 12, 2018, https://www.mercurynews.com/2018/09/11/verdict-in-de-la-salle-football-player-rape-case/.

199 *"What's going on with men?":* Jackson Katz, "Violence Against Women—It's a Men's Issue," TEDxFiDiWomen, November 2012, https://www.ted.com/talks/jackson_katz_violence_against_women_it_s_a_men_s_issue?language=en#t-1043825.

203 *"if he was going to be told day after day that they're all rapists":* This is one reason bystander intervention programs have become so popular on college campuses: they're palatable. Nobody wants to be treated as a rapist. Another reason they're popular on college campuses is because they are mandatory: in 2013, Congress passed an updated Violence Against Women Act that required colleges to train all students and employees in preventing sexual assault and dating violence, including by teaching the definition of consent and "safe and positive options for bystander intervention."

Bystander programs have important limitations. Even when they work, they do so by changing the conditions around aggressive people—they don't actually decrease aggression itself, a problem given that some researchers estimate that more than 80 percent of sexual assaults take place behind closed doors, where there are no bystanders to intervene. And we don't know much about bystander intervention in the real world. None of the research touting the benefits of bystander intervention accounts for the fact that bystanders are often drunk, says Dominic Parrott, who studies sexual violence at Georgia State University. Women who have been sexually assaulted have reported in surveys that when other people were around prior to the assault, those people were usually drinking. In lab simulations, Parrott has found that drunk men are much less likely

ENDNOTES

to intervene to stop sexual abuse. "We need to know, do programs which aim to promote bystander intervention actually work when people are drinking?" Parrott said. "We have no idea." Michelle Haikalis, Ruschelle M. Leone, Dominic J. Parrott, and David DiLillo, "Sexual Assault Survivor Reports of Missed Bystander Opportunities: The Role of Alcohol, Sexual Objectification, and Relational Factors," *Violence Against Women* 24, no. 10 (July 2018): 1232–54. https://doi.org/10.1177/1077801218781941. Ruschelle M. Leone and Dominic J. Parrott, "Acute Alcohol Intoxication Inhibits Bystander Intervention Behavior for Sexual Aggression Among Men with High Intent to Help," *Alcoholism: Clinical and Experimental Research* 43, no. 1 (January 2019): 170–79, https://doi.org/10.1111/acer.13920.

CHAPTER EIGHT: BOY-FRIENDS

207 *less likely than other athletes to abuse their dating partners:* The program was first shown to be effective among high school boys. Elizabeth Miller et al., "One-Year Follow-up of a Coach-Delivered Dating Violence Prevention Program: A Cluster Randomized Controlled Trial," *American Journal of Preventive Medicine* 45, no. 1 (2013): 108–12, https://doi.org/10.1016/j.amepre.2013.03.007.

    In 2020, a team led by the same researcher, Elizabeth Miller, published a study showing that the program is also effective among middle school boys. Elizabeth Miller et al., "An Athletic Coach–Delivered Middle School Gender Violence Prevention Program: A Cluster Randomized Clinical Trial," *JAMA Pediatrics* 174, no. 3 (January 2020): 241–49, https://doi.org/10.1001/jamapediatrics.2019.5217.

208 *the friend groups a young man chooses:* Kevin M. Swartout, "The Company They Keep: How Peer Networks Influence Male Sexual Aggression," *Psychology of Violence* 3, no. 2 (2013): 157.

209 *a video game called* Chicken: Margo Gardner and Laurence Steinberg, "Peer Influence on Risk Taking, Risk Preference, and Risky Decision Making in Adolescence and Adulthood: An Experimental Study," *Developmental Psychology* 41, no. 4 (2005): 625, https://doi.org/10.1037/0012-1649.41.4.625.

209 *When they played alone:* Steinberg's research along these lines is summarized in Dustin Albert, Jason Chein, and Laurence Steinberg, "The Teenage Brain: Peer Influences on Adolescent Decision Making," *Current Directions in Psychological Science* 22, no. 2 (2013): 114–20, https://doi.org/10.1177/0963721412471347.

209 *In another study . . . eighteen- and nineteen-year-olds:* Ibid.

211 *accustomed to being called a "fucking fag":* C. J. Pascoe, *Dude, You're a Fag: Masculinity and Sexuality in High School* (Berkeley, CA: University of California Press, 2012), Kindle edition, 67.

211 *"To call someone gay or fag is like the lowest thing":* Ibid, 55.

211 *"I did her so hard":* Ibid, 103.

211 *"Get raped! Get raped":* Ibid, 100.

212 *saw in data she collected from thousands of middle school students:* Dorothy L. Espelage et al., "Longitudinal Examination of the Bullying-Sexual Violence Pathway Across Early to Late Adolescence: Implicating Homophobic Name-Calling," *Journal of Youth and Adolescence* 47, no. 9 (2018): 1880–93, https://doi.org/10.1007/s10964-018-0827-4.

212 *The data she has collected:* Dorothy L. Espelage et al., "The Bully-Sexual Violence Pathway Theory Among Early Adolescents: Moderating Role of Traditional Mas-

ENDNOTES

culinity, Social Dominance, and Dismissiveness of Sexual Harassment," manuscript in preparation.

212 *more likely . . . to be sexually coercive and physically abusive:* Dorothy L. Espelage, Sabina K. Low, Carolyn Anderson, and Lisa De La Ru, "Bullying, Sexual, and Dating Violence Trajectories from Early to Late Adolescence," 2014, https://www.ncjrs.gov/pdffiles1/nij/grants/246830.pdf.

212 seven times *more likely to physically abuse a dating partner:* Dorothy L. Espelage, Sabina Low, Carolyn Anderson, and Lisa De La Rue, "Relation between Bully & Teen Dating Violence Perpetration across Early to Late Adolescence," 2013, https://www.apa.org/news/press/releases/2013/08/bully-dating.pdf.

213 *Initial (and, as it turned out, incorrect) media reports:* Dave Cullen, *Columbine* (New York: Twelve, 2009).

213 *By eighth grade, it's too late:* David Scott Yeager, Carlton J. Fong, Hae Yeon Lee, and Dorothy L. Espelage, "Declines in Efficacy of Anti-Bullying Programs Among Older Adolescents: Theory and a Three-Level Meta-Analysis," *Journal of Applied Developmental Psychology* 37 (March 2015): 36–51, https://doi.org/10.1016/j.appdev.2014.11.005. http://www.sciencedirect.com/science/article/pii/S0193397314001385.

218 *a review of more than 200 programs:* Joseph A. Durlak et al., "The Impact of Enhancing Students' Social and Emotional Learning: A Meta-Analysis of School-Based Universal Interventions," *Child Development* 82, no. 1 (January 2011): 405–32, https://doi.org/10.1111/j.1467-8624.2010.01564.x.

219 *The few studies that measured impact on academic achievement:* Rebecca D. Taylor, Eva Oberle, Joseph A. Durlak, and Roger P. Weissberg, "Promoting Positive Youth Development through School-Based Social and Emotional Learning Interventions: A Meta-Analysis of Follow-up Effects," *Child Development* 88, no. 4 (July 2017): 1156–71, https://doi.org/10.1111/cdev.12864.

219 *The CDC lists social-emotional learning:* Kathleen C. Basile et al., "Stop SV: A Technical Package to Prevent Sexual Violence," 2016, https://www.cdc.gov/violenceprevention/pdf/sv-prevention-technical-package.pdf.

219 *56 percent decline in homophobic name-calling:* Dorothy L. Espelage, Sabina Low, Joshua R. Polanin, and Eric C. Brown, "Clinical Trial of Second Step© Middle-School Program: Impact on Aggression & Victimization," *Journal of Applied Developmental Psychology* 37 (March–April 2015): 52–63, https://doi.org/10.1016/j.appdev.2014.11.007.

219 *"Emotional learning will be the downfall of society":* Teresa Mull, "Emotional Learning Will Be the Downfall of Society," *Townhall*, March 10, 2018, https://townhall.com/columnists/teresamull/2018/03/10/emotional-learning-will-be-the-downfall-of-society-n2458912.

219 *his teachers' relentless focus on seven skills:* Five of these skills (empathy, optimism, persistence, resilience, and flexibility) come from a book that refers to them as "stances": Kristine Mraz and Christine Hertz, *A Mindset for Learning: Teaching the Traits of Joyful, Independent Growth* (Portsmouth, NH: Heinemann, 2015). Duckett and Sparrow adapted this approach, adding two more stances for their classroom: courage and consistency.

220 *Roots results in less aggression and bullying:* Kimberly A. Schonert-Reichl, Veronica Smith, Anat Zaidman-Zait, and Clyde Hertzman, "Promoting Children's Prosocial Behaviors in School: Impact of the 'Roots of Empathy' Program on the Social and Emotional Competence of School-Aged Children," *School Mental Health* 4, no. 1 (March 2012): 1–21, https://doi.org/10.1007/s12310-011-9064-7.

223 *a turning point in the global fight for gender equity:* Shari L. Dworkin, Paul J. Fleming, and Christopher J. Colvin, "The Promises and Limitations of Gender-Transformative Health Programming with Men: Critical Reflections from the Field," *Culture, Health & Sexuality* 17, no. 2 (May 2015): 128–43, https://doi.org/10.1080 /13691058.2015.1035751.

223 *helping men challenge rigid ideas about masculinity:* Shari L. Dworkin, Sarah Treves-Kagan, and Sheri A. Lippman, "Gender-Transformative Interventions to Reduce HIV Risks and Violence with Heterosexually-Active Men: A Review of the Global Evidence," *AIDS and Behavior* 17, no. 9 (November 2013): 2845–63, https://doi.org/10.1007/s10461-013-0565-2.

223 *From South Africa to Canada:* Rachel Jewkes, Michael Flood, and James Lang, "From Work with Men and Boys to Changes of Social Norms and Reduction of Inequities in Gender Relations: A Conceptual Shift in Prevention of Violence Against Women and Girls," *The Lancet* 385, no. 9977 (November 2014): 1580–89, https://doi.org/10.1016/S0140-6736(14)61683-4.

223 *programs focused on challenging norms of masculinity:* Dworkin, Treves-Kagan, and Lippman, "Gender-Transformative Interventions to Reduce HIV Risks and Violence with Heterosexually-Active Men: A Review of the Global Evidence," 2845–63.

224 *We still need more evidence about what works:* Ibid.

224 *"prove themselves to be 'real men,' often at great cost":* "Working with Men and Boys to End Violence Against Women and Girls: Approaches, Challenges, and Lessons," U.S. Agency for International Development," 2015, https://www.usaid.gov/sites/default/files/documents/1865/Men_VAW_re port_Feb2015_Final.pdf, 10. USAID issued another report in 2018 highlighting the success of "gender transformative" programs—those that seek to promote gender equality by challenging traditional masculinity—in generating support among men for safer sex and family planning: "Essential Considerations for Engaging Men and Boys for Improved Family Planning Outcomes," U.S. Agency for International Development, 2018, https://www .usaid.gov/sites/default/files/documents/1864/Engaging-men-boys-family -planning-508.pdf.

224 *"Offering men a positive vision":* Ibid., 6.

226 *Studies of the program's impact in eight countries:* "Program H|M|D: A Toolkit for Action/ Engaging Youth to Achieve Gender Equity," Promundo, Instituto PAPAI, Salud y Género and ECOS, Rio de Janeiro, Brazil, and Washington, D.C., 2013, 72–77, https://promundoglobal.org/wp-content/uploads/2015/01/Program-HMD -Toolkit-for-Action.pdf.

226 *thirteen-hour curriculum:* Promundo-US and University of Pittsburgh Medical Center, Manhood 2.0: A Curriculum Promoting a Gender-Equitable Future of Manhood, Washington, D.C., and Pittsburgh, 2018, https://promundoglobal.org /resources/manhood-2-0-curriculum/?lang=english.

227 *Trump administration suddenly announced it would yank the pregnancy prevention funds:* Elizabeth Chuck, "Trump Administration Abruptly Cuts Funding to Teen Pregnancy Prevention Programs," NBC News, August 25, 2017, https://www.nbc news.com/news/us-news/trump-administration-abruptly-cuts-funding-teen -pregnancy-prevention-programs-n795321.

227 *"very weak evidence of positive impact":* Jacqueline Howard, "Why the Trump Administration Is Cutting Teen Pregnancy Prevention Funding," CNN, August 17, 2017, https://www.cnn.com/2017/08/17/health/teen-pregnancy-prevention -programs-funding/index.html.

ENDNOTES

227 *Trump appointed a leading advocate for abstinence-only sex education:* David Crary, "Advocate of Abstinence-Only Sex Education Gets High HHS Post," Associated Press, June 7, 2017, https://apnews.com/5d547535a37948ec9578eb4562 db1b06/Advocate-of-abstinence-only-sex-education-gets-high-HHS-post.

227 *A federal judge agreed:* Jennifer Hansler, "HHS Loses Another Court Battle over Teen Pregnancy Prevention Grant Funding," CNN, June 4, 2018, https://www .cnn.com/2018/06/02/politics/hhs-teen-pregnancy-program-dc-district-court /index.html.

227 *A look just at the impact on boys in Pittsburgh:* Elizabeth Miller, personal communication, July 3, 2019.

229 *Many other activists and scholars:* Elizabeth Miller, "Reclaiming Gender and Power in Sexual Violence Prevention in Adolescence," *Violence Against Women* 24, no. 15 (2018): 1785–93, https://doi.org/10.1177/1077801217753323.

231 *"The campaign's tips":* Dana Bolger, "It's on Us to Go Beyond 'It's on Us,'" 2014, http://feministing.com/2014/09/22/its-on-us-to-go-beyond-its-on-us/.

232 *twenty-six Kentucky high schools:* Ann L. Coker et al., "RCT Testing Bystander Effectiveness to Reduce Violence," *American Journal of Preventive Medicine* 52, no. 5 (2017): 566–78, https://doi.org/10.1016/j.amepre.2017.01.020.

232 *more effective for straight than for sexual-minority boys and girls:* Ann L. Coker et al., "Bystander Program Effectiveness to Reduce Violence and Violence Acceptance Within Sexual Minority Male and Female High School Students Using a Cluster Rct," *Prevention Science* 21, no. 3 (January 2020): 434–44, https://doi .org/10.1007/s11121-019-01073-7.

234 *social norms approach:* Alan Berkowitz, "An Overview of the Social Norms Approach," in Linda C. Lederman and Lea P. Stewart, eds., *Changing the Culture of College Drinking: A Socially Situated Prevention Campaign* (New York: Hampton Press, 2004). http://www.alanberkowitz.com/articles/social%20norms%20 approach-short.pdf.

234 *Men tend to believe that other men aren't as bothered:* Alan D. Berkowitz, "Fostering Healthy Norms to Prevent Violence and Abuse: The Social Norms Approach," in *The Prevention of Sexual Violence: A Practitioner's Sourcebook,* ed. Keith Kaufman (Holyoke: NEARI Press, 2010), 147–172.

EPILOGUE

242 *"tests of masculinity/femininity":* Mihaly Csikszentmihalyi, *Creativity: Flow and the Psychology of Discovery and Invention* (New York: Harper Perennial, 2013), 70. Hat tip to the website Brainpickings, where I first saw this quote: Maria Popova, "Why 'Psychological Androgyny' Is Essential for Creativity," Brainpickings, 2014, https://www.brainpickings.org/2014/11/07/psychological-androginy-creativity -csikszentmihalyi/.

243 *"masculine" or "feminine" instead of simply "human":* Bernice Lott, "A Feminist Critique of Androgyny: Toward the Elimination of Gender Attributions for Learned Behavior," in Clara Mayo and Nancy M. Henley, eds., *Gender and Nonverbal Behavior* (New York: Springer, 1981), 171–80.

243 *efforts to "inoculate" her son:* Sandra Lipsitz Bem, *An Unconventional Family* (New Haven, CT: Yale University Press, 1998), 125.

243 *being the parent "on duty":* Ibid., 95.

243 *"intense discussion of the inner details of life":* Ibid., 181.

243 *"If you were doing it all over again":* Ibid., 189.

243 *"I get to be a complete person":* Ibid., 190.

Index

INDEX

INDEX

About the Author

Emma Brown is an investigative reporter at *The Washington Post*. In her life before journalism, she worked as a wilderness ranger in Wyoming and a middle-school math teacher in Alaska. She lives with her husband and two children in Washington, D.C.